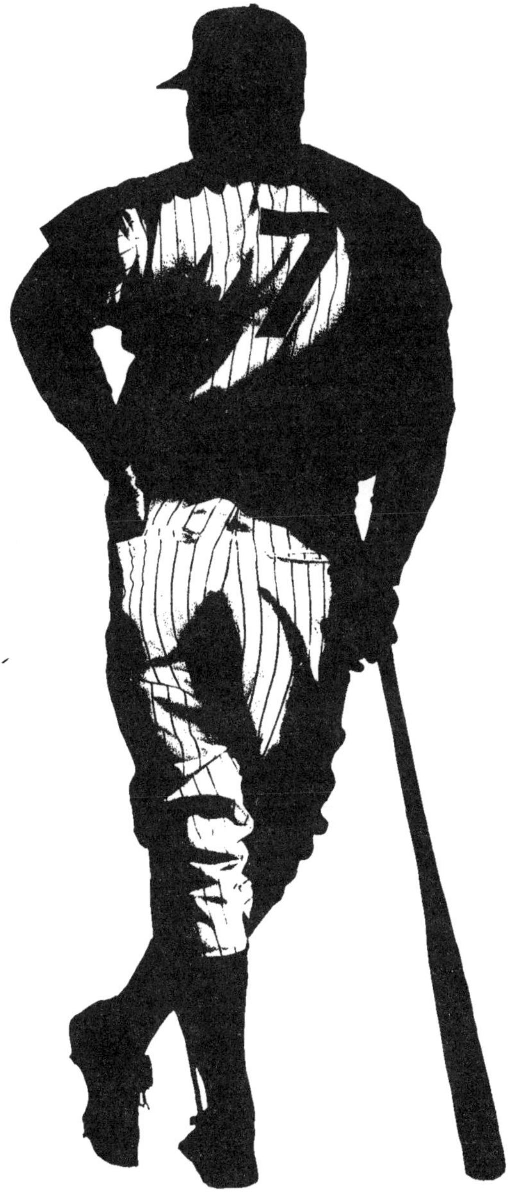

Mutt's Dream
Making the Mick

Howard Burman

Copyright © 2020 by Howard Burman

ALL RIGHTS RESERVED. No part of this book may be reproduced or transmitted in any form by any means, electronic or mechanical, including photocopying and recording, or by any information storage and retrieval system, except as may be expressly permitted in writing from the publisher.

Requests for permission should be addressed to: Ascend Books, LLC, Attn: Rights and Permissions Department, 7221 West 79th Street, Suite 206, Overland Park, KS 66204

First Edition
10 9 8 7 6 5 4 3 2 1

ISBN: print book 978-1-7344637-0-5

Library of Congress Control Number: 2020933279

Publisher: Bob Snodgrass
Editor: Mark Fitzpatrick
Publication Coordinator: Molly Gore
Sales and Marketing: Lenny Cohen
Dust Jacket and Book Design: Rob Peters

The goal of Ascend Books is to publish quality works. With that goal in mind, we are proud to offer this book to our readers. Please notify the publisher of any erroneous credits or omissions, and corrections will be made to subsequent editions/future printings.

This novel is inspired by actual historical events but is not intended to replicate those events. The author altered certain details for the sake of the narrative, while striving to be true to the realities of the era. The characters, story and dialogue are entirely fictional and the products of the imagination of the author. Any resemblance to actual persons, events or locales is entirely coincidental. This book is not affiliated with, endorsed, or licensed by any league, team, other institution or entity.

Printed in Canada

Mickey and Elven "Mutt" Mantle at home in Spavinaw, Oklahoma. Circa 1933.
(Courtesy Getty Images/Bettmann)

For Karen,
without whose support and
encouragement this book would not
have been possible.

Introduction

There is a time when all the important choices in our lives are before us. A time pregnant with the excitement of adolescence and the promise of adulthood. This story is about that time.

Baseball fans, even the casual ones, know something of Mickey Mantle—the tape-measure home runs, the blazing speed, the nagging injuries. His story of becoming The Mick is part of American lore—the ultimate baseball father creates a legendary player.

Mickey became a great baseball player, one of the best ever, and certainly the finest switch-hitting slugger of all time. As legendary sportscaster Bob Costas said in his eulogy for Mantle, "There was a greatness about him, but vulnerability too." Those qualities not only brought him the adoration of millions, but also gave his fans reasons to excuse his shortcomings.

Mickey often told a story in which St. Peter meets him at the pearly gates and says, "Mick, we checked the record. We know some of what went on. Sorry we can't let you in. But before you go, God wants to know if you'd sign these six dozen baseballs."

In his eulogy Costas characterized him as "... a fragile hero to whom we had an emotional attachment so strong and lasting that it defied logic. Mickey often said he didn't understand it, this enduring connection and affection—the men now in their 40s and 50s, otherwise perfectly sensible, who went dry in the mouth and stammered like schoolboys in the presence of Mickey Mantle. Maybe Mick was uncomfortable with it, not just because of his basic shyness, but because he was always too honest to regard himself as some kind of deity..."

"... Mickey Mantle got from America something other than misplaced and mindless celebrity worship. He got something far more meaningful. He got love—love for what he had been, love for what he made us feel, love for the humanity and sweetness that was always there mixed in with the flaws and all the pain that wracked his body and his soul. We wanted to tell him that it was OK, that what he had been was enough. We hoped he felt that Mutt Mantle would have understood..."

How does an extraordinary life emerge from ordinary beginnings? In Mickey's case, one must look at how another person dreamt and then shaped that life. Mickey and his father, Mutt, must be considered together, for without Mutt, The Mick most likely would never have been.

The threads of Mickey Mantle's unsettled adult life, his athletic feats and persona, real and claimed, mythic but true—rube, legend, drunkard—can be found in the alkali fields, the chat piles, and the parched earth of rural Oklahoma.

Prologue

In my end is my beginning.
In my beginning is my end.
—T.S. Eliot, Four Quartets

May 28, 1995. The Mick is 63. He has been retired from baseball for 27 years. He calls his son David, says he has been suffering stomach pains, and asks David to drive him over to Baylor University Medical Center in Dallas.

"Probably nothing to worry about. Just want to get it checked out," he tells his son. He doesn't admit that for days he's been doubled up in bed. Nauseated, too sick to get up.

Doctors immediately diagnose Mickey's illness. His yellowed skin and eyes tell them it is caused by liver failure. Tests indicate his kidneys are also failing. Formal diagnosis: end-stage liver disease.

Mickey has been a heavy drinker for years. He's had his share of driving accidents, quarrels, public scenes, periods of confusion, memory loss, blackouts. Never a mellow drunk, he often turned loud, obnoxious, rude. He drove recklessly and insulted fans. He neglected his wife and sons.

Little was made of it. After all, he was The Mick.

A year and a half earlier, Mickey had checked himself into the Betty Ford Clinic, determined to quit drinking. He did. But it was too late. Afterward, when he made public appearances he always said, "Here's a role model for you. Don't be like me."

They run scores of tests: CTs, ultrasounds, MRIs. More bad news. Mickey also has a tumor in his liver. Doctors assume it is malignant, but there is no evidence it has spread. Additional tests follow. They determine Mickey is also infected with hepatitis C.

Mickey is barely conscious when they tell him that a liver transplant is the only way to extend his life. Mickey assures them he is a fighter. "I never give up," he tells them.

On June 6, 1995, Mickey's doctors contact the United Network for Organ Sharing (UNOS) with a report of their patient's medical condition. The network classifies Mickey as a Status 2 patient, a ranking only surpassed by those not expected to live more than a week without a transplant. Mickey's doctors believe he can be stabilized for two to three weeks.

"We're one of the top liver transplant hospitals in the country," they tell Mickey at the Baylor Medical Center. "Seventy percent of our transplant patients have survived for at least five years." Mickey says he'll take a .700 batting average any time.

Mickey doesn't want the public to know. He's a sports hero. He's a legend. Legends don't command pity. But word gets out. Mickey Mantle is in the hospital. Mickey Mantle needs a transplant. Mickey Mantle may not make it.

Reporters descend on the hospital. A news conference is hastily arranged. Dr. Robert Goldstein stands behind a battery of microphones.

"I can tell you he will not get out of the hospital without getting a transplant," he says.

He thinks that without a new liver, Mickey might not survive another two days. While the doctor is speaking to the reporters, Mickey slips into a coma.

Later that evening, a hospital spokesman releases a statement that a liver donor may have been found. An anonymous young man. Athletic, popular, still trying to figure out what he wanted to do with his life, he died after a blood vessel burst in his brain. His family has donated his organs, so something good can come from his tragedy. Six people are expected to receive his organs: a truck driver, a farm manager, a resort operator, an electrical lineman—and a famous ex-ballplayer.

As soon as the announcement is made, a storm of criticism erupts. Surely Mantle's celebrity status has vaulted him to the front of the transplant queue. Obviously, he is receiving preferential treatment. The hospital's phone line is jammed with irate callers.

"He's a boozehound. An absolute guzzler. Has been for years. A famous lush. How the hell does he get special treatment?"

"I had a liver transplant, but I had to suffer in agony for almost a year before I got mine."

"Somebody else will probably die because a celebrity jumped the transplant line."

"Many extremely ill children and adults die while waiting for organs, but a retired baseball player gets his within a day."

"The average waiting time for a liver transplant is 135 days. Mantle gets his in one. It's disgraceful."

Many people had read the stories. Mickey's drinking had gotten heavier each year he was with the Yankees. After he retired in 1968 and found himself without the purpose he had worked for since childhood, his drinking became an essential part of his daily life. He drank often and heavily. It was how he maintained his self-esteem.

His health deteriorated. He became severely undernourished.

He had often said he didn't expect to live past 40 anyway. The father he loved died at that age. The grandfather he admired and two of his uncles also passed away well before their time.

The hospital administration scrambles to limit the damage to its sterling reputation. His doctors claim there is no celebrity favoritism—that Mickey had been classified as Status 2, according to the standards of UNOS. Still, many argue he doesn't deserve a liver. He has caused his own problems by drinking heavily for more than 40 years.

Prior to the transplant, doctors also find that Mickey has an inoperable type of liver cancer, which further necessitates the need for a transplant. The surgery lasts for six hours, but the prospects for recovery aren't good.

Mickey is sent home, put on chemotherapy.

A month later, he is back in the hospital. The cancer has spread. His doctor gives him the news.

"I'm not going to get better, right?" Mickey asks.

"No, and in terms of time—"

"I don't want to know."

Two months after his liver transplant, Mickey is dead.

Chapter 1

In **Spavinaw,** Oklahoma, static crackles from the Philco Baby Grand radio in the small living room. Mutt Mantle winces and smacks his hand against its side. France Laux's voice clearly reverberates off the yellowed wallpaper.

"Hello folks. This is France Laux coming to you from beautiful Sportsman's Park in St. Louis. We have a dandy of a game for you today between the St. Louis Cardinals and the Philadelphia Athletics. It's Game Five of the 1930 World Series, which is all knotted up at two games each."

Mutt knows he should be outside. He should be working on the county road east of town, but surely his foreman will understand. He knows Mutt is not going to miss the game. These are "his boys"—the Cardinals. Besides, it's 110 degrees in the Oklahoma sun. Not a good day for physical labor.

In a house short on luxuries, the Philco stands out. Sure, money is scarce, but the radio is a must-have. Mutt fiddles with the knobs, trying desperately to balance out the irritating noise with Laux's seductive baritone. But cranking up the volume only makes the static louder.

"We have quite a matchup in store for us today, folks. Burleigh Grimes will take the hill for the Cardinals and George Earnshaw for the Elephants."

As always, Mutt is pulling for the Cardinals, but there is one Philadelphia player he can't help but root for – Mickey Cochrane. The best catcher in the game. Fierce, fiery, irresistible. From humble beginnings. "Just like me," Mutt thinks as he looks at his bare walls.

Cochrane combines his competitive passion with a potent personality. The fifth of seven children of Irish and Scottish immigrants, Cochrane endears himself to those in similar situations during the Great Depression. Mutt imagines himself as another Cochrane. He's 18, fit, and clearly a much faster runner. And he too is certainly from humble beginnings. If Mutt ever had the chance, he could be a Major League catcher in the mold of Cochrane. Well, maybe he could, but it's probably a hollow yearning. Nobody from Major League Baseball ever comes to the tri-county area to scout for prospects. You have to be in the right place at the right time, and Mutt understands he isn't. Still, the hope, as fuzzy as it is, never completely fades.

Mutt leans forward on the edge of a hard chair and, as he usually does when he's nervous, he lights a cigarette, then checks the pack to make sure he has enough to last him through the next two hours. Just enough. But what if the game goes extras?

His father must have some in the house somewhere. He can't see getting through the game without them.

"The big right-hander, 30-year-old Earnshaw, won 22 games for the Athletics during the regular season. Grimes is in his first season with St. Louis after featuring for many years with Brooklyn and the Giants. We'll be back with the first pitch after this message from our sponsor."

Cochrane, as superb as he's been, has never been better than in 1930, batting a career-high .357. He is the team's natural leader, driving and haranguing his teammates.

Mutt has followed the 1930 baseball season closely. Every morning, he scans the box scores with the meticulous attention of a jeweler studying watch components. Then he reads the baseball news of the day. It's about all he ever reads. If there's something about Cochrane, he takes particular note. Every time Cochrane is mentioned, it seems he's referred to as "fiery." Teammate Jimmy Dykes claims that if Cochrane breathed on bread, it would turn into toast. Mutt respects fiery.

It's been a remarkable season—a great respite from the gloom of the developing Depression. The regular season saw an eruption of offense. The batter was king. Men like Babe Ruth, Lou Gehrig, and Jimmy Foxx were the unquestioned titans of the diamond. The St. Louis Cardinals and their gaudy .314 team batting average were the National League champs. Mutt has followed them all the way to the Series.

Their pitching staff has been led all season by "Wild Bill" Hallahan and Burleigh Grimes, the last pitcher officially permitted to throw the spitball. After falling 12 games behind the Cubs in August, the Cardinals went 39-10 down the stretch to win the pennant.

Mutt loves the up-and-down storylines in a 154-game season. Loves stories of the interesting characters who play the game. Characters like pitcher Flint Rhem. In mid-September, the Cardinals found themselves in Brooklyn for a three-game series. Rhem stumbled into his hotel room, red-eyed and hungover. This was his explanation: he had been kidnapped. While minding his own business, he was pushed into a car and driven to a remote area of New Jersey, where he was forced to guzzle Prohibition booze all night. The kidnappers, he explained, were gamblers who didn't want him to pitch against the Dodgers. The very thought of a ballplayer drinking before a game repulses Mutt. Cochrane would never put up with such things. Too bad he isn't playing for St. Louis.

"Settle in folks, this should be a doozy."

Mutt rubs his eyes as if he were watching the game. Watching baseball on the radio. He sees everything. The players. The plays. The flight of the ball against the blue sky.

The game is tense. By the ninth inning, Mutt has gone through the entire pack of Lucky Strike cigarettes. The game is scoreless – a pitching masterpiece. Then, in the top of the ninth, Cochrane gets on by a hard-earned walk.

"With his 37 home runs, Jimmie Foxx steps in. Cochrane leads off first. Grimes eyes him carefully. Cochrane is not what you would call a prolific base stealer, but he does have five on the season."

Mutt thinks if he were on first with his speed, he'd be able to swipe second easily.

"Here's the pitch, and there it goes, deep to left and... gone. A two-run homer."

The Cardinals fail to score in the bottom of the ninth, and that's the game. Philadelphia is one win away from back-to-back championships.

"Damn it all," Mutt mutters as he goes in search of more cigarettes. "Damn it all."

———◦●◦———

For all the passion he shows for baseball, Mutt remains a quiet man. A man without airs. Laconic when it comes to anything other than the game he loves.

As always, the Saturday night dance is crowded, smoky, loud. Mutt isn't much of a dancer. Or a conversationalist. An observer mostly. He'll take a nip of Tennessee whiskey. Or two. Seldom more.

On this night, he's been paying particular attention to one young lady: Lovell Richardson.

He's attracted to her animated personality, her lively disposition, her sardonic sense of humor. Her air of briskness. He likes her bright, clear eyes. The way her hair flies wildly when she dances. She's shorter than Mutt. Her face is rounder. More handsome than beautiful.

Mutt likes the way she can carry a conversation when he gets stuck between thoughts.

The question sounds as simple as he intends it to be.

"You like baseball?" he asks her.

"I guess I do," she replies, airily fanning herself.

Mutt grins and shoves his hands in his pockets.

"Maybe you could come to my game Sunday."

"Sunday?"

"In the afternoon. So, if you go to church—"

"No, I could come anytime, but are you sure you wouldn't rather ask my sister?"

"I'm sure."

"Because she'll be expecting you to."

"The game starts at one," Mutt says with a suggestive wink.

Elven Charles "Mutt" Mantle and Lovell Thelma Richardson Davis seem to have little in common. He is 18; she is 26. He has seldom dated; she is a divorcee with a young son and daughter. He is quiet; she is a hellcat. He is invariably polite; she can be cheeky.

Mutt had been seeing Lovell's 16-year-old sister, Dulsa Annie. Surely, she seems more appropriate for the taciturn man. Mutt's father, Charlie, wonders whether his son is looking for a wife or a mother.

No matter. A mutual interest in baseball is enough. So what if she's divorced? So what if she has a couple of kids? So what if most folks around here see that as offending their religious sensibilities? Mutt doesn't care a whit about religion anyway. Lovell's father may be a deacon in the Methodist church, but she doesn't share his concerns about preparing for the hereafter. So, she's free on Sundays. That's not a bad thing in Mutt's world. She does care about Mutt. He's serious, sober, fit. Nothing like her first husband, Bill Davis. He wasn't any of those things.

Mutt is working on a construction crew, fixing county roads while living with his father. He's sinewy, slim-hipped, and tan, but not sun-weathered. His eyes are dark pools with a glint of light at the bottom (at least that's how Lovell describes them to her sister). His carriage suggests the athlete he is. Suggests the promise of the man he will become.

Mutt and Lovell go on a few dates, squeezed in between work and baseball. He is attentive but not particularly affectionate. It's not in his nature. She doesn't seem to mind.

Then one Sunday, after a game in which he gets three hits including a game-winning double, Mutt is feeling exuberant.

While walking Lovell home, he says, almost casually, "Why don't we get married?"

She stops in her tracks.

"Married?"

"Why not?"

He offers no romantic affirmations, no expressions of love. Mutt is a pragmatist. Romantic whimsies have no place in Depression Oklahoma.

"Made that mistake once," she says.

"I haven't."

"And you don't want to."

"I've got a job. We won't need a place of our own for a while. We could live with my father."

"Do you know how many people are getting laid off these days?"

"I can always get another one."

"That's what everybody thinks, but it ain't happening. Not around here anyways."

Mutt takes her hand. "Come on, it will be fun."

"Fun? That's it?"

"Well, maybe a little more."

"Mutt Mantle, you're hopeless."

"You give me hope."

"You know what people will say. I'm too old for you. I'm too … divorced for you."

"I don't care."

What Lovell doesn't say is that she has had her eyes on Mutt for some time. Had he not proposed, she probably would have.

"I'll have to think about it," she says.

Then, after a pause of no more than two seconds, "OK, I've thought about it."

Mutt stares at her. "And?"

She breaks into a big smile. "I guess I have nothing better to do. So yes, Elven Charles Mantle, I'll marry you."

"Good."

When Mutt tells his father of his marriage plans, Charlie isn't surprised. He knows Lovell has been chasing his son, even if Mutt doesn't.

"Better be good to her," Charlie says. "She's got a couple of big whiskey-running brothers."

"What they say."

Mutt was eight when his mother, Mae, died of pneumonia a month after giving birth to her fifth child. She was 30. Mutt has only a few spotty memories of her. Charlie raised him and his two brothers and sister without remarrying. He did a little tenant farming, but mostly he worked as a part-time butcher to support his family.

And he passed on his love of baseball. He played on local amateur teams during the summers. In winter, he and Mutt would put a ball and their gloves in the oven to warm them up. Then they'd go outside to play catch. Every day, all year long. This was their connection, what they had to share. A willing father and an eager son playing catch.

"There are only two things I know to teach you," he once said to Mutt.

"Treating others with the same respect you'd want from them. Your ma was a good woman. Always tried to do the right thing no matter what it cost her. She'd want me to teach you to do the same. And I can teach you a little about baseball. That's about it. Oh, I guess I could teach you some butchering skills, but I'm not sure you'd want that. Not a lot of call for that these days."

Charlie is a perpetually agreeable man. A gentle man who works hard when he has the work, takes care of his family, stays out of trouble.

"So, I suspect you're gonna want to move in here," he says to Mutt.

"I suspect so."

Lovell's son, Theodore, and daughter, Anna Bea, can stay with their father. For now.

Not much else is said about the pending marriage. Getting married at 18 in these parts isn't unusual; getting married to an older divorcee is. But Charlie figures that if it's what Mutt wants and he is willing to accept the consequences, then it's no bother to him.

Besides, there's not a lot else to look forward to around here, other than raising a family and earning enough to feed and clothe them in a house that doesn't leak and has a good stove in winter. People around here mostly don't have dreams of different and better lives. The future looks mostly like the present. Dusty and poor.

But Mutt does have a dream. Soon he will share it with his bride-to-be.

As is the local custom, the wedding ceremony is small and simple. There are no thoughts of a honeymoon, no thoughts of taking time away from his county job. Mutt lives on his weekly paycheck.

Lovell will move in and begin her expected homemaking duties. She will do the wash and the cooking while the men are off working. This is what wives do. When Mutt gets home, he will always find dinner ready. Every morning he will put on a clean shirt—one with sharply-pressed creases.

There isn't much talk about planning for anything better. This is how it is and will always be. Still, Mutt is concerned about his job. The situation is getting bad. Men are being laid off. Without much tenure on his crew, Mutt knows he could be next. On any morning he might show up for work, just to be told he should go home. He's seen it happen more than once.

"What then?" Lovell asks as she hands him a cup of bean soup.

"Soup's good," he says.

"If you get laid off?"

"Farm, I guess."

"Do you know a landlord? So you could sharecrop, I mean?"

"I'll find someone."

"I know you will because you're a good worker."

"As long as I get Sundays off."

"Naturally."

"There are limits to a man's sacrifices."

Chapter 2

Mutt and the bull-necked man he knows as Ox are sitting on the side of a dusty road. It's their lunch break. Both men are eating bologna sandwiches prepared by their wives.

As usual, the conversation is baseball. Ox is a big first baseman who sometimes plays on the same team as Mutt. For a man his size, he shows little power. When he does get on base, he's such a slow runner that he clogs the bases for faster runners like Mutt.

"Who's the slowest player in the majors?" Mutt asks.

"Easy. Ernie Lombardi. Even slower than me."

"I wonder. Who's the fastest?"

"I dunno. Maybe that guy for Cincinnati."

"Didn't he steal something like 30 bases or something?"

"Swanson."

"That's him."

"I'd say probably Chapman."

"Yeah, you're probably right. Chapman." Mutt chomps down hard on an apple. "Smartest?"

"Moe Berg."

"Biggest drinker?"

"I hear Jimmie Foxx."

"Best nickname?"

"How about Stinky Davis ... or Rocking Chair Johnny Murphy?"

"Twinkletoes Selkirk."

 "Mutt Riddle."

"Careful there."

"How'd you come by it? Your name?" Ox asks as he lights a cigarette.

"Beats me. I've always had it as far as I know. Who's the toughest player?"

"Can't go wrong with Pepper Martin. Or maybe Leo Durocher."

"Yeah, they're both pretty tough, but nobody measures up to Mickey Cochrane," Mutt says, throwing his apple core across the road as if trying to nab a runner at second.

"Could be."

"In my book, anyhows."

"A competitive son of a gun, no doubt about it."

Mutt takes Ox's cigarette to light his own. "You know why he's called Mickey?"

"Yeah, because his parents named him that."

"Except that ain't his name."

"Sure it is."

"It's a nickname. Because he's a mick. See, he's Irish. Or maybe Scottish. I don't know. Anyways, one of them."

"Then what's his real name?"

"Gordon Stanley Cochrane," Mutt says with a little amused smile.

"Gordon?"

"Yep."

"How do you know that?"

"I read it."

"Where? Where'd you read it?"

"Picked up a paper when I was in St. Louis. They had this story about him. Gordon Stanley Cochrane, they said."

"But you gonna name the kid Mickey?"

Mutt shakes his head emphatically. "Yeah."

"You got any Irish blood in you?"

"Not as far as I know."

"Then you'd better call him Gordon."

"He's Mickey. End of discussion."

"How about Gordon Mickey Mantle?"

"Nope. Mickey Charles Mantle. Charles for my father."

"Mickey's a nickname, not a real name."

"It is now."

"Just because he's a catcher—Cochrane."

"He's a catcher, I'm a catcher, my son's going to be a catcher."

A truck rumbles by, throwing up enough dust that both men have to duck their heads to avoid getting it in their eyes.

After waiting a few seconds for the dust to clear, Ox asks, "What if he hates baseball?"

"He won't."

"Or hates being a catcher?"

"He won't."

"How the hell do you know?"

"I won't let him," Mutt says, emphasizing each word.

"You can't make somebody like something they don't."

"Why wouldn't he like baseball? Everybody likes baseball."

"No, everybody don't."

"Well, they damn well oughta."

"Why, because you do?"

"Because it's American."

"So is football. What if he wants to grow up playing football?"

"Baseball. It's a road outta here. Away from the mines, the dust, the …"

"What are you talking about?"

"Professional baseball."

"Oh, so you think not only that he'll have to like baseball because you like baseball, but he'll be good enough to go pro?"

"That's what I think," Mutt says with enough force to show his irritation.

"And make enough money to do what? Buy a pack of Camels?"

"Major League players make plenty. Ruth makes 80 grand a year. That'll buy a lot of smokes."

"Mutt, you're dreaming."

"And that's the dream."

"Do you know what the chances are?"

"Not interested."

"A million to one—maybe. Besides, nobody comes down here looking for baseball players. Miners and farmers maybe. Not baseball players."

"If a boy is good enough, people will know. Teams want good players. If they find them, they'll sign them ... and for good money."

The foreman waves for them to get back to work. They pick up the axes they will be wielding for the rest of the afternoon.

"You used to say you were good enough," Ox says as they walk back to the shallow ditch beside the road they're expected to finish. "What happened?"

"Maybe I didn't have anybody to push me hard enough—or to get me seen."

"Face it, you're a good player, all right. Nobody can deny that. But just maybe you ain't quite good enough for the Cardinals."

"Could be. But what if I would've been ... I don't know what you want to call it ... trained ... brought up to be a better player?"

"How old are you, Mutt?"

"Nineteen."

"You still have time."

"Nope. I'm gonna give Mickey my dream, and I'm gonna give him everything he needs to make it come true. And he's gonna get out of here and have a great life, and maybe get the rest of the family out of here, too."

"For your sake, Mutt, I hope so. But you could be in for a great disappointment."

"We'll see."

"What if it's a girl?"

"Watch your mouth."

The morning of October 20, 1931. Mutt awakes to a faint staccato noise. Little more than a pecking. A bird at the kitchen window.

Still dark. Still early.

He's awake now. Might as well get up. Make coffee.

MUTT'S DREAM: MAKING THE MICK

In the kitchen, he spreads yesterday's paper across the table. The sports section brings welcome news. Frankie Frisch, the Cardinals' second baseman, has been named the National League's Most Valuable Player. Mutt is pleased.

Later in the day, he is at the hospital, where he receives even better news.

"It's a healthy baby boy," the young doctor tells Mutt.

Mutt beams. "I knew it."

"You can go in and see them in a few minutes."

"He's going to be a baseball player, you know, my boy, Mickey. Can you tell if he's left-handed or right-handed?"

The doctor laughs. "It's a little early for that."

—◆●—

Mutt holds a new baseball to his nose. It smells of fresh-cut grass. Powdery resin, maybe. It's perfect. The size it should be. The shape it must be. Made to be thrown.

Mutt cradles it in his strong right hand. The stuff of dreams.

The new ball is slick, its shine yet to be worn off.

Mutt holds the ball up in front of his 12-hour-old baby.

"Here, son. A baseball."

Mickey doesn't open his eyes. Mutt frowns.

Mutt knows the baseball is a perfect object. The size it should be. The shape it must be. Mutt cradles it in his strong left hand. The stuff of dreams.

Within a few days, Mutt begins Mickey's "training."

He has a bag of dime baseballs that he lobs into little Mickey's cradle. They're lighter and smaller than regulation baseballs. The baby pays little attention, but Mutt continues to throw them—albeit softly. Mickey may not see the fun in it, but Mutt sure does.

Eventually, and quite by accident, Mickey actually grabs one of the 10-cent balls and promptly puts it to his mouth. Mutt is so overjoyed that he lets out an uncharacteristic gasp.

"I'll bet Cochrane wasn't half that good at his age."

A rainy winter's afternoon. The worst time of the year. It will be another couple of months before the local baseball teams begin playing again. Mutt knows baseball dies every winter only to be born again in the warming days of spring.

He is standing next to the makeshift crib, looking down at the baby. Imagining what he will become. Then, taking a big step back, he glances over his shoulder to make sure Lovell isn't looking. She's in the next room folding laundry.

The coast is clear, Mutt. Do it.

From his right pants pocket, he takes out a real baseball. Worn, grass-stained. Showing the results of countless bat strikes and errant throws into the baked Oklahoma dirt. But Mutt has had it a long time, and he'll keep it as long as it has life left in it. That's how Mutt sees it. A good baseball has its own life.

He gently lobs the ball into the corner of the crib. It nestles softly into the cottony bedding.

Mutt smiles. No, more than a smile. An all-over glow.

The baby noticed the ball. Mutt is sure of it. He noticed. OK, Mickey didn't change his bewildered expression, but Mutt can tell, like any observant father could, that little Mickey is aware of the ball. Tracked its short flight. Knows it has its own life.

Mutt retrieves the ball, again checks over his shoulder, gently lofts it back into the crib.

"See that, Mickey? That's a baseball. Remember? There is nothing else quite like it in the world. Beautiful, ain't it?"

Again, and again, he sends the ball into the crib.

Mickey doesn't cry. Why would he? He's being shown into one of the great pleasures that the world has waiting for him. A father's introduction to ... a way out.

Mutt whispers, "Someday, Mickey. And it won't be too long either. You'll see."

Then, not so quietly, Lovell's voice: "What the dickens do you think you're doing?"

"Nothing. Just—"

"Are you out of your mind?"

"I ain't gonna—"

"You could really hurt him."

"Hurt him."

She takes the ball like a schoolteacher extracting a dangerous slingshot from a daydreaming student. "Don't you know any better?"

"Apparently not."

When she's gone: "Don't worry, Mickey Charles, I got another one."

Lovell continues to quarantine every ball she can find around the house. Mutt keeps coming up with more.

Although they have little money for "life's extras," Mutt seems always able to get more balls. Lovell won't say anything about it. This is Mutt's dream, after all, and for the sake of their relationship, she knows better than to say anything. But if it's a question of buying milk for the baby or a new baseball, Mutt will opt for the ball, Lovell for the milk.

"You expect him to eat that?" Lovell has been known to ask.

"Maybe," Mutt says without suggesting that he is kidding.

When Lovell is watching, Mutt uses balls of her knitting yarn.

"That's more sensible," Lovell says.

"Except he's gotta learn early not to be afraid of the ball. That's important. Guys who are afraid of the ball, well, they ain't never going to become good players."

"He's gotta learn early?"

"Yeah."

"At six months?"

"Better late than ..."

"You're impossible."

"Here you go, little fella," Mutt says, tossing another yarn ball. "This will do until she's gone. Then we'll get the real ball."

Mutt is becoming a little frustrated. How many times has he lofted the ball in Mickey's direction without the baby tracking it with his eyes? Shouldn't he at least be tracking it with his eyes?

Mutt throws the yarn ball time after time without getting the hoped-for reaction from the baby.

"Maybe something's wrong. He shows more interest in his bottle than the ball," he acknowledges to Lovell between throws.

"Yeah, well he needs the milk to grow, don't he?"

"I guess he does."

"Gotta develop those muscles."

"Except he should at least recognize the ball, shouldn't he? Maybe something's wrong with his eyes."

"Ain't nothing wrong," Charlie assures him. "He's just showing signs of being a slow learner."

"Maybe. Was I a slow learner? When I was his age, did I respond to a ball?"

"Don't think I ever throwed you one at that age."

"How old was I before you did?"

"Throw a ball into your bed? I dunno."

"But I knew early, didn't I?"

"Probably did."

"Maybe if we took the bottle away for, I dunno know, a few hours. Maybe if he got real hungry, he be more likely to pay attention?"

"I don't know about that."

"Here you go, little Mickey," Mutt says as he lofts another yarn ball toward the baby. The ball hits Mickey in the eye, causing him to cry. "Hey, don't cry. Everybody gets hit by the ball once in a while. Best to get used to it now."

The sound of crying brings Lovell into the room. "What are you two geniuses doing to the kid now?"

"Training," Mutt says.

"That's great. Hit him with the ball enough, and he'll hate the sight of one," she says as she picks the baby up and takes him into the kitchen.

"You're right," Mutt says. "Maybe just a slow learner."

"But that don't mean he won't learn," says Charlie.

"Nah, he'll learn."

"You got any real balls hidden?"
"Just one."
"We can use it tomorrow. A real ball's better."
"Better, yeah."

Mickey is one.

The Cardinals-Pirates game is on the radio.

"Pepper Martin settles in. He's two for two today with a double and a single. Bill Swift looks in, gets the signal, and ..."

Static overwhelms the result. Mutt cranks up the volume.

"He slides headfirst into second. It's close, but he's safe. His second double of the game."

"Mutt, for Pete's sake, would you please turn that down," Lovell calls from the kitchen. "Mickey's trying to sleep."

"It's tied in the ninth."

"Babies have to have their sleep."

"Pepper's on second."

"I don't care if he's on the moon."

Mutt turns the sound knob down. Slightly. It doesn't make much difference.

"Why don't you take Mickey outside for a while," he calls. "Babies need sun, don't they?"

"It's 110 degrees. I'm not taking him out," Lovell says as she finishes drying the morning's dishes.

Mutt turns the knob another fraction. Moves closer to the speaker.

Lovell throws a dishtowel at him. He brushes the towel aside with an annoyed swipe.

"Well, folks, it looks like we going to have more baseball to enjoy today. We're heading into extras. Stay with us."

"Don't worry," Mutt mumbles. "I ain't going nowhere."

Two innings later and the game still tied, Mickey wakes up with a piercing wail.

"You woke him," Lovell says as she picks up the crying baby and holds him out to Mutt. "You take care of him."

"I didn't wake him."

"No, but your radio did."

"You got the kid wrong, hon," says Mutt. "I don't blame him for screaming. Mickey ain't sick or hungry. It's just that he knew the situation called for a bunt instead of swinging away, and in my opinion, he's a lot smarter than the manager."

"Here, you rock the little genius back to sleep," she says, plopping the baby onto Mutt's lap.

For the next half-hour, Mutt rocks Mickey back to sleep to the mellifluous baritone play-by-play of France Laux.

"He may be the first baby in history whose first lullaby is a radio broadcast," Lovell says as she sits down to listen to the end of the game.

"It's good for him."

"Says you."

"It's all sinking into his brain as he sleeps. The idea of the game. He's picking up the finer points."

It never occurs to Mutt that Mickey might resent his father forcing the game on him. Mutt is a most uncomplicated man. As he learned to love the game from Charlie, so will Mickey learn to love it from Mutt. Isn't that the way it's supposed to be? Fathers passing on their passions and skills to their sons.

Mutt doesn't have a lot he can teach his son. He's not well-educated, not a musician, not a scientist. He's not good with figures. He can't draw. What he can do is work hard. And he can play baseball. That is what he can pass on. That and being a good man, fair and honest. Those things he will pass on.

That will do it, folks. The Cardinals win it in 13.

Chapter 3

The country is in the Great Depression, brought about by the sharply unequal distribution of wealth, creating an unstable economy and extensive stock market speculation. Or so say the papers. Not many people around here know anything about these things. What stock market crash? They're poor. Always have been. Likely always will be.

What they do know about is the red dirt that blankets everything when the wind blows, and it seems the wind is always blowing. Sometimes, the skies darken for days. Even the best-built homes have thick layers of dust on the floors and furniture. Outside, the dust can drift like snow.

As the winds and drought continue, the ground cover that holds the soil in place is disappearing. Farmers are worried. They plant and plow. Still nothing grows.

It's hard not to see the world as cheerless and drab, spiritually void and forever mired in dusty gloom. A greige world with nothing to suggest coming change. A monochrome that is the absence of color.

To Mutt, and many like him, baseball is the great escape. They call it the national pastime for a reason. It provides diversion, and a summertime remedy to the pervading feeling of hopelessness. It offers hope. Always. No matter how poorly a team or player is playing, there is always hope that in tomorrow's game, things will be better. The team will win. The player will break out of a slump. This is Mutt's faith.

Mutt follows his Cardinals now more than ever. Never misses a day either on the radio or in the papers. They lift his spirits. They win games. They have winning players like Pepper Martin, who came from Oklahoma. Mutt has heard the stories. How he once eluded a patrolman, jumped on a train, and rode as a stowaway to spring training. After a brief stay with the Cardinals in 1928, he was sent back to the minor leagues for most of the next two seasons. But he earned his way back to the big-league club in 1931, when he arrived in Florida and introduced himself as their 27-year-old rookie savior.

As if the team needed one. What a brash kid.

That year the Cardinals won the World Series.

From the moment he stepped off the Hobo Express, Martin proved himself a relentless force on the basepaths, in the field, and at bat. Mutt loves the way he plays. Loves the daring, the cannonball attitude. Loves picturing his headfirst slides. His rascally persona sets the tone for the new breed of Cardinal players who will become known as the Gashouse Gang. Led by their skipper, Gabby Street, the Gang always offers excitement, a whiff of audacity at a time when that is so very welcome. An escape.

Even if he can't be at the park to watch the Cardinals games, Mutt can envision every play as he "watches" on the radio. He can see Pepper slide headfirst into home with the winning run. When he can't listen to the games, he reads the box scores in the morning paper. For those who know how to read them, they tell the complete story of a game. They're little two-by-three-inch boxes of names and numbers buried on an inside page of a local Oklahoma newspaper, but oh the stories they tell to those with imagination and baseball acumen. Mutt has both.

When he's listening to games, Lovell often joins him. She doesn't share her husband's level of passion and commitment, but she's perceptive; the more she listens, the more she begins to appreciate the finer points of baseball strategy. Sometimes she picks up on small things Mutt doesn't. Because he is so emotionally involved, Mutt can't analyze the game as impartially as Lovell.

Mutt loves that she loves what he loves.

MUTT'S DREAM: MAKING THE MICK

Mutt is unsure how much longer he can hang on to his job with the county. If he does lose it, his only recourse is farming, but farmers aren't faring much better.

Everyone seems to be concerned about jobs. Mutt even reads about a special three-team benefit series to aid the unemployed. The Brooklyn Robins (later Dodgers), the New York Yankees, and the New York Giants played a round-robin competition.

The paper reports: *It was a superb show, taken in the right spirit and taken in the right way. Two games, an attractive series of athletic events, music by three bands, a homer by Lou Gehrig, superb weather, and unexampled personal appearances by the headmen of the town. What more could a baseball fan want? And what better way to raise funds for those who need aid?*

In addition to the games, they held several field events for players. Lefty O'Doul, a Robin outfielder, proved best at bunting and running to first base. His time was 3.3 seconds. Ethan Allen of the Giants was fastest circling the bases—13.8 seconds. The Yankees' Ben Chapman threw the ball the farthest—392 feet. Babe Ruth of the Yankees hit a fungo 421 feet, 8 inches.

Mutt notes the times and distances with the meticulous detail of a watchmaker. He records them in a little notebook, so they won't be forgotten. A truly skillful player might be able to achieve all three elements—the speed, the arm, the power—if he trained for all three. Really trained for a long time. If there were a plan and an unrelenting commitment, it might just be possible. What an accomplishment that would be—a player who could run like O'Doul, throw like Chapman, hit like Ruth. A unique player.

Is Mickey able to swing a bat and connect with a thrown ball earlier than most boys? Mutt can't say for sure, but he thinks so. It's a habit, and habits can be learned early, can't they? Repetition, that's the key.

Mutt has the patience to lob the ball toward Mickey for hours. Not surprisingly, Mickey's patience is considerably more limited.

His attention easily wanders.

"That's natural," Charlie assures Mutt. "Kids, they don't have the same attention as we do."

"He'll develop that."

Mutt lofts the ball toward Mickey, who stands with a little bat in his hands. He doesn't move.

"You got to swing the bat, son. Like I showed you."

Mickey grips the bat tighter. Mutt throws the ball underhand in his direction. Mickey swings well after the ball has passed him.

Mutt smiles. "That's it," he says. "Good job."

"Yeah," Charlie says. "Good job."

Mutt throws a few more with the same results. With each successive throw, little Mickey loses more interest.

If Mutt is exacting an emotional and physical toll on his young son, he doesn't notice. It's not something he thinks about now. Nor will he ever. Of course Mickey will want to become a great athlete. Why wouldn't he? Mutt would. If the boy can use that to get away from the trap of a dispirited culture, it will be worth it. He'll thank his dad someday.

But what if Mickey doesn't have the talent?

Mutt is an athlete, and to a lesser extent, so is Lovell. In high school, she was a good runner, a sprinter. She says she never lost a race. Grandpa Charlie is a decent baseball player. Athletic ability is in the family. There's no doubt about that.

What if Mickey doesn't have the desire?

When he's old enough to understand what eking out a living in this part of the world is like, what having nothing else to look forward to is like, then he'll appreciate what his dad did for him. The desire will follow naturally.

What if it's not in his nature?

Mutt doesn't even entertain the thought. His obsession trumps all.

The odds against any young boy growing up to become a professional athlete are astronomical. If pressed, Mutt would agree, but don't all great things come from overcoming great odds?

MUTT'S DREAM: MAKING THE MICK

It never occurs to Mutt that perhaps he's doing psychological harm to his son, although others will claim so. Helping the boy to become good at something like baseball isn't harmful. Trying to earn a decent living in these conditions is.

"Come on, Mickey, pay attention now. We're not going in for dinner until you hit at least two in a row."

Lovell sticks her head out the kitchen window. "Mutt, he's two years old."

"Yeah, and next year he'll be three. "Keep your eye on the ball, son."

―――●●―――

Mutt has had a long day under the punishing August sun. Part of a crew working on a long, flat stretch of a county road south of Commerce. They've been out there all week patching holes, cleaning up the shoulders, clearing debris. With his shift almost over, all he is thinking about is getting home, taking a shower, and playing with little Mickey. It's what he thinks about as the end of every shift nears.

Mutt is still adjusting his eyes to the bright Oklahoma sun when Bixby, his shift foreman, hands him the envelope he has dreaded seeing but always expected.

"Sorry, Mutt," Bixby says. "You know how it is."

"Yeah."

"I wanted to keep you on. You're a good worker. I argued for you, but you know how it is."

"I know how it is."

"Maybe in a couple of months …"

"Yeah."

Mutt has seen some men become agitated when they got the ax, but he figures there's not much point. For all the spirit he shows while playing and watching baseball, he remains at heart a placid man.

"You can pick up your last pay any time after Monday. Check back, from time to time," Bixby says.

Mutt nods and heads home.

He doesn't have to tell Lovell. She can see it in his face.

"I guess we shouldn't be surprised," she says.

"Only a matter of time," he says as he pulls off his work boots and tosses them across the kitchen.

"So ..."

"See if I can hook up on a farm."

"Farming, yeah."

"Can't be worse than working on the roads."

"Better. I'd say better."

"If I can grade a road, I can sure as hell push a plow."

"The mines ..."

"No. Anything would be better."

"Yeah."

"Because being stuck every day down there in the dark, I don't know if I could do that."

Mutt picks up Mickey, who has been crawling on the floor. "Just gives me more time to play baseball and to play with you, being out of work and all. If I can get a job as a farmer, maybe you could learn to ride a horse. What do you think of that?"

Mutt, Lovell, and Mickey are living in Spavinaw, Oklahoma, a town of about 200 in the flatlands at the heart of Cherokee Indian country, about 35 miles southwest of Commerce. This is the hub of the tri-county mining district. The borders of Arkansas and Kansas are only a few miles away.

Theirs is a two-room, unpainted house sitting atop a little hill on the north edge of town. No street leads to it. At the bottom of the hill, a narrow dirt road winds past fields of withering wheat and corn.

Not far away is Route 66. Route 66 leads to California. California leads to ... a better life. At least that's what some folks around here say. Mutt is not so sure.

"The McMurtrys went last week. Did you know that?" Lovell asks late one night when the blistering temperature refuses to give in. They are sitting on the ground in front of their house.

"Not surprised. He's talked about it. Teddy said something about it a while back."

"Hard to make it as a sharecropper these days."

"Sometimes, yeah."

"Most times, I'd say."

This is not the first time they have thought or talked about this. So many folks are packing it up and heading west. They call them Okies. It is not a term of endearment. The widespread feeling is that California is a promised land. The weather is better. The farm fields of the Central Valley are more bountiful. Still, the effects of the burgeoning Depression are not unknown to Californians either.

Mutt lights a cigarette as he looks to the starry night sky in the west.

"I dunno about it," he says. "A whole bunch of people have come back, too."

"Some," says Lovell. "We need to think about it."

"Mostly they had relatives already there. We sure as hell don't."

"But look around. It's got to be better than what's facing us."

"Maybe. Maybe not. Anyway, even if we did decide to go, how would we get there? Walk?"

"I'm just saying we should think about it, that's all."

"Everything we know is here. Everybody we know is here—our folks, our friends. I don't know how we'd get by."

"We'd figure it out. They play baseball in California, don't they?"

"I imagine."

"You'd make friends playing ball. You always do."

"I don't know."

The local economy has hit rock bottom. The question on everyone's mind: Will it ever get better? Nobody has the answers.

Unemployment is so pervasive that tent cities are springing up for those unable to afford proper housing. Shacks and caves have people living in them, too. A few local restaurants are handing out table scraps. Hospitals are operating soup lines.

Tenant farming looks to be the only way to keep an income, but that too is tenuous. Tenant farmers make up the majority of the farming community, but the drought is making it more and more difficult for farmers to show a profit. The governor has approved distributing free seeds to farmers. But with no water, that's not proving to be a solution. With the situation becoming more dire all the time, the governor finally proclaims martial law to halt the rise of farm foreclosures, and suspends oil production to boost petroleum prices.

Nothing seems to help much.

Despite the deteriorating conditions, Mutt manages to get work as a tenant farmer. He will have 80 acres to plow and farm. Whatever he manages to grow, he will turn over to the landlord, who will then see what he can get by selling the crops. Any profits will be split with Mutt.

Mutt doesn't mind the work. It's better than fixing roads. He's up early every morning and comes home for lunch, which Lovell always has waiting, then returns to his fields. Sometimes Lovell goes with him to help while Charlie stays home with Mickey.

There are some advantages to farm work. He sets his own hours, doesn't have to worry about a bellicose foreman. He can play baseball on his own schedule. He has time to be with his young son.

As is the custom, Mutt's tenancy arrangement with the landlord is an oral contract for one year only. To thwart the development of an established tenantry, most landlords encourage their tenants to move on after one year. Because there is a constant surplus of tenants, at the end of each crop year landlords can easily take on new men willing to work their land.

Mutt's landlord, as is generally the case, provides nothing but the land. Poor land. Eroded and exhausted land. Mutt is struggling to produce enough to survive. Like all the sharecroppers, he is at the mercy of the tri-county's drought, insects, high winds, frost, hail, and plant disease.

Lovell is bundled up against the spring chill that doesn't seem to be showing any signs of letting up. Carrying a jar of water she has brought for Mutt, she walks out across the dusty field that should be greener by now. Despite the bite in the late afternoon air, Mutt is sweating profusely.

Lovell can see the effort her husband is putting in with so little to show for it.

"Ain't looking good, is it?" Lovell says, stating the obvious.

"A little early to say, but no, probably not."

Mutt sits while he guzzles the water. Lovell sits next to him.

"I'm going to talk to him," Lovell says, referring to the landlord.

"No, don't."

"Eighty acres is more than any one man can handle with so little—"

"He don't care. None of them do. Maybe with spring rain … who knows?"

She looks up into the cloudless sky. "Rain?"

"We'll see."

"He could at least make you a share tenant."

"Yeah."

They know about the tenancy ladder. A sharecropper on the bottom rung like Mutt could climb to become a share tenant. They keep two-thirds or even three-fourths of the crop, depending on how much they can furnish. If a share tenant can produce bumper crops, he can move up another rung and become a cash tenant, who pays a fixed rent and keeps all the proceeds from the crop. But to move up at all requires that the sharecropper accumulate his own equipment and money for seeds and other expenses. Mutt doesn't have it.

Mutt can work toward getting his young family into a better situation. He can hope and dream of becoming a successful cash tenant, or maybe, if nature gives them a break, he could even save enough to buy his own small farm. But he doesn't hope or dream any of those things. He dreams of training Mickey to become a baseball player.

Lovell wonders if that's part of what's holding them back. Maybe without the passion to succeed at something, success will always be elusive. And Mutt, although he works hard at farming, clearly doesn't have that. He likes the work well enough. He likes physical exertion, likes being outside. But "likes" may not be enough.

"I'm going to talk to him," Lovell says, again referring to the landlord.

"You can't do that, hon."

"Why, because you're too proud?"

"It's not the way it works."

"Well, it should."

Being so assertive is not in Mutt's makeup; it is in hers.

She gets up, takes the empty jar. "When are you coming home? Not after dark again, I hope."

"I dunno. Couple of hours, I guess." As she turns to walk away, he adds, "Don't do anything to embarrass me."

Dinner is soup made with scraps from the week's meals. There's some bread to sop it up. It's not much, but it will have to do. Mickey gets all he can eat; Mutt, Lovell, and Charlie settle for less. They're not starving, but each week it seems as if the portions are diminishing. There is a limit that is understood if not acknowledged.

After dinner Mutt throws tennis balls to Mickey, most of which go uncaught, but not all. Mutt can see the improvement.

"I caught it," Mickey says after each successful catch.

"Yes, you did. Very good."

Mickey is learning.

Mutt lays out a baseball infield on the floor, using a salt shaker for home, a pepper shaker for the pitcher's mound, and cutout squares of cardboard for the bases. "What is this?" he asks, putting his finger on the pepper shaker.

"Catcher," Mickey says, proudly.

"No, that's the pitcher," Mutt says. "Remember, he's the one who throws the ball to the batter."

"Yeah."

Pointing to the catcher's position. "What's this?"

"Catcher."

"That's right. That's what your daddy is. I'm a catcher. Someday you'll be a catcher, too."

"You trying to turn him into a salt shaker?" Lovell quips.

"Isn't that what every father hopes for his son?"

"This is great," says Lovell with a forced smile. "He doesn't have a clue about his ABCs, but he knows the positions on the baseball field."

"Important things first."

"Only you would say that."

"And I did."

"What else is on your 'important' list?"

"Listen to me now, Mickey. George Washington was the first president. Know why? Because he could throw. There's a lesson for you."

"What are you talking about?" Lovell asks.

"He threw a dollar across the Potomac or something. I think it was a curve."

"And he chopped down a cherry tree. What does that tell you, he had a good swing?"

"Absolutely."

"The twisted education of Mickey Charles Mantle."

Chapter 4

Mickey is turning three.

Mutt figures it's time for him to be completely outfitted in a baseball uniform made from genuine baseball material. Of course, there's no money to buy a real uniform, so Mutt sacrifices one of his.

Lovell agrees to cut it up and fashion a little uniform for Mickey. She'll sew it together, allowing extra room in the seat for the diapers that Mickey still wears because of his bed-wetting habit.

"You mean sliding pads," says Mutt.

"Yeah, sliding pads with safety pins."

It takes her several hours to fashion the "uniform."

"What do you think, Mickey?" she asks.

"Good," he says.

"Try it on, so your father can see it when he gets home."

When Mutt walks in that evening and sees Mickey in that uniform, he breaks into an amused smile. So do Mickey and Lovell.

It's a little moment of pure joy at a time when there are few such moments for the struggling Mantles.

The temperature has soared above 100 degrees for 35 consecutive days. Yesterday, it reached 117. No rain in sight. On the skin the ever-present dust feels like a file with a grit strong enough to sting.

Mutt rubs Vaseline in his nostrils as a filter. The damn wind.

The plow he is pushing is heavy in the parched earth devoid of soft topsoil. If nothing else, it's strengthening his arms, legs, and shoulders. Never a bad thing for a catcher. But as he looks out over the field he has been working for months, he sees little growing. It's dispiriting. He sinks to his knees.

He can't put in more effort than he has been. He's already working at his full powers. Lovell is doing a great job stretching what they have to the maximum. But Mickey can't grow up to become a proper athlete without enough food to build his muscles.

If he can't make this work, then what? California? He can't see himself leaving the only part of the country he has known. Starting over in a strange place, working with strangers? And maybe that won't work out either, and they'll be stranded in California, even worse off than they are now.

He is losing sleep.

The only other possibility is something he has been dreading. The mines.

Mickey is four.

The Mantles move to Quincy Street in Commerce, where Mutt has resolved to look for a job in the mines. He feels like it's a defeat but insists they'll come back in the next inning (his words).

The house is like all the others in the area: a small sand-scarred dwelling. Barely more than a shack, really. There are blocks and blocks of them, all with patched roofs and raggedy weeds in the front yards that remind the locals where they are. The Mantle house is some 100 yards off the main road at the end of a gravel track. It has two small bedrooms, a basic kitchen, a postage-sized front porch. It is unpainted and unheated. In the winter, the north wind will come howling across the plains and whistle through cracks in the walls.

A wooden garage held together by rusty sheet metal panels stands away from the house. If they had a car, it would barely cover it. But Mutt, as soon as he spots it, doesn't see a garage. He sees a baseball backstop. He sees Mickey standing in front of it, swinging at pitches, sending the ball soaring over the roof of the house, raising his arms in triumph. What a blast! That Mickey Mantle, he sure can hit them like nobody else.

Charlie moves in with them. The house is already crowded, and they are expecting additions to the family in the not-too-distant future. They'll just have to make do.

Commerce is a town of almost 2,000 people with a seven-block-long main street. Some people call it North Miami because it is only four miles from Miami, a considerably larger town. This is Ottawa County, once part of the Quapaw Indian land. The Quapaws had resided for hundreds of years in the territory that became Arkansas. Then, after being removed by the federal government, they settled in Oklahoma.

In the early years of the century, immigrants arrived in the area around Commerce and began mining. They built a railway line between Miami and Commerce to serve the mining industry. With it came thousands of men willing to work underground for a living wage.

It is an insular world, homogeneous as many parts around here are. The indigenous population is Native American, although that is not what the locals call them. After dark, blacks are not welcome on the streets—an informal policy enforced by the police and sheriff's deputies. If there are Jews among them, no one admits it.

The Sahara-like panorama of the area around the town is dotted with hundreds of mammoth spent chat piles—fragments of siliceous rock, limestone, and dolomite waste from the lead-zinc mines. Some more than 100 feet high. Thousands of acres of dust and chat and entrances to shafts leading to the stygian depths laced with lead and zinc. It is a dusty, thirsty part of the world, catacombed with tunnels below and canopied by leaden skies above.

This is zinc country, lead country—a place full of holes, smokestacks, trucks trundling back and forth across dusty roads, and spindly trees standing next to chat piles like skeleton hands reaching up from the underworld.

Mutt and Lovell don't talk about it, but they know. Everyone around here does. Working in the mines is dangerous. Deadly dangerous. Nary a day goes by when they don't hear the whining siren of the little white ambulance. People hold their breath. Particularly the wives. They listen, trying to determine if the "death wagon" is coming toward them or going away.

The local paper carries names of the dead. Lovell will soon be checking the list regularly.

The Blue Goose Mine, the biggest in the area, has had its share of injuries and deaths. More than its share. Many families have moved here seeking a better life by working in the mines, only to have the mines kill them.

Still, the area is booming with a growing population, almost all of whom owe their livelihoods to zinc. It is the most productive lead-zinc mining field in the country, producing more than 50 percent of the lead and zinc used during World War I.

The lead, when smelted, is used for plumbing pipes and various containers. In paint and as bullets and shot. The zinc goes to making galvanized wire and sheet iron for roofing and stoves. In dyes and fireworks.

If hired, Mutt will be one of almost 10,000 men making a living in the mines. All American-born. All white. Almost all raised on area farms. Despite the collapses, explosions, accidents, stale and dusty air, polluted water, and diseases, they will spend most of each day deep in the underground. And they will do it for relatively low wages. But the wages are steady and more reliable than trying to eke out a living by farming the dry, parched land.

Mutt climbs to the top of the highest chat pile in the area. A 20-story behemoth built from more than 13 million tons of chat. From the top, no matter in which direction he looks, he sees wisps of smoke, trains crisscrossing a maze of tracks, trucks, horses, and wagons. He sees a veritable land of machines, small and large. Unadorned buildings with people constantly shuttling between them. And this is all he sees.

MUTT'S DREAM: MAKING THE MICK

There is never any serious thought of the dangerous chemicals that hide in the waste. At least these monstrous piles offer some protection from the tornadoes that return to Oklahoma each spring.

Dust is everywhere. It hangs heavy in the air. It covers metal rooftops, and settles on parched fields and baked roads.

Millions of tons of ore have already been brought to the surface; millions more are waiting. What will happen when the ore eventually runs out? No one is thinking about this now. Just so long as there is wealth to be extracted, the Eagle-Picher Lead and Zinc Mining Company will send down men who are willing to bring it out, and there are many who are. What else can they do in this otherwise empty land?

This is Dust Bowl Oklahoma, a colorless world, a world punctuated by piles of chat. The "Chatanagey" Mountains.

The little office is crammed with parts. Probably pump parts, Mutt thinks. A little man with mousy hair sits behind a wooden desk, the most dominant feature of which is a big scrap metal iron ashtray overflowing with ash and butts.

Without looking up, the man takes a sheet of paper from a stack of similar papers. "Name?"

Mutt picks uneasily at a stain on his shirt sleeve. "Mutt Mantle."

"Name?"

"Mutt Mantle."

"That ain't a name. Mutt."

"Elven Mantle."

"Age?"

"Twenty-two."

"Negro?"

"What?"

"You ain't colored, are you?"

"Do I look like it?"

"I dunno. Does it look like I'm looking at you?"

"No, I'm not colored."

"Foreigner?"

"Well, we come from Missouri down to …"

"All I need to know if you're an American. Gotta be American to work here."

"Yeah, I am."

He pushes the paper across the desk. "Sign here. You can sign, right? You can write?"

Mutt signs. "Yeah."

"You're hired."

"That's it?"

"What do you want, a congressional investigation?"

"When do I start?"

"How long will it take to get your ass over to the Blue Goose?"

"I don't know what the …"

"It's a mine. You're a miner. Go see George when you get there."

"How will he know I'm hired?"

"You got two feet, two arms. He'll know. Next!"

That evening, when Mutt walks in the door, he startles Lovell. "You must be in the wrong house. We don't have any darkies here."

"Not funny."

"You're as black as the ace of spades."

"But I have a paycheck. Or I will have a paycheck."

"How much?"

"The paycheck?"

"Yeah."

"I dunno. I didn't ask."

"Don't you think that might have been a good thing to know?"

"A dollar a week would be more than I was making on the farm."

"You on every day regular?"

"Didn't say I wasn't."

"What did they have you doing?"

"Mining."

"I figured that."

Mutt pulls his shirt off. "Shoveling."
"All day?"
"All day."
"You must be exhausted."
"Not too beat to throw to Mickey."
"Well, wash your face first, or you'll scare the hell out of him."
"Mickey don't scare."
"Wash."
"Oh, and they have a baseball team—the Blue Goose Mine. Plays the other mines in the area."
"Goody."

As Mutt comes to learn, the Eagle-Picher Lead and Zinc Mining Company has mines in every corner of the Tri-State district. An oft-repeated claim is that you could go 20 miles underground from where the Mantles live all the way to Joplin, Missouri, without ever seeing the sky.

Miners ride the great hooks into the mines. Day and night, they use heavy picks to chop away at the rock walls. A constant staccato echoes down the endless dark corridors. And always, rock dust hangs heavy in the choking air. The deadly rock dust.

Mutt begins as a shoveler. He scoops up the rocks broken by the screen apes with 16-pound sledgehammers, and puts up to 300 pounds of them in cans to be hauled away by mules pulling them along tracks. The cans are eventually chain-hoisted to the surface. At the end of each shift, he rides a can to the surface, his eyes blinking at the glaring light. It takes several minutes before they adjust to sunlight.

Mutt works the mines six days a week, shoveling hard, breathing hard, sucking the fine dust into his lungs.

"That can't be good, the dust," Lovell says.
"Comes with the job."
"Don't they have jobs up top? In the air."
"Dusty up here too."
"And what happens if you get sick from that? The dust."

"You get fired."

"That ain't right."

"It's how it is."

Mutt is even more eager now to give Mickey the skills he can use to avoid ever having to ride the hook into a hole.

He begins a tradition he will continue for many years. Every day after work, he will pitch to Mickey against their garage/backstop. Every day. It's the repetition that will lead to positive results. Sure, there will be days Mickey won't want to practice. Maybe lots of them, but Mutt is determined that there can't be any break in the daily practice routine. Not ever, because just as soon as that happens, it will always be in the boy's mind. No, Mickey must understand that every day he will practice regardless of how he feels. Don't let him think there is even the remotest possibility of skipping a day. Someday Mickey will thank him.

Mutt's obsession with teaching Mickey baseball is clear and constant. Like a steady flame.

If Mutt hasn't come to this understanding before, he certainly does now. He will go down 300 feet into the ground most days for the rest of his working life. There isn't much else. He will try to do the best he can. He always does. It's what he must do; it's all he can do. He will never make a lot of money. He understands that.

In this world, the future is the mines if you're lucky enough. If you want or need more, well, that just makes you a hopeless dreamer. Mutt's dream will always be about Mickey, not a better life for himself. That is not in his future.

Mickey can escape the cycle in which Mutt finds himself, a poverty-stricken existence chained to farms or mines. For boys in this part of Depression America, there are only two realistic routes out: baseball or boxing. For some, it might be college, but the Mantles have no experience with or interest in higher education.

Mutt has a brother who has flashed some pugilistic abilities: Eugene, better known as "Tunney," after world heavyweight champion Gene Tunney. According to a story that everyone in the family knows how to tell, he once put out a man's eye. It seems Tunney and Mutt found themselves in a situation where they were outnumbered by a belligerent group. In defense Tunney struck one of his assailants, causing him to lose the eye. That's the story.

It often goes unmentioned that Tunney hit him with a shovel, not his fists. Nevertheless, he would always boast he never lost a fight, including that one.

Family fisticuff experiences notwithstanding, Mutt wouldn't know how to teach Mickey to box. He does know how to teach him to play baseball.

As they are gathering up their gear to head out to the garage to do some hitting, Mickey asks, "What's it like down in the mines?"

Mutt is going to make it sound as bad as he possibly can, although there is not much exaggeration in what he has to say. "You'd hate it. It's dark and dirty and hot and real loud all the time. You get so sweaty, you can hardly get enough to drink. Your clothes stick to you. You're breathing in dust with every breath you take. Men are always coughing and spitting out the black soot that's coating their lungs. And it's dangerous. Many men get hurt. It's a terrible, terrible place. You never want to go down there."

"Then why do you do it?"

"So that we have enough to buy groceries and pay the rent on the house."

"But Grandpa doesn't."

"No, but we all help out the best we can. Even Grandpa. Now go get in position. And be ready. Always be ready for the ball."

"Can I go down with you sometime?"

"You wouldn't like it. Now get up there and hold the bat like I told you."

Chapter 5

Water and ice are regularly delivered to the Mantle house by a truck that serves all the houses in the area without running water. On the bed of the truck a tank sits on two beams that stick out beyond the rear of the vehicle.

Mickey squats outside the house. Mutt is at work. In the backyard, Lovell is hanging wash. Mickey watches the truck come up the road, stopping at each house as the grumpy, bearded driver makes his deliveries. When he gets in front of the Mantles', he fills a bucket from the tank and carries it to the house.

"Hey, kid," he says. "Thirsty, are you?"

"No."

Climbing back onto his truck, he says, "Gonna be hot. You'll want water."

As he starts to drive off, Mickey slips behind the truck. He jumps up, holds on to one of the rails, and goes for a ride. In half a block, he loses his grip and drops off, letting out a yelp as he hits the road.

Lovell, hearing this, comes running out from behind the house. "Mickey Charles Mantle, what in the world do you think you're doing?"

She lifts him up. He has a few scrapes on his arms and legs, but otherwise doesn't appear to be injured.

"Wait till your father hears about this, young man! How stupid can you be? You could get seriously hurt with a stunt like that. You could get killed."

"Don't tell him, please."

"Of course I'll tell him!"

When Mutt hears of his son's water truck ride, he positively shakes with anger. Looking around the yard, the only thing he can find is a length of baling wire, which he immediately and forcefully takes to Mickey's rear end. "If I ever catch you doing something so stupid again, there ain't gonna be enough bailing wire in the state to teach you better."

Mickey, who is already developing a pronounced stubborn streak, does everything he can to avoid crying, with only sniveling success.

"Go to your room. Now!" Mutt shouts.

It's the first time Mickey has to be punished. It won't be the last.

———•———

Mutt has always favored catching because he sees the position as being in the center of everything – the most important man on the field. From his squatting position behind the plate, the catcher scans the entire field. He tells the pitcher what kind of pitch he wants, he calls out to infielders to tell them who should take a high popup when two or more are coming together, he signals to everyone how many outs there are. And he must be tough. Tipped fast pitches will come back and nail him; all manner of wild pitches will carom and strike him. Black and blue marks, broken fingers, and sore knees from constant squatting come with the position. Battering and bruising are to be expected. Only hard men put on the catching gear. Mutt is a hard man.

Catchers also need to be among the most skillful players. They must have lightning-fast reflexes, great hands, a powerful and accurate throwing arm. Few players can claim such a troika of skills. Mutt has them, and he is determined Mickey will learn them.

"Now, you watch me today," Mutt says to Mickey as they are getting ready to leave for Mutt's game.

Mutt will be catching for the Spavinaw team against a group of miners from Grove.

During the game, Lovell sits on the ground behind home plate, doing her best to corral her roving son.

Mutt becomes annoyed when it appears that Mickey isn't paying as much attention to the game as Mutt thinks he should. When he hits a long drive down the left field line, the ball rolls so far on the hard dirt that Mutt makes it all the way to third—then decides he'll try for home. As he runs, he looks up to see if Mickey is watching his speedy father make the game-winning dash. He is. Mutt slides hard into the Grove catcher, sending him sprawling backwards.

Mutt pops up, thrilled that his son has seen what kind of intrepid ballplayer his father is. That's how you play the game, Son. That's how Mickey Cochrane and your father play the game. That's how you'll play.

"Well, well, what have we here?" Lovell asks as she spreads the morning paper across the table. "Looks like Commerce has hit the big time."

Mutt seldom gets past the sports page. "How's that?" he asks.

"We've been visited by celebrities."

"Why? They get lost?"

"Bonnie and Clyde."

"In town?"

"Yep."

"Rob the grocery store or something?"

"Says they crossed the Red River from Arkansas and got stuck in the mud."

Lovell reads: "Convinced that Clyde Barrow, fugitive killer, and his companions will seek to backtrack into this area under cover of darkness, scores of officers guarded highways and bridge heads near here Friday night. Officers are determined to halt, once and for all, the ruthless and brutal slayings of the Barrow Gang. From four states came operatives of the Federal Department of Justice who took up posts assigned to them. Barrow and his cigar-smoking woman, Bonnie Parker, have friends in the vicinity."

Lovell looks up from the paper. "Now, who do you suppose that could be?"

"Maybe your sister?"

"Not likely."

Lovell goes back to the paper. "Sheriff Watters expressed his hope and his conviction that the trio, who killed another peace officer Friday morning, will come back during the night. 'If they do, we'll be ready for them,' said Waters.

"Cal Campbell, 60-year-old constable, and Police Chief Percy Boyd met the fugitives at a mudhole where their car was stuck. Campbell died emptying his pistol at the outlaws, who cut him down with machine gun bullets. Boyd was wounded, bullets striking his face and shoulder, and then was forced into the outlaws' car and taken for a ride to an undetermined fate. They are believed to still be in the area."

"I don't know what they'd want to hang around here for, anyway," Mutt says. "There ain't enough money in these parts to pay for their bullets."

"The paper lists twelve people they say they've murdered."

Mickey, who had listened to his mother read the story, asks, "Are you going to get murdered, Daddy?"

"Nah, don't worry, we're safe here."

Still, Mickey is scared. He stays awake most of the night, insisting he is not scared. He doesn't want to think about living without his father, so he forces himself to think about something else. Anything else. When concern edges into his mind, he sings a little song in his head—over and over. He cannot now, nor will he ever, be comfortable handling what he perceives as threats. All his life, Mickey will be a self-protectionist, and his protection will generally take the forms of flight or disavowal. Working underground in this part of the world will always mean danger. How many men down there are killed or seriously injured every year? Nobody knows, or at least nobody is saying. So many daddies are lost to their sons. Young Mickey is forever anxious.

More times than he cares to remember, Mutt is called during the night to go back down the mine to rescue trapped miners. Once, he is called to go down to fight a raging fire.

Lovell can sense the angst in her son. She knows enough to take it seriously, so she responds to Mickey in a calm and reassuring way. Despite his young age, she affirms the hard reality. No sugar-coating here. She talks to him about how everything and everyone will die someday. Unfortunately, she uses the term "going to sleep" for dying. Perhaps this is the cause of Mickey's sleep problems. And his bed-wetting, too.

Mickey can see that so many of the men in the area die young. They die from mining accidents. From breathing the foul air. Many from lung cancer.

When Mickey asks what happens when someone dies, Lovell responds as positively as possible without getting mystical. She doesn't want to fill his head with ideas of ghosts or the belief that parents die because they have chosen to go off to a better place and leave their children behind. She talks to him about the ways people live in others' memories. There are no religious messages here. She prefers to think she is explaining reality, not make-believe.

Despite Lovell's best intentions, the idea of death is never far from Mickey's mind. He wishes his father could be anything but a miner. He knows it's killing him, and that one day, maybe soon, he will be gone. Mutt is underground eight hours a day. Every time he takes a breath, the dust and dampness enter his lungs. At night, he coughs up gobs of phlegm. Mickey thinks he should see a doctor. Mutt shrugs off the idea. What for? He'd only be told it's miner's disease – which is what everybody calls it – although the proper medical term is silicosis caused by the inhalation of crystalline silica dust.

His likely fate is cancer or tuberculosis. Many local men die before reaching 40.

"What the hell, live while you can," Mutt would say as he lit another cigarette.

Most men in the Mantle family had died young. Mickey is convinced he will, too. This is a lingering thought that will always haunt him.

One night, when his parents think he is asleep, Mickey overhears their conversation.

"You know Ted, don't you?" Mutt asks. "Ted Burgess?"

"I remember he came to pick you up once to go fishing or

something," Lovell says.

"He's real sick. Coughing all the time."

"Who isn't?"

"Except his skin's turning blue, and he's feverish. You know what that means. The docs will check him out, and if they find spots on his lungs, they'll hand him a check and send him on his way."

"Mutt, I can't stand it. You guys give your lives to the company—literally—and then they buy you off."

Mutt stares out the window for a long time before replying. "If you can hit a curve ball …"

Lovell has a present for her husband. While in town, she picked up a copy of *Time Magazine*. The entire cover is a photo of Mickey Cochrane in his catching gear. He's in a partial squat, his right hand held to his side in a fist. His left hand holds a big, padded catcher's mitt. He peers straight ahead through the bars of his mask, and looks as if he is on the brink of breaking into a smile.

Mutt loves the present.

"Look at this, Mickey," he says. "The great man on the cover of a magazine that usually has pictures of presidents and popes and, you know, real important people, and here he is, a baseball catcher. That just goes to show you what can happen if you work hard enough at it. You could be on a magazine like that someday in your catcher's gear. What do you think of that?"

"Then I'd be famous, too."

"Just like your namesake."

Mickey puts the magazine in his dresser drawer. Some things are just too valuable to leave around the house.

Late at night under a full moon, Mutt sits on the front steps. He has brought home a broken bat from one of his games. Using a whetstone, he carefully sharpens Lovell's big kitchen knife. Then, with the care of a skilled artisan, he goes to work on the bat. He takes inches off the barrel, shaping the handle to make it Mickey-sized. He is at it for several hours, and although he must go down into the mining hole at the soon-to-arrive daybreak, he doesn't mind. This brings him great pleasure.

When he returns from work this day, he presents the bat to Mickey. "What do you think?" Mutt asks.

Mickey takes it and strikes a hitting pose. "It's just like yours."

"It is mine. I made it so it would be the right size for you."

"Thanks."

"So, today is a big day. Wanna know why?"

"Why?"

"Grandpa Charlie and me, we're gonna start a new game with you."

"What game?"

"You'll see. Now come on with me."

They go into the backyard, where Charlie is waiting.

Mutt juggles tennis balls. "I don't suppose these will hurt him," he says to Charlie.

"Nah," Charlie agrees.

"Now, I want you to stand over there by the side of the garage," Mutt says to Mickey. "Take your bat. Me and Grandpa are going to pitch to you, and you try to hit the ball. Try to see if you can hit the ball far enough to reach the house. Don't worry, we're only going to throw tennis balls. Nice, soft balls."

Charlie adjusts Mickey's stance a little. "There, that's it, now. That's how you want to be ready for the pitch."

"These balls ain't gonna hurt you none," Mutt says as he throws one that purposely hits Mickey in the stomach.

"Ow, yes they do. That hurts."

"Nah, that didn't really hurt now, did it? See, that's why I threw it at you, so you'd know that it wouldn't really hurt if it hit you on accident like. OK, now get ready to swing."

Mutt lobs the tennis ball underhanded. Mickey swings wildly and late.

"OK, that's the way. Now keep your eye on the ball."

Another throw and another wild miss.

"Good. You're getting the hang of it."

After several more pitches with similar results, Mickey tosses the bat down. "I don't want to do this anymore."

"Pick up the bat, now. We're not done."

"I can't hit it."

"Sure, you can. It just takes practice, that's all."

"I don't want to practice."

"Don't you want to be a good ballplayer like your old man and Grandpa?"

"It's hard."

Charlie picks up the bat and holds it out for Mickey to take. "Not too hard for a Mantle. We're all good players. You are, too. Don't get discouraged. You're gonna do good, too."

After several more futile attempts, Mickey manages to make enough contact to send the ball back to Mutt on the ground.

"Good going," says Mutt. "That's the idea."

"Now can we go in?" Mickey asks.

"Nope. And don't ask again."

"Now comes the fun part. Grandpa will throw the ball to you left-handed and you're gonna swing right-handed since that's the way you always do everything. But when I throw, I want you to turn around and swing left-handed."

Mutt demonstrates swinging left-handed. "Now this might be a little hard in the beginning, but the more you practice, the more you'll get the hang of it."

Mickey makes occasional contact right-handed but doesn't come close left-handed.

"It's too hard that way," Mickey whines.

"Stay with it—you'll get it."

They keep going for another half hour. Mickey makes occasional contact; thus starts a ritual that continues every day for many years: Mutt, Charlie, and Mickey taking batting practice. Regularly. Virtually every day. A little snow doesn't stop them, nor some light rain. Nor birthdays, holidays, or overtime workdays.

This defines Mickey's younger years. Everyday practice with his father and grandfather.

Chapter 6

On a sultry spring night, Mickey is sitting on the front step. His mother and father have gone with a relative up to Tulsa to visit someone in the hospital. Mickey doesn't know whom. They had intended to take Mickey, but he is showing early symptoms of a cold, and they think a hospital, with all its germs, is not a good place to take him. Besides, who wants to sit on a bus all the way to Tulsa just to see a sick person you don't know lying in a bed? It would be better to leave him with his half-sister, Anna Bea. She's almost 17. Old enough to look after the kid until Mutt and her mother return later that night.

It is an unusually sticky night, and as Mickey has been instructed not to leave the house, he waits dutifully on the porch in an old wicker chair. Mutt is always promising to paint it but never has. Its big arched back and wide arms seem to envelop the young boy who sits in it bare-chested with shoeless feet that don't come anywhere near the floor. His tan shorts, which someone had given to his mother, are too big.

Anna Bea, who is also not supposed to leave the house, does. She tells Mickey she will only be gone a few minutes and that he should wait right there for her. She will be right back, so he is not to move.

"You understand that, don't you, you little twerp?"

"Yeah, you big twerp."

The young boy is restless, as young boys tend to be when left alone on warm spring nights. There is nothing to do on the porch other than look at the stars, but young boys aren't interested in stars. He might have listened to the sounds of the crickets or the birds, but he isn't interested in them, either. He thinks Anna Bea has been gone a long time, not the few minutes she promised. He grows apprehensive.

Years later, when he finally tells the story of this night, he says he waited an hour, but it was more like fifteen minutes until Anna Bea returns as promised. She has with her two of her friends – simpering high school girls Mickey has seen before but doesn't like. They make him feel like a toy. A Mickey doll they can make do things. They like to boss him around. They would send him into another room when they had secrets they didn't want him to hear. Mickey hates the bossing. He hates them. Mostly, though, he hates Anna Bea when she is with them.

Sometimes, he can run away to the tacit protection of his mother when he sees them coming, but now he is trapped on the steps. His parents will be home soon, but how soon?

The giggling girls come running onto the porch. They call him "Little Mickey." Anna Bea makes him stand up on the rickety chair so that he is almost her height. Then, after a knowing nod from her friends, she pulls his shorts down and plays with his penis. The other girls move in to get a better look. Mickey stands there as if frozen. Mute. Confused. Frightened. The girls titter. They say things to one other, but Mickey hears none of it. The titters turn to loud laughter. Thunderous laughter to a frightened, humiliated little boy on the front porch, when his parents are away on a hot spring night.

When Anna Bea's friends have laughed enough, she stops and tells him to pull up his pants.

"Don't tell anybody, or you know what," she says.

"I'm not gonna," he whimpers.

And he won't, not because his half-sister told him so, but because he is ashamed. He feels guilty and will do whatever he can to hide that feeling.

Later that night when his parents return, his mother tells Mickey about the visit to Tulsa and about the sick relative he doesn't know. Then she puts him to bed because he looks flushed. Probably a cold coming on.

The pattern of abuse continues for several years. Saturday nights are dreaded like no others. Mutt and Lovell like to go to the Saturday night dances in town, and often Charlie will go with them. As the weekends near, Mickey becomes more tense. His parents see Anna Bea as a perfectly acceptable babysitter. Mickey would hide if he could, but the house is far too small to offer hiding places. And he certainly can't tell anybody.

When he yells at the girls to leave him alone, they just laugh. When he tries to run off, they chase, and even with his speed they eventually manage to corner him. Two girls grab his arms to stop him from squirming and lift him up onto the chair while Anna Bea pulls his shorts down.

Anna Bea and the other girls howl with laughter and derision every time he gets a tiny erection, which they take turns putting in their mouths. To Mickey, the girl's tittering sounds are more like deafening shrieks.

Eventually, the molestation and teasing stop, but the traumatic scarring will last a lifetime. Perhaps it is the source of Mickey's many unhealthy relationships, affairs, and one-night stands as an adult. Maybe it accounts for the crude and vulgar language he would exhibit when he drank too much, as he so often did.

For many years no one knows of the molestations. Like other abused children, Mickey feels the shame, knows the guilt. It eats away at him from the inside, but goes outwardly unexpressed. Anger and frustration are easier for him to express than guilt or shame. His guilt becomes a defense mechanism designed to prevent further damage, by hurting himself before others get the chance. Seeds of anxiety have been planted, but none of self-compassion. Mickey will always find it easier to avoid stressful situations than to confront them.

Mickey is starting school. Mutt, although his education is minimal, insists school learning is important, but not as important as baseball learning.

Classes are small at Central Grade School in Commerce. Mickey is the shortest boy in his class. "Little Mickey," his teacher, Mrs. Potorrof, calls him. She is a large woman, so much so that when she is not watching the boys in her class make fun of her bulk by miming a fat woman toddling. But they actually like her, and she loves the youngsters, especially little towheaded Mickey. She likes his grin, crowded with the teeth she thinks look too big for his mouth. He is somewhat timid, but she likes that he is respectful.

As a kid, Mickey is a little pigeon-toed, and bashful. A shy boy who comes to class every day in cowboy boots. Some of the kids in class are barefooted, but Lovell makes sure he has the boots. The Mantles are poor but not destitute, she insists. She reminds Mutt that if he can find money for baseball equipment, she can damn well find money to send Mickey to school properly shoed and with freshly pressed shirts. As soon as he comes home from school, he has to take off his school shirt so she can iron it, making sure the sleeves have sharp creases down their entire lengths.

When Mrs. Potorrof meets Mickey's parents, she likes them as much as she does Mickey. "Very humble people," she describes them to the principal. "They seem to accept things as they come along."

Among Mickey's school friends is a tall, gangly kid named Bill Mosley. Mickey and "Mose" hit it off right from the start. They both like baseball and will come to play important roles in each other's lives as they grow older.

Chapter 7

It has been a particularly bad year for the area in what is becoming a long string of poor years. The three words on everybody's lips are "if it rains."

If it rains, some farmers will get wheat crops.

If it rains, fresh row crops may flourish.

If it rains, pasture and range for livestock may be restored.

If it rains, fields quickly turned into wind-resisting clods may stop the dust.

If it rains … it always has.

But it doesn't.

Clouds of black dust, spectacular and menacing, choking and blowing out tender crops, last without mercy for days. Dust clouds have even been known to derail trains. The area hit the hardest is west of Commerce, but the feeling is that the worst may yet be moving east. They have already seen three years of drought. The damned dust in these parts is nothing new.

The storms leave drifts of powdery sand along the highways and fences, sometimes drifting as high as the eaves of farm buildings. It can't be kept out of the house. On the worst of days, Lovell washes the dishes six times. Before and after every meal.

It's not just the dust coming off the flat fields, though. Down in the mine, the drilling, blasting and shoveling naturally produce dust. Three times a year, officials come in and take dust samples. Workers wash down the walls before every shift. Ventilation sweeps away some of the dust that wetting down doesn't settle. That helps some, but it doesn't stop the dust from swirling in the air as each work shift continues.

Mutt coughs a lot. All the miners do. Coughing death stalks the town like a wolf.

"What are they going to do, kill me?" Mutt says every time Lovell brings up the subject.

"At least we still ain't farming, and you got a steady."

They both know they have no choice. Dust or not, Mutt would much prefer to be outdoors all day than 300 feet underground.

But Mickey will have a choice. Mutt is determined that he will.

Mutt is an artist; his medium is his son. He is creating a baseball player in the manner of a sculptor working with clay. With every spare moment, he coaches, inspires, shapes. Baseball is Mickey's destiny. Mutt is sure of it. It is what his son is meant to do. Perhaps it is even stronger than destiny. Perhaps it is Mickey's fate. Something out of his control, something ordered, inevitable. Unavoidable.

Mutt is not a religious man, but if he was he might say Mickey's fate was divinely inspired.

Every day, when Mutt returns from the mine at four o'clock, Mickey is waiting for him. Practice begins almost immediately and goes on until nightfall. As expected, with continued practice comes continued improvement. But Mickey still struggles when trying to hit left-handed.

After one particularly exasperating session, Mutt explains to Mickey that right-handed hitters generally have more success against left-handed pitchers, while left-handed hitters usually do better against right-handed pitchers.

"See, that's on account of right-handed pitchers' curve balls breaking away from right-handed-hitters. That makes them harder to hit, and the other way around for left-handers. At least it makes it harder to hit the ball with the sweet spot of the bat."

"Do a lot of hitters do that, switch-hit?"

"Not a lot, but some of the really smart ones do. Like Frankie Frisch on the Cards. And he's a really great hitter. Max Carey was, too. But he's retired now. And George Davis some years back. There are a few others, but I know if you can do both, well, that's going to make you more dangerous."

"I hate it. I can't do it."

"Sure you can. You do it already. Maybe not as well as right-handed, but it will come. It will come."

So Mutt and Charlie continue pitching to him, and Mickey continues to switch sides of the plate. And he continues to whiff on most pitches when hitting from the left side.

They have been at it for almost five hours when Lovell calls them to come in for dinner.

"OK, in a few minutes," says Mutt.

"Mutt, do you know what time it is?"

"Nope."

"Do you care what time it is?"

"Nope."

"Do you want your dinner?"

"Yep."

"Before the sun comes up?"

"Maybe."

"Can't you see it's getting dark?"

"The ball is white."

"And if we had floodlights, you'd probably be out there all night."

"Probably."

"You know you're pig-headed, don't you?"

"Yep."

Two in the morning, and Mutt is unable to sleep. He sits on the front step. The wind blows. The moon hangs yellow and gibbous, throwing the chat piles into eerie silhouettes

Somewhere in the distance, a dog howls. Is he crying out to the moon?

Otherwise, the night is dreadfully silent: no engines, no voices, no mine elevators. No sirens. No men on their way to work. Not even birds. Just the wind causing branches to scrape against the side of the garage.

Then something else.

Something whispering ever so softly in the distance. A baseball soaring high into the cloudless night. Mutt knows the sound, loves the sound. Isn't surprised to hear it.

Now Mutt is playing for the Cards. He comes to bat in the bottom of the ninth inning with two outs in a tie game. The World Series is at stake. He digs in and stares out toward the mound, his face set as in granite. The pitcher delivers the ball. Mutt swings and drives the ball high and deep into center. It keeps going up and out until it clears a 100-foot-high chat pile. As he circles the bases, Mutt morphs into Mickey, who rounds third and jogs home. The dog's wail becomes the sound of thousands of cheering fans. Then, just before he reaches the plate, Mickey's leg gives way, and he ends up sprawled on the ground a few feet from home.

This is not the first time Mutt has imagined this scene. Why can't he complete it with Mickey as hero? Surely he can will it so. Maybe he's not outside but in bed dreaming? But he is not.

———•●•———

Mickey is at home with Grandpa Charlie waiting for his parents to return from the hospital in Miami. The Cardinals game is on the radio, but he is only listening half-heartedly. Regardless of the reason, the idea of anyone in the hospital makes him nervous.

The game is just concluding when Mutt returns. "Twins," he says.

"Twins? Really?" says Charlie.

"Two boys."

"Healthy?"

"Seem to be."

"Lovell?"

"Tough as nails, she is."

Mickey can't imagine having one brother, let alone two. He's always been Mutt's focus. Now he'll have to share that. It's an odd feeling. Uncomfortable. Scary even.

"Could be a good keystone combination," Mutt says. "A real double-play combination."

"But I'll still be the catcher, right?" says Mickey.

"Sure. Ain't nobody taking that away from you."

Mutt doesn't throw balls into the twins' crib as he did shortly after Mickey was born. Doesn't talk to them about the Cardinals before they even understand what the word means. When the time comes, he'll introduce them to the game, but Mickey is, and shall forever remain, the centerpiece of his dreams, a place where there is not a lot of room for others. The twins, Ray and Roy, will have to take their place on the dream's edge.

Mutt can't believe what he is reading in the morning paper. They say the great Mickey Cochrane has had a nervous breakdown. He may never play again.

Two seasons ago Cochrane was named the Tigers' player-manager, and under his leadership Detroit reached the World Series in 1934, and won it all in '35. Prior to the 1936 season he was also named the club's vice president, which added the responsibilities of player acquisitions and contract negotiations. On June 3rd, after going hitless in five at-bats in an 11–7 loss, Cochrane went home, but apparently stayed awake all night. The next day, in his third at-bat, he lofted a ball to deep center. It ricocheted off the scoreboard. While the outfielders gave chase, Cochrane raced around the bases for an inside-the-park grand slam.

Fueled by adrenaline, the exhausted Cochrane returned to the dugout. When the inning ended, he put on his gear and headed to his position. Huge dark spots appeared in his eyes, and his heart was racing. He nearly collapsed at the plate, but managed to wobble to the clubhouse.

The team doctor looked at him and said he was on the verge of a nervous breakdown.

Cochrane tried to play the next few games, but suffered several similar spells. When the team traveled to Boston, near his parents and childhood home, he went to St. Elizabeth's Hospital. The paper reported: *Cochrane looked bad. His dark eyes, hollow and vacant, bulged. His shoulders sagged. His face harbored deep furrows. It is painful to watch the creeping shadow of a man's sunset.*

A doctor confirmed the earlier diagnosis—a complete nervous breakdown. He ordered rest. No baseball at all for the great catcher.

One writer described Cochrane's prematurely creased face and smoldering eyes as a window into "a soul of torment."

Naturally, the news upsets Mutt. His hero has always been a fierce competitor. It's hard to picture him breaking down emotionally. Maybe it was the physical demands of his 11-plus years as a catcher or his days as a boxer, when the 160-pound "Kid" Cochrane had taken his share of abuse from heavyweights. Maybe his fiery nature and acknowledged flaming anger simply got the better of him. Maybe the stress of the multiple roles with the team was proving to be too much.

Mutt commiserates with his idol and can readily imagine the pressures of living up to the standard of greatness Cochrane has placed on himself. Where most players have to take the field and perform the best they can, the great ones always have to be great. They expect it of themselves. The fans expect it of them. That pressure can build up to be so overwhelming that it must be released. Nervous exhaustion is one way, alcohol another. One day, Mutt's oldest son will find that out for himself.

An oppressively hot Saturday afternoon. No breeze. No clouds. No relief in sight. Mickey's mom, with a towel neatly wrapped around her head, stands in the kitchen ironing. As determined as Mutt is to pitch to Mickey every day, so is Lovell determined to iron his shirts. But there is more going on than putting crisp edges on sleeves. She is monitoring the Cardinals on the radio. They are in St. Louis, playing two with Pie Traynor's Pirates.

If Mutt weren't deep in the mine, he'd be listening. Mickey is playing at a friend's house, or he'd be listening. Since they are where they are, she'll deliver a present-tense recap of the games when they're both home. If she didn't, they'd have to wait for the next day's paper, and who knows how much detail that will include?

That evening, as is the family's custom, they sit around the table in the kitchen, tucking into a steaming plate of meatballs while she recounts the day's action with remarkable accuracy and detail. She has a head for such things.

"The game has hardly started before the Pirates jump to a four-run lead. Their center fielder, Jensen, cracks a homer with Lloyd Waner on. Then Paul Waner singles and Arky Vaughan reaches on a bunt. Gus Suhr walks to load the bases. Then Waner scores on a slow roller, and Vaughan slides home on Young's foul popfly. Jensen also hits for the circuit in the second."

"How long Diz go?" Mutt asks.

"Until the sixth, and then they bring in Si Johnson. Ryba comes on in the eighth, but by then the game is pretty much over. The Cards end up losing 9–4."

The account of the second game has to wait for the busy mother to wipe the faces of the young twins.

"Lefty Bob Weiland turns in a fine performance in the second game. Only a series of misplays by our infield keeps him from throwing a shutout."

"They're doing that too damn often," says Mutt. "The errors."

"Maybe you should teach them," says Mickey.

"I sure as hell could."

"Johnny Dickshot, the Bucs left fielder," Lovell continues, "scampers to third from first in the third inning on an attempted double play when Stu Martin fumbles a grounder near the bag and then throws wild. That lets Dickshot score on Suhr's long fly ball. It's the only run they get."

"How'd we score?" Mutt asks.

"Hold your horses. I'm getting to that," she says as she continues to spoon cereal into the mouths of the hungry twins. "In the first, Gutteridge blasts a Brandt fastball into the left-field bleachers. Then in the fifth, Pepper Martin scores from third on Mickey Owen's single. Weiland whiffs seven. Best of all is when he strikes out Dickshot with two out in the ninth and the tying run on second."

"So, that should keep us in third place, right?"

"I suspect so."

"We'll catch them," Mutt says to Mickey.

"Sure we will," says Mickey. "We'll catch 'em."

"Atta boy. That's the attitude."

It's Sunday afternoon at the Black Cat Café, a small restaurant on the main street of Commerce. It's been drizzling steadily all day. All games cancelled. Mutt and Ox sit at the crowded bar, enjoying their beers but ruing the rain. Sunday is the only day of the week they don't have to shovel rocks.

"It ain't right," says Ox.

Mutt takes a long swig. "What's that?"

"Rain on Sunday. Don't God know that we gotta have Sundays dry?"

"Guess not."

"Maybe he's not a baseball fan."

"I can't imagine that."

"Nah. I mean, he invented the game, didn't he?"

"I wouldn't know about that."

"Because he invented everything."

"Including raining Sundays."

On the jukebox, Bob Wills and the Texas Playboys are singing something about a lost love in San Antonio, but nobody is paying much attention.

"Still trying to get Mickey to switch-hit?" Ox asks.

"Yeah, but he ain't taking to it too good."

"I think you should give it up."

"Is that what you think?"

"That's what I think."

MUTT'S DREAM: MAKING THE MICK

"Think again. Anybody can develop into a switch-hitter if they start early enough. It ain't no different from learning how to write. Any left-handed kid can be taught to write right-handed if he starts out that way."

"That so?"

"Seems like."

"A waste of time."

"It ain't. Someday, every big-league manager is gonna shift his hitters around on account of the game situation. See, they're gonna have their left-handers bat against righties and right-handers against lefties."

"How much have you had to drink, Mutt? You see them doing that? I don't see them doing that."

"They will. It's coming."

"So, now you can see the future?"

Mutt lights a cigarette from the stub of one almost dead. "If a guy can hit from both sides, he's gonna be much more valuable to a manager. The game, it's always changing, and this is one of the changes I see coming."

"Yeah, what else do you see?"

"I see two more beers coming."

"I like your predictions."

"Didn't I predict the end of Prohibition?"

"Not that I recall."

"Well, I did."

"So you say."

Mutt waves to the bartender. "Two more Hamms."

"You still throwing to Mickey every day?"

"Every day."

"For how long?"

"From four till it gets too dark."

"Like nine o'clock?"

"This time of the year, yeah about that."

"You like that, don't you?"

"I like that."
"But does the kid?"
"He loves it."
"How do you know that?"
"I know that."
"Because he tells you?"
"Because I know it," Mutt says firmly. "I can see it."
"You think he'd tell you if he didn't?"
"Yeah, he would."
"He wouldn't dare."
"What the hell you talking about?"
"Have you ever given him a chance?"
"He could say it any damn time he wanted. He could say he don't want to hit no more. But he don't because he don't want to."
"What would you do if he did?"
"He won't."
"But if he did?"
"Dammit Ox, you're becoming a pain in the ass."
"He can't live your life just to keep you happy, you moron."
"Oh, I'm the moron? What do you know about it?"
"I know you're blind to anything that don't jibe with your ... I don't know, your big ego thing about turning your son into something that maybe he wants or don't want, and you're going to do it no matter what. It's not about him; it's all about you, ain't it?"
"He'll thank me. Someday, you bet your ass he will."

The men continue in a similar vein until, on orders from Lovell, Charlie comes in to fetch Mutt home. It's not the first time, and it won't be the last time, he's sent on such an errand.

———◆●◆———

Mickey is now hitting regulation baseballs. Since a tennis ball curves more than a real baseball, Mutt figures the tennis balls he has been hitting have given him a good eye for the breaking ball.

Now the break on a regulation baseball looks much easier to hit, and both Mutt and Charlie can throw mean curves.

Mutt is still bringing home used bats from his games and cutting them down to Mickey size. No sense in swinging a bat that's too heavy. Nothing would be accomplished.

Mutt devises some "scoring rules" for their practices. A ground ball, pop-up, or strikeout counts as an out. A line drive off the side of the house is a double; off the roof a triple. A shot that lands in the trees in the adjoining lot is a homer. They play consecutive nine-inning games, with Charlie responsible for tallying the runs scored.

They're at this so often and so long that some of the neighbors, curious about what is going on every day at the Mantle place, start to come and watch.

Mickey has his first audience. And he doesn't like it. He's shy, concerned about what people think every time he strikes out or looks bad swinging—especially when Mutt makes him bat left-handed. He thinks people are laughing at him. They're not. In this respect, he is like his father. Both are reluctant to draw attention to themselves. Both are self-effacing. Mickey always feels a little uncomfortable when he is around people he doesn't know. If given the chance, he will avoid such situations. Always.

He still thinks about Anna Bea and her friends watching him with his pants down. He's the center of attention then, too.

Regardless of his wishes, watching the little kid hit has become a welcome afternoon diversion for the Quincy Street neighbors.

"Sorta like a trained monkey."

"He's such a runt. How's he do that?"

"Hey, he ain't bad for such a little squirt."

Mickey's small stature makes his batting accomplishments that much more impressive. He will remain smaller than most boys his age, until changed years later by the unexpected consequences of an injury.

Her three boys are all asleep. Lovell is finishing up the dishes after a dinner eaten even later than usual. Mutt had insisted on throwing to Mickey until he managed to get one over the roof hitting left-handed.

"He's still wetting his bed," Lovell says to Mutt. "I have to change his sheets almost every morning."

Mutt lights a cigarette, blows a distorted smoke ring. "He'll get over it."

"When?"

"When he's ready, I guess."

"Wetting your bed has nothing to do with being ready. Know why he's wetting his bed?"

"Yeah, he's young."

"He's nervous. All the time he gets nervous when you pressure him with all them people watching. He don't like it."

"He never told me that. Anyway, he'll get used to it."

"Maybe he will. Maybe he won't."

"Of course he will. Anyway, I think he actually likes the attention."

"Says you."

"Deep down he does."

"Don't you realize that maybe he don't complain to you because he's afraid to? Afraid of what you'll say. You know, he's got this thing that he has to please you. All the time he has to have your approval, and you act sometimes like it don't matter what he does, you always want more from him. You keep pushing him like that and … I don't know, maybe you'll push him too far and he'll snap or something."

"Aw, he won't snap, but he'll become a lot stronger."

"Maybe, but in the meantime, you can wash his damn sheets every damn morning."

―⁂―

Mickey is now seven. It's a Saturday night. Mutt and Lovell are in town at a barn dance. Charlie is taking care of the kids. Ray and Roy are already asleep when Mickey takes out a book they are learning to read in school. The story is about a frog who's lost his voice. While it's mostly pictures, it has a few tough words that Mickey asks Charlie about.

"What's this?" he asks, pointing to *lily pad*.

"'Lily pad.' I think that's something a frog sits on."

"Like a chair for frogs."

"I guess you could say that."

The story tells of the frog's family coming from a pond far away.

"Sorta like our family," Charlie tells him. "The Mantles of Brierley Hill. That's over in England. On the other side of the Big Pond. That's what they sometimes call the Atlantic Ocean—the Big Pond. Anyway, it was mining country, too. I guess we can't never get away from that. That part of where we come from was all collieries and ironworks."

"What's collieries?"

"Coal mines and things like that. They used to say about it that it was black by day and red by night. That was on account of all the smoke in the daytime and the fires at night. That's what my grandpa told me. Anyway, your great-great-granddaddy—his name was George—he brung the family over here to America, looking for a new life away from the dirty coal mines. Kind of funny, isn't it? He left the mines to find something better, and here we are in the mine business again."

"You're not."

"No, but your daddy and just about everybody around here is."

"Why didn't they go someplace else then?"

"Well, at first they did. They got to New Orleans after a long boat trip from England. Took them like a month to get there, and it was real hard going in them days. They was on a boat called the Sailor Prince, and when the wind stopped, the women in the family, they started doing the washing up on the deck. Then this big storm came along, and all their clothes and pretty much everything else they had washed overboard. So, when they landed, they had almost nothing. Maybe that was a sign of things to come. Anyway, they got on this riverboat and sailed up the Mississippi to St. Louis. George and his sons found work there. Guess what they were doing?"

"I dunno."

"Coal mining. They just couldn't get away from it. I guess it's in our blood. A couple of years later, they wanted to get away from the coal mining again. So, they packed up and headed west to Osage County in Missouri, so they could try to make a living above ground as farmers and grocers. Well, they did for a while, but then guess what?"

"They went into the coal mines."

"Not coal, but mines. Like your dad's doing now. But you, young man, you won't have to because of what your dad is giving you. He's giving you a chance. That's a big present. I hope you appreciate that."

"Sure I do."

"But you gotta learn to read, too, or else you'll never be able to understand that big contract they're gonna give you someday. So back to the book."

Mickey squints hard as he looks at a page. "What's this word?"

"Now you're joshing me. You know that word."

"No, I don't."

"Ball."

Chapter 8

When **Mutt** isn't home by four o'clock, Lovell and Mickey are worried. Other men may stop off at the Black Cat Café for a few beers after work. Not Mutt. He won't miss an opportunity to throw to Mickey.

Lovell knows the only thing that could delay him is an accident in the mine. She listens for the sound of the death wagon. Mickey stands in the open doorway, looking for the white ambulance. He knows what it means.

"We're doing this too damn often," Lovell mumbles under her breath. Too many men are getting hurt. Too many are getting killed. The mine owners don't seem to care. As long as the buckets come full to the surface, nothing else matters. Somebody is making piles of money in these hard times, but it sure as hell isn't the miners.

When she hears the whining siren, she drops the plate she has been drying. She tells Mickey there is nothing to worry about. Mickey doesn't believe her. He can see the fear in his mother.

With so many stories of miners being killed, Mickey worries that one day, maybe Mutt won't come home. Despite assurances from his parents and grandfather that he shouldn't think about such things because Mutt is very careful, his anxiety doesn't subside. It's a fear of abandonment that he carries in the back of his mind. An uneasy sensation that never quite abates. Of course, most miners don't die in the mines, but since some do ...

It's a little after six when Mutt finally shows up.

"Grab your bat," he says the minute he walks in the door.

"What happened?" asks a visibly relieved Lovell.

"Merrill Masters."

"The boxer guy?"

"Yeah."

"And?"

"We were just about to close up for the day. He was working as a dummy on a machine near me. Bending over when a slab came loose, hit him in the small of the back. Me and another guy, we had to carry him out to the ambulance. They slammed the doors shut behind us, so I was stuck going to the hospital with him—Miami Baptist. He was a mess. Bleeding from the chin and hips. But the worst part was that he said he couldn't move his legs."

"What did the doc say?"

"They didn't tell us nothing. It ain't good, though, I can tell you that. I seen these kinds of things before. I don't know if he'll ever walk again. I doubt it."

"You don't know that."

"I do though."

"I know the company will just cut him loose, won't they? Chuck him out."

"That's about the size of it. Come on, Mickey, let's go. We still got time."

Mutt is looking at a picture in the paper. A group of anxious young boys is waiting outside the hospital for word of Mickey Cochrane. He had been hit in the temple by a pitched ball. The caption says that at every opportunity, they ask hospital staff "How's Mickey?" Physicians give Mickey an "even chance."

As Mutt reads the story of the beaning, the bright sun is shining through the window. It sparkles in a little tear on the cheek of the normally stoic amateur ballplayer/miner.

Without a doubt, Cochrane is nearing the end of a brilliant career. He turned 34 just before the start of the season. That's particularly old for someone who plays the game's most demanding position.

Cochrane will never play another game.

MUTT'S DREAM: MAKING THE MICK

Baseball may not be as dangerous as working in the mines, but Mutt knows that a ballplayer needs to make the most of his abilities when he can because injuries can put a stop to them at any moment.

"Let's go, Mickey, time to work."

The next morning brings reports that Cochrane has made progress in his fight for life. He has spent a comfortable day in a New York hospital after suffering a triple skull fracture, resulting from a beanball thrown by the Yankees' Bump Hadley. Cochrane had homered against Hadley in his previous at-bat, but Hadley insisted the beaning was not intentional, and Mickey and his teammates absolved the pitcher of any blame.

"That Hadley fella is about as wild as they come," Mutt tells Mickey. "Led the league in walks a couple of times."

"Cochrane's gonna be OK, though, isn't he?"

"All Mickeys are tough. Comes with the name."

"Yeah."

Mutt isn't going to miss a chance to use this as a teaching point.

"But you gotta learn the right way to get out of the way of a high hard one. See, you gotta turn back, away from the ball. Now, your instincts might tell you the opposite, but with enough practice, it will become second nature. Like this."

Mutt assumes his natural hitting stance and mimes avoiding fastballs coming at his head.

"Now you try."

For the next twenty minutes, Mickey ducks and dodges imaginary high pitches and tennis balls thrown underhand by his father.

"That's it. It just takes practice."

When his mother sees this she says, "For Pete's sake, Mutt, what are you throwing balls at his head for?"

"Can't learn too early to duck."

"Maybe you've taken one too many to the head yourself."

A couple of Mickey's schoolmates have started coming over during the afternoon baseball activities in the Mantles' yard. Jackie Leland Ferguson, whom everyone calls Nick, and LeRoy Bennett.

At first, they come just to watch the goings-on, but after a few viewing sessions Mutt involves them as well. It adds variety to the practices. Mutt doesn't mind the audience. It's good for Mickey. It keeps him interested.

Mutt and Charlie pitch to all three. Soon, all the boys are switch-hitting. LeRoy even goes a step further. A natural right-hander, he begins throwing with either hand. But when Mickey wants to try it, Mutt won't allow it.

"You're a catcher, Mickey. Catchers don't throw left-handed."

"Why not?"

"They just don't, seeing as how most batters are righties, and so they're hitting where it would make it harder for the catcher to throw. Much harder if they gotta throw to third."

"Are there some lefties in the majors? Catchers?"

"Been very few—way back in the early days. But today it would be a real exception."

"Maybe I could be an exception, too."

"Believe me, you want to throw right-handed."

Nick and LeRoy show signs of becoming good players. Maybe not Mickey good, but good enough that the three boys can play together without any of them feeling out of place. It's not long before they are spending time together most days before Mutt gets home to throw to them.

For the most part, Mickey is as quiet and reserved as his father, but when challenged he can be as pugnacious as his mother. His friends quickly learn that making fun of Mickey's left-handed strikeouts brings Mickey to a boil.

"That pitch was too high. Nobody could hit it, Nick, so shut up."

The boys become fast friends, though, and will remain close for many years. In addition to playing together, they have something else they share—interest in Major League Baseball. Every morning during the season, each of them scours the sports pages in the local paper.

"We could each pick a team," LeRoy says one day as they are walking home from school. "And then we could, you know, pretend to be players on that team when we bat."

"OK, but I got dibs on the Cards," Mickey says quickly.

St. Louis, with the Browns and the Cardinals, has the only Major League teams west of the Mississippi, and the city overlooks that mighty river. It's also the closest Major League city to Oklahoma. Most interest in the area is on the Cardinals. The Browns are such a bad team that they have few followers.

"We could flip to see who gets the Cardinals," Nick says.

"I called it first, so I get them," Mickey says.

"That ain't fair," Nick counters.

"First who says it gets it."

Eventually, they come up with their teams. For LeRoy, it's the Red Sox. For Nick, the Yankees. Mickey gets the Cardinals.

With baseball as the common denominator, the boys quickly become inseparable. Nick lives up the street on Quincy, LeRoy on Vine Street about eight blocks away. They often play together at one or another of their houses. In their games, Mickey bats left-handed for Johnny Mize, right-handed for Pepper Martin and Mickey Owen. Nick gets to be Lou Gehrig and Joe DiMaggio. LeRoy is always Jimmie Fox, Joe Cronin, or Pinky Higgins.

"Who's the best player in the world?" Nick asks.

LeRoy shakes his head. "I dunno. Who do you think?"

Nick is the brainy one among them, so the boys often look to him for answers to life's most pressing questions. "Lou Gehrig," he says with authority as he assumes his interpretation of the Iron Horse's batting stance. The baseball-obsessed boys have all studied pictures of Major League players that they have seen in the papers.

Some days, they play pitch and catch or Annie Over. Sometimes, for a little variety, they sneak off looking for new adventures. Like climbing fences or walking along the fouled creek.

Since few residences have proper sewer systems, most just dump their raw sewage into the creek. When the creek backs up, the boys see the "Baby Ruth candy bars" floating back to town.

"Those are for my grandfather," Nick says.

"What are you talking about?" Mickey asks.

"He's a honey bucket man. That's his job. Picking them things up."

LeRoy giggles. "So, that's what you have for dinner?"

"No, we don't have them for dinner, stupid," Nick says as he hits LeRoy on the arm.

"Yeah, what does he do with them, then?"

"He sends them to your mother."

"Ha, ha."

Occasionally, they go down to Chandler's Drugstore on Commerce's main street or take in a Saturday afternoon matinee at the Coleman. Sometimes, they just lie on the ground watching the cloud formations, trying to pick out shapes that look like animals. As they see it, doing nothing is sometimes a very good thing for a young boy to do.

Then shortly before four o'clock comes the call they all expect: "Mickey Charles!" It's Lovell's reminder that Mutt will be home soon.

A neighbor cracks, "Time for Mickey to stop playing and start practicing."

———•●•———

Lovell looks up from the sink, where she is scouring an old pot, to see Mutt coming up the dirt path to the front door. It's early afternoon. Mickey is still at school; the twins are napping. There are only three possible reasons Mutt is home this early. Either he was fired, injured, or …

"Strike," he says as he steps through the door.

"Damn. How long?"

"How would I know?"

"Guess."

"Not long."

But it is. And it turns ugly. Violence erupts in several towns, including Commerce, and the men of Eagle-Picher are in the thick of it. Almost all the workers are members of an independent union determined to prevent the Congress of Industrial Organizations from unionizing the territory. In nearby Galena, eight men and a boy are wounded by gunfire from the headquarters of the international union. The shootings climax a bloody weekend of beatings and attacks with pick handles.

Mutt stays away from the altercations. He's a member of the independent union because he has to be. The other men in the mine would hold it against him if he didn't stand with them, but he has little interest in the politics of union infighting. He attends the meetings to show his support, if not his enthusiasm.

The president of his union, Reid Robinson, announces, "We're definitely going to keep fighting the CIO in the lead and zinc fields. I regret tremendously that anyone was hurt, but you know we didn't retaliate until they forced us to protect our lives and property in Galena. Now I'm told they got two of the shooters, Charles Aldridge and Price Reiner, in jail."

When Mutt gets home from the meeting, Lovell asks him what Robinson told them.

"I dunno."

"What do you mean, 'you dunno'?"

"I didn't pay a whole lot of attention to tell you the truth."

"For Chrissake, what were you paying attention to?"

"Sunday's game. I'm batting leadoff, and Audie Ware is pitching, and he's got a hell of a curve, so I'm thinking—"

"This is important, Mutt. This strike, if it goes on for too long, I don't know what we'll do."

"Oh, and I think he said we're going back soon."

"You *think*?"

"Anyway, everybody's in the same boat as we are. We all gotta go back."

"Even when people are getting shot over this? Promise you'll stay away from the violence."

"I wouldn't want to hurt my throwing arm, so yeah, I'm not going anywhere near the fighting."

"By all means, protect that arm."

"Anyway, as long as we're out, I can always use extra time to work with Mickey and his buddies."

"Would I expect anything else?"

The strike is over in a few days. Nobody expects it will be the last one.

※

"Your father don't ever yell at you, does he?" asks LeRoy one day as the boys wait for Mutt, who has been catching in a game for the Blue Goose Number One mine team.

"Nah, not much."

"Not never, I'd say. When you do something bad, he don't even then?"

Mickey shakes his head. "He doesn't have to. It's how he looks."

Mutt is strong, austere. Six feet tall. Lean and well-muscled with thick reddish-black hair. His gnarled hands are the products of his strenuous mine work. Yet, it is that Mutt glare that the boys notice most, and to which they respond. He is a quiet man, but he can freeze the boys with a look. He seldom raises his voice even when he is angry. That look says it all. Otherwise, he rarely shows any outward emotion.

Mickey, who is about as close to his father as a boy can get, is adopting similar habits. He too seldom lets on how he feels. He can't now, nor will he ever, open up freely to people. Some will mistake his reticence for rudeness. When he can't deal with his feelings, he buries them. He will eventually pay a high price for that.

But now he will do about anything to please his father. When he does something particularly good, Mutt will drape an arm over Mickey's shoulder. Maybe give him a little hug. He never says "I love you" to Mickey. The hug suffices.

To the boys, Mutt's grin says he approves of what they just did. He doesn't whoop and holler if one of them hits a ball over the house. He flashes the grin. If they do something wrong, he flashes the Mutt glare. Either way, they are in his thrall.

When Nick's mother asks him how Mutt is treating him, he explains that Mutt doesn't usually tell him what to do, because they just want to do what he wants. Mutt, as quiet as he is, has that effect on most people. They instinctively want to please him.

Chapter 9

When Mickey is eight, the family adds a new member—a baby girl name Barbara.

"Well, there goes any idea of an all-Mantle infield," Mutt says after they bring Barbara home from the hospital.

"What do you think, Mickey? A little sister."

"Good."

The house is already crowded. Now there is another mouth to feed, but Mutt has developed some seniority at the mine and is bringing in a few extra dollars playing semi-pro ball. To get to all the games, however, he needs a car. One morning, with Lovell home taking care of her new daughter, Mutt loads Mickey and the twins on a wagon pulled by two horses he had picked up earlier. Ray and Roy ride with Mutt while Mickey sits on the back, his feet dangling off as they make the 20-mile trip to Afton. It is slow going. Behind the wagon stack up agitated automobile drivers, impatiently waiting for a chance to pass on the busy, winding two-lane road.

Originally a thriving farming and railroad community, Afton, like many other towns in the area, has seen a recent decline in population. On a corner along Route 66, which runs through the center of town, Mickey jumps down. He is excited to think they might be riding home in a car. Mutt had tried to temper his enthusiasm by telling him he wasn't sure what he could get in exchange for the horses and wagon.

A young boy is dusting a shiny, bright two-seater in the front row of the crowded lot. Mutt spots it right away. He tells Mickey to watch the twins.

"Mighty good-looking car you got there, kid," Mutt says to the boy.

"Thirty-seven Ford," the boy says proudly as he slaps a fender. "A real dandy. You interested? I'll go tell Mr. Fuiez you're interested."

"OK, sure."

"A fine car, a fine car," the boy says as he leaves to inform the lot owner that he has almost talked a customer into buying the Ford.

"You gonna buy that?" Mickey calls.

"We'll see."

"Hello there, partner," the cheery owner says as he approaches Mutt. "I hear you like that Ford. It's a swell car. Can't go wrong with a Ford. Can't never go wrong with one of them."

"What is the—?"

"I can make you a real good deal on it. New it sells for $749. This one is a year old, but very few miles on it. Owned by a farmer who went bust. You know how it is. His bad luck can be your good luck. I could let you have it for $600. How's that sound?"

Mutt is uncomfortable in situations like these. He knows nothing about cars. Nothing about negotiating. Nothing about what the lot owner expects from him. He doesn't want to be taken advantage of, but he also doesn't like arguing with anyone. "Well, actually what I want to do is trade in my wagon and two fine horses," he says, hoping that won't sound ridiculous to the salesman.

"Your wagon and horses?"

"Yeah, those over there," Mutt says, pointing to his potential trade-in.

"That's a different story, partner."

"Do you take trades?"

"Depends on for what."

"What cars do you have that you might trade?"

"Well, let me see," he says as he goes to the wagon. He walks completely around, examines it, and checks on the horses. He doesn't look too pleased, which makes Mickey nervous. His heart is set on a car; now it looks like maybe they'll have to make the long trip home back in the old wagon.

"Well, I don't know. I guess I could think about that spiffy LaSalle over there," he says, pointing to a car in the back row. "It's got some years on it, I got to tell you. But then, don't we all? Got some miles on it, too, but I mean, it's a LaSalle. You probably know that's a real good car. A luxury car made by the same people who make the Cadillac. An almost-Cadillac, I like to say. Runs good too. Runs real good. Smokes a little, but that don't hurt nothing."

Mutt looks at the LaSalle. He has rationalized that he needs the car if he is going to continue playing semi-pro games all over the area, and he needs to play games to make extra money. That he probably won't make enough to pay for the gas, oil, and upkeep is ignored, but such is the nature of rationalization. So, after some time looking and talking, the two men come to an agreement. One wagon and two horses for a '30 LaSalle that smokes.

Mickey is thrilled. He climbs into the front seat next to his father. The proud owner of an almost-Cadillac. The antsy twins climb onto the back seat as the lot owner points to all the controls and explains what they do.

Mickey is pleased that they can get home in a much shorter time than they took to get there. But Mutt drives so slowly that frustrated drivers, waiting for a chance to pass, again bunch up behind them.

"Can't this car go faster?" Mickey asks.

"What's the rush?"

"I could walk faster."

Mickey assumes his father just needs time to feel comfortable driving and once he is, he'll speed up. He never does.

On most Sundays for the rest of the summer, rather than dressing up and going to church as most of their neighbors do, the Mantles pile into the LaSalle and drive—albeit slowly—to wherever Mutt will be playing. They drive to games in Salina, Jay, Grove, Vinita, and Spavinaw.

To Mickey, his father is every bit as good as Pepper Martin or Mickey Cochrane. He can play any position, bat from either side of the plate, hit for distance. And he has a shotgun arm. The best player in the area. Mickey is sure of it. Others agree he is a good player, but maybe not the best. It is a son's prerogative, however, to see a father as shining in a brighter light than reality suggests.

Mutt likes to park the LaSalle along one of the foul lines, so Lovell can stay inside with Barbara and the twins. If there is a Cardinals game being broadcast, Mickey watches his father from the front seat as he listens to the game on the car radio.

Mutt's brother Tunney is also on Mutt's team. Sometimes, the Brothers Mantle form the battery. Mutt pitching, Tunney catching. One Sunday, Tunney calls for a curve. Mutt unleashes a fastball. Tunney is steamed. Both players slam down their gloves, meet midway between the mound and the plate, and exchange punches. Other players quickly pull the feuding brothers apart.

Mutt, the stoic, surprises everyone by showing this much fire. But then, this is baseball. If Mutt gets fired up about anything, this is it.

That night, the feuding brothers bowl for their Cardin Yards bowling team. The fight is never mentioned.

They call it simply "the alkali." A flat plain dotted with abandoned mine shafts and chat piles, some higher than a house, that in the early morning cast shadows a mile long. Dry summer winds pick up dust from the tops of the piles and scatter it across the plain. Nothing grows on the flat, hardpacked, dust-coated alkali. A barren landscape. A wasteland.

And a place for young boys to play.

Ever since she was a young girl, Lovell has heard the stories about the alkali's abandoned mine shafts, about how young boys have fallen in and died in the black holes. True or not, those are the stories she passes on to Mickey.

The caved-in old mine shafts are closed off by sagging fences. "That's all that keeps someone from falling in," she tells him when she hears he's been playing there. "Rusted, broken fences. And do you know how deep some of those shafts are?"

Mickey just shrugs.

"They're very, very, very deep. You fall in, you're never going to come out alive. You understand that, don't you? You understand how dangerous they are?"

Another shrug.

"I heard one boy fell in and was never seen again. He just disappeared down there and was gone forever. Maybe more than one boy. Maybe lots, but people, they don't want to talk about them. The mine company should do something about them. Fill them up or something, or at least put something up around them that stops kids from falling in, but of course they don't. They don't care about disappearing kids, only how much money they can make. So, you're not to go anywheres near them. You hear me?"

"OK," Mickey mumbles.

"Stay away from them. Don't play out there in the alkali anywhere that's near them. You hear me?"

"I heard you."

"You go near them, and you'll get your britches tanned like you never have before."

Where Lovell sees a dangerous trap just waiting for unsuspecting victims, the boys see a flat and level baseball field. Using sticks, they draw baselines. They find gunnysacks for bases. An old rusted beer sign for home plate. That takes care of the infield, but the outfield presents a problem. There are no streams, trees, ditches, or embankments to stop a hard-hit grounder. Balls seemingly roll forever.

Still, on most summer Saturday afternoons, the alkali beckons.

"Looks like it's going to Tulsa," Nick observes after Mickey sends a ball in that direction. "You go get it."

"I called left; I ain't going after it."

When Mickey, Nick, and LeRoy play without enough other boys to make a complete nine, they are supposed to go by the agreed-upon "ground rules." A batter must call either left or right field before he swings. Then when he hits a ball, it must be on the left or right side of second base, depending on which side has been called.

Hit it to the wrong side, it counts as an out, and the batter has to chase and retrieve it. Even if it gets to Tulsa.

"That's right. You called left, but it went to the right of second."

"Did not."

"Did too."

"I seen it. We all did."

"Then you're seeing things."

After a show of hands, the consensus is Mickey is wrong, so he reluctantly jogs after the ball. He had hit it hard. It will be a long chase. He runs slowly to make his point that he has been wronged. The wind suddenly picks up, throwing huge clouds of dust into the air. Into his eyes, his mouth. He can't see more than two feet in front of him. As he jogs on, he is unaware that he has veered from his intended direction and is no longer on the path of the wayward ball. The wind and dust don't let up, but he knows if he stops every time the wind comes up, they'll never get a game in, so he runs on. Suddenly, he crashes into part of a broken fence, which sends him sprawling on the hard ground a few feet short of an abandoned shaft. His pants are badly ripped, his leg gashed, his shirt covered in gritty dust particles.

He remains on the ground for several minutes, waiting for the wind to die down. When it does, he goes back to the other coughing boys. "Somebody else has got to go find it," he says. "I gotta go home."

The torn pant leg and cut tell Lovell everything she needs to know. The leg ends up hurting less than the tanning of his britches she had promised—and delivers.

On a balmy fall day, Mutt takes Mickey hunting along the banks of the Neosho River. Mickey carries the single-shot .22 caliber rifle Charlie had found for him.

When they spot a rabbit scurrying out from under a low bush, Mickey raises his rifle and fires. The rabbit scurries on.

"You're shooting right-handed," Mutt barks.

"That's because I am right-handed."

"No, you're both-handed. You gotta think that way because

that's what you are. Next rabbit we see, you shoot left-handed. Hit it square, and you can go back to your right."

"What if it's a right-footed rabbit?"

"Don't be a smart-ass."

"Dust storm derailed a train up in Kansas," Lovell says, pointing to the headline in the paper she has spread across the kitchen table.

"That so?" Mutt mumbles without looking up from the Cardinals box score he has been studying.

"According to the paper."

"Didn't notice."

"Yeah, they probably didn't cover that on the sports page."

It was early on a faultless Oklahoma Saturday evening. The kind of crisp early fall weather made for baseball.

"Hey, Mickey, let's go outside," Mutt says. "I want to show you the finer points of playing the catcher's position. You ready for that?"

"Yeah, good."

Lovell throws her hands up. "I've got dinner almost ready."

"Won't take long," Mutt says.

"Now, why don't I believe that?"

"No idea."

Mutt and Mickey walk out to the garage/backstop.

"The first thing you gotta make sure of is that you got a good wide, comfortable stance behind the plate. Like this," Mutt says as he demonstrates.

He is gratified that his son is paying attention.

"You want your left foot about four or five inches out farther than your right. That'll give you good balance. See, you don't want to have both feet on the same plane. That ain't good. But with one foot in front of the other, you can shift your balance more easy, and you won't waste motion for taking the ball or throwing. Make sure you don't never take a step after you catch the ball. That's what loses time, and every little bitty part of a second is what counts. Now, you show me your position just like I did."

Mickey does his best impression of Mutt's setup.

"OK, that's real good. It don't matter if the ball is coming above or below the waist, you want to remember to keep your left foot forward and let your arm go way back and throw with the same motion as your body going forward. See, that's the important thing—having your feet ready to shift easy and quick like. Now, if there's runners on base, here's what you gotta do. You gotta receive the ball already in a position to try to nab a runner trying to steal a base. Now watch."

Mutt mimes receiving the ball while in his crouch, then rising and throwing in one coordinated effort.

"Now you show me."

"Like this?" Mickey asks, mimicking his father.

"That's it. Now let's keep doing it. Repetition, that's always the key. You know that. Keep doing it until it become natural … like without thinking."

"Yep."

They continue miming throws even after Lovell's "third and final" call for dinner.

Mutt is overjoyed to be passing on to his willing son the one thing in the world that he knows he does well.

When they finally go back into the house, Lovell, the twins, and Barbara have already eaten, and Lovell has cleared the table.

"Where's dinner? Mutt asks.

"You missed it."

"You didn't save anything?"

"Nope. You had your chance. You could have either played or eaten. Which is more important? Don't answer that."

"We're hungry."

"Too bad."

So, Mickey and Mutt go to bed hungry, but pleased with the baseball lesson. There are priorities after all.

MUTT'S DREAM: MAKING THE MICK

There aren't many games played by the Eagle-Picher baseball team that Mickey doesn't watch. His father and Uncle Tunney always play. They are reliable, staunch, committed players who can always be counted on. These games are a staple of their Sunday afternoons.

On this afternoon, however, Mickey stays home. He doesn't like it. It is important to please his father. Always. Without exception. No excuses. Going to his father's games shows Mickey's love for his father. Mickey is sure of it.

As Bill Mosley would later explain, "Mickey's desire to please his father at all costs controlled him. He was obsessed by the need. It wasn't so much that Mickey wanted to be a good player himself that pushed him to practice so much; rather, it was that he couldn't stand to let his father down. I mean, I think he'd break out into sweats if he ever thought his father was disappointed in him. It wasn't the desire to be a good player that drove him; it was the desire to be a good son. And I could see that from the first time I ever met him, when he was still so young. Mickey had to please his father, and I do mean *had to*."

Earlier in the day, Mickey had been playing out in the alkali with his friends and had lost track of the time. Mutt had gone off alone to the game in the LaSalle. Since Mickey wasn't back by the time Mutt had to leave for his game in Salina, Lovell had stayed home with Barbara and the twins to wait for him. She wouldn't leave with Mickey out in the alkali. Anything could happen to the boys out there. Oh, sure, they were responsible enough, but they were also kids. Taking foolish chances is part of being young. And being a boy.

"Relax, Mickey. You don't have to go to every one of his games," Lovell says between bites of her coffee cake.

"Yes, I do."

"Don't be ridiculous."

"He wants me there."

"Yeah, and he wants a million dollars, but that ain't ever gonna happen neither."

"How do you know?"

"I think it's a pretty good bet. You're dirty, covered with dust. Time for a bath."

"I don't want a bath."

"I don't care what you want; you're gonna take a bath."

"Ah, come on, I'm going back out to play with Nick and LeRoy."

"No, you're not."

"I'm going."

"The only place you're going is into the tub."

"I don't need a bath."

"And I don't care if you're as clean as a just-washed pot; you're going into the tub."

Although natural gas is available, water heaters are still a luxury. Anyway, the Mantles don't have inside plumbing, so Lovell heats water on top of the kitchen stove, then dumps it into an old galvanized tub that once served as a horse-and-cow-watering trough. The only good thing to come from an early Sunday bath for Mickey is that being in first means that the water is still hot and cleaner than it will be later for the twins and his sister.

When Mutt gets home, he tells Mickey he has had one of his best games. Stole a base, hit two doubles, slugged the game-winning home run. On this Sunday, he is the hero of the Eagle-Picher team. Even carried off the field by his teammates. Naturally, Mickey is excited by the news, but he can't help feeling more than a little guilty. He may be clean, but he should have been there to watch his remarkable father, and he worries that Mutt will be angry with him. Mutt is not angry; he is disappointed. He does his best not to show it, but both Mickey and his mother know better.

Over dinner Mutt, still basking in the euphoria of his game, is more talkative than usual as he recounts the details of his on-field accomplishments.

"There was no wind neither. That home run, it was a wicked line drive that sailed over the left fielder's head like it was shot out of a cannon or something. I mean, I really got all of it."

MUTT'S DREAM: MAKING THE MICK

Mickey, trying to get him to change the subject, asks about the mine work. He prefers to forget about the game. Forget about how he let his father down.

"Pretty much the same every day," Mutt says, a little surprised that Mickey doesn't want to hear more about his heroics. "Well, I do different things. Mostly, I work as a shoveler, breaking up rocks to put into a skip."

"Because you have really strong arms."

"I suppose I do. Spent a little time, too, as a screen ape, swinging a heavy hammer."

"You wear a lamp every day on your head? I seen pictures of that."

"A carbide lamp, yeah. We all do. I'd rather be wearing a catcher's mask, though."

"You do other things in the mine too."

Mutt looks at Mickey strangely. "Why so interested in the mine?"

"I dunno. Someday maybe I'll need to know about those things."

"No, you won't, not never," Mutt says, his voice rising to a level he seldom uses. "You ain't going down no mines. I don't even want you to think about that. I go down in the hole every day, so you won't ever have to."

"Don't get angry, hon," Lovell interjects. "He's just interested, that's all. It's a natural thing for a boy to be interested in what his father does."

With an edge of annoyance, Mutt explains, "There are hoistermen, who operate the machine for lifting the full tubs, and roustabouts. They're the unskilled laborers who carry the equipment and do other simple things in the mine and on the surface. There are pigtail men who tram the ore cans from the drift or the lay-by or switch point, where a string of cars are collected and pulled to the shaft for hoisting. We got mule skinners and powder monkeys. They take care of the explosives. And then there are Bruno men who … oh, never mind."

Mutt pushes back from the table. "Who cares about any of that? Who gives a damn?"

Now the father and the son are both upset.

"Anyone have room for dessert?" Lovell asks. "I got some muffins in the oven."

Chapter 10

Late August. Raining on and off, with "on" dominating as it has been for several days. The farmers are happy. The boys cooped up in the Mantle house aren't. They're restless, frustrated.

"You mother gotta be some kinda saint," Mosley says. "Putting up with all of us all the time."

"Aw, she likes it," Mickey says. "She likes having people around ... even you."

"A real saint, I tell you."

The boys are used to coming over most days to have Mutt and Charlie pitch to them, so it seems only natural to be here on other days too. It is the closest thing they have to a clubhouse.

Mickey, Mose, LeRoy, Nick, and Mickey's half-brother Theodore, all squeezed around the wooden kitchen table, play various card and board games. Sometimes, a game of dominoes can go on for hours. The kitchen is always a lively, febrile place of camaraderie and occasional game-related friendly squabbles. Mostly, the house is filled with the exuberant chatter of young boys enjoying themselves.

On this day, they are engaged in a prolonged game of Monopoly. Usually, a game can be wrapped up in about two hours, but not when a Cardinals game on the radio periodically takes their attention from the board to Sportsman's Park in St. Louis.

"Well, it sure looks like the Cards have their hitting shoes on today. That's their third home run already, and we're only in the second inning."

"Can't beat that," says Mickey.

"Between Medwick, Slaughter, and Mize, they oughta get at least a hundred," Nick says.

"Maybe more," Mose adds.

During the break between innings, the boys turn their attention back to the Monopoly board.

"You can't do that," LeRoy says.

"Like hell, I can't," Nick says. "I can do that if I want."

"Watch your language, Nick," Lovell calls from the bedroom.

"You gotta play by the rules," LeRoy says, "not what you want. You can't just make up rules for the hell—heck of it."

"It ain't for the heck of it. It's so I can win."

LeRoy sighs. "If we're not going to play by the rules, then I quit."

"You can't quit," Mickey says. "Then we'd never know what to do."

LeRoy will always be known as the smart one. He always gets the best grades in school, is always favored by his teachers because of the attention he gives to his studies. He had promised his dying father that he would take his schoolwork seriously, and he has invariably abided by that promise. Like so many other miners, his father's dying admonition came as he struggled with the miner's disease, desperately wanting his son to avoid having to work in the death-trap mines as he had. "Your brain is your way out," he had told his son. "Use it. Use it to get out of here. Don't be like me. You're too smart for that."

Avoiding a life in the mines is the priority of so many miner fathers. LeRoy isn't a bad athlete, but he is not Mickey, so where Mutt pushes his son in athletics, LeRoy's parents have always pushed him scholastically.

"You read the whole rule book or something?" Nick asks, glaring at LeRoy.

"Or something, yeah."

"Nobody's ever read the whole rule book. Who would do that?"

"I did."

"What a waste of time."

"Anyway—"

"We play like we play, anyway. House rules." Nick laughs. "Mantle house rules. Right, Mickey?"

"I guess—"

"Except that when you land on free parking, you don't get the fine money from the middle of the board."

"OK, genius, what do you get?"

"Absolutely nothing."

"That's stupid."

"It's a rest place, so you can … I don't know, count your money or something."

"I've counted it. I don't have any."

"That's not surprising."

"So, I'll borrow some. Mickey, want to loan me some money? You got piles."

"You can't do that," LeRoy says, throwing up his arms.

"I can if Mickey wants to. Right, Mickey? You'll lend me some."

"Yeah, sure. How much you want?"

LeRoy slams his palm down on the table, "You can only borrow from the bank. You can't borrow from another player."

"Mantle house rules say I can."

A game of acquiring wealth in these Great Depression days might be intriguing for many, but the world of high finance is hardly a world any of these boys know. Still, all have competitive instincts, and all the indoor activities they share give them another chance to compete. Mickey is particularly good at cards, but not Monopoly. The idea of working toward immense wealth and prosperity is not something he ever thinks about.

"The Sox just paid $40,000 for Joe DiMaggio's brother, Dom," Mose says. "That's real money."

"Probably borrowed it from Mickey," Nick said.

Prompted by France Laux's rising baritone voice, Mickey gets up and moves closer to the radio.

"Well, that's it, folks. The Cardinals nose out the Chicago Cubs 6-5 in 10 innings—a great game witnessed by 8,000 fans on Ladies Day."

Making pretend money is one thing; the Cardinals' season is quite another.

The rain doesn't let up, so neither does the Monopoly quest to become the richest player.

"You can't collect rent when you're in jail," LeRoy says, glaring at Nick.

"Who says?"

"The rules."

"That ain't in the rules. Everybody knows that."

"No, they don't know that. Idiots just think that."

"You calling me an idiot?"

"If you don't know the rules—"

"I thought this game was supposed to be fun," Mose says.

"Apparently not," says LeRoy.

"Yeah, only one guy wins, and everybody else goes home pissed off," Mickey says.

"Hope it don't rain tomorrow," Nick adds, summing up the feelings of everyone.

As usual for a weekday afternoon, Mutt and Charlie are pitching to Mickey with Nick and LeRoy waiting their turns. Mutt seems to be throwing particularly hard and frequently up-and-in to Mickey, who has to duck to avoid getting hit in the head.

"Hey," Mickey finally says. "Watch it!"

The next pitch again comes whistling in, grazing Mickey's shoulder. He ends up sprawled on the ground.

"Focus. You're not concentrating," Mutt says.

"I am too."

"If you're complaining, you ain't concentrating," Mutt says as he throws another up-and-in ball. "It's scary, I know. A ball coming at your head is scary. That's baseball. It's gonna happen, but you know what? You gotta face your fears. Face them like a man, like a real baseball player. Now get your butt up and stand in there. Get mad at me if you want, but don't back down. Don't never back down from a wild pitcher because you're scared. If you do, he wins. Always."

MUTT'S DREAM: MAKING THE MICK

Mutt and Charlie continue to alternate pitching to Mickey, each occasionally throwing purposely inside. Mickey, determined to heed his father's instructions, gets hit several times.

"When you get hit," Mutt says, "don't never show it. Don't let the pitcher think he can get to you. Be even more determined to drive the ball hard."

When Mickey takes a short break, Nick and LeRoy take their turns hitting. Neither gets balls inside. Neither gets what LeRoy calls "the Mickey treatment."

When it starts turning dark, the friends head home for dinner. Mutt continues to pitch to Mickey. "He must have a rubber arm," Nick says.

"When the ball comes in so high and inside, what do you think comes next?" Mutt asks.

"Low and away," Mickey answers.

"Always be ready for that."

Finally, when darkness gets the better of them, they go in for dinner.

Lovell may not be able to pitch to him, but she wants to contribute to Mickey's baseball experiences too.

"I'm thinking it's time for you to have spikes," she says.

That night, she stays up late. Using screws, she fashions makeshift cleats on the soles of an old pair of shoes. When Mickey comes in for breakfast, there they are—homemade spikes—sitting on his chair. He immediately puts them on and goes outside to run around the yard. Lovell is pleased; Mickey is thrilled.

Nick, LeRoy, and Mosley ride their bikes over to the Mantles' house, which has become a daily meeting place for the boys. Even before Mutt gets home from the mine, they know they'll likely find that Lovell has made fresh lemonade. Maybe some still-warm cookies, too.

"Let's go down to the Stepps Ford Bridge and go swimming," Mosley says. "It's hot as hell."

"Yeah, OK," says Mickey as he goes out to the garage to get his old, rickety bicycle. Mutt isn't interested in buying him a new one. Any extra money has to go for baseball equipment.

The boys ride four abreast to the Neosho River. Mosley, easily the tallest, rides on one end; Mickey, easily the shortest, rides on the other. Nick and LeRoy ride between them.

The Stepps Ford Bridge, the first bridge to cross the Neosho, had been over another river, but in the early 1920s it was disassembled, transported, and reassembled here. It is next to a deep watering hole into which a boy can dive if he is able or jump if not. Mickey is the only one in the quartet who can't swim, so he always wades in from the shore. But never too far. He takes some kidding from the others, but that's better than taking needless chances.

"Don't go in over your ankles," Nick says before jumping in.

Mickey wades in. "You think there's alligators in here?"

The boys enjoy the bracing water on this muggy afternoon. Nick shows off his diving, even though the drop from the bridge to the water isn't very far. LeRoy's cannonball jumps provide water sprays that reach the banks on both sides of the river. They are at it for some time before Mosley returns to the sandy river's edge, where he has left his shirt, pants, and bicycle. He reaches into a front pocket of his jeans and takes out his watch. He's the only one who ever carries one, so it's up to him to keep track of the time. When he looks at it, he realizes they have been there for longer than he thought.

"Hey, Mickey," he calls, "It's a couple of minutes before four."

Mickey, who had been sitting on a partially submerged log, jumps up as if there really were an alligator after him. "Dammit!" he yells as he quickly gathers up his clothes, gets dressed, and makes a running mount onto his bicycle. He races as fast as he can toward home. If Mutt gets there before he does and sees that Mickey isn't ready for practice, he will be displeased. Mickey never wants to displease his father.

He races into his yard, skids to a dusty stop, and throws the bike down just as his father comes up the path to the house.

"Why are you so sweaty?" Mutt asks.

"It's hot."

"Get your bat; I'll be right out."

Charlie, who has seen the last-second speedy arrival, gives Mickey a wink. "Hot enough to go swimming, don't you think?"

"Nah," Mickey says.

"That's what I'd do. I'd go swimming on a day like this if I was your age."

———◦•◦———

Mutt pushes back his chair and takes his dinner plate to the sink. "Mickey, what do you say we go up to Joplin to see a game?"

"What game?"

"The Springfield Cardinals and the Joplin Miners."

"Yeah, sure."

"We could go tomorrow. I don't have a game, and the weather is supposed to be good. It's a C-level league. They're a St. Louis farm club, the Springfield Cardinals. Joplin, they're a Yankee farm."

"Yeah, I know that, Dad."

Lovell is expecting again, so she stays home with Barbara and the twins. Charlie is there should she need any help. Joplin is only 29 miles away, but with Mutt's excessively cautious driving, it takes over an hour.

They drive up into Kansas, passing near Galena and the huge ordnance works producing ammonium for the war effort. Then they cross into Missouri.

"Seven miles to heaven," Mutt says.

"What do you mean?"

"You'll see."

With each mile they travel, Mickey's excitement ratchets up.

Joe Becker Stadium in Joplin is the first professional baseball stadium Mickey has ever seen. Mutt buys two tickets. "We'll sit in the top of the bleachers," Mutt says. "We'll get the best view from there."

After they climb up, Mickey looks down on a manicured field as green as a shamrock. It's perfect. The symmetrical infield, the foul lines seemingly leading off to infinity. The beautifully manicured green grass looks greener than any green could be. He takes in the scene as if it were a technicolor fairytale, a field where magic happens and reality fades away. To a transfixed young boy, it is both mythical and mystical. A place of dreams and legends.

A green cathedral. A field of dreams. An unspoiled diamond. There are scores of metaphors. All are inadequate.

Someday, other young boys will look out onto this field from the top of these bleachers, and their fathers will say to them, "This is where the great Mickey Mantle began his professional career in 1950. He hit .383 with 26 homers." And the boys will gaze in awe.

For now, Mutt and Mickey will watch a game between the Joplin Miners and the Springfield Cardinals. Mutt buys two hot dogs. He wants Mickey to have a great time.

"I want you to keep your eyes on George Niedson," Mutt says. "He's the catcher. By the end of the game, I want you to tell me what's so special about him."

But it is not Niedson who catches Mickey's eye. Nor Mutt's. There's a young kid, an outfielder, who is flying around the field with graceful speed and heightened baseball instincts. On one play, he races far into foul territory to track down a looping liner, catches it as he makes a full somersault, then pops up, turns, and makes a perfect throw to second base in time to nab a runner who had tagged up at first, thinking there was no way he could be thrown out. At the plate, this kid has three hits. All line drives. Mutt looks him up in the program he bought to keep as a souvenir of Mickey's first visit to a professional game.

"Kid's only 20," Mutt says. "Name's Stan Musial."

From this moment on, Mickey's favorite player is, and always will be, Musial, who like Mickey himself will come to be regarded as one of the game's all-time greats. His easy smile, unassuming demeanor, and obvious talent are appealing. Mickey closely observes his unique left-handed batting stance. He wants to adopt it when he and the boys are aping the stances of the professional players.

MUTT'S DREAM: MAKING THE MICK

On the drive home, Mutt says, "That Musial kid's gonna be in the Major Leagues someday, I can tell you that right now. Did you see how he was so balanced when he swung the bat? You see that?"

"Yeah, he was pretty good."

"How he didn't swing at them pitches that were up around his eyes? Strikes. He was always looking for strikes."

"Just like Joe DiMaggio."

"Except Joe D. is a righty, the kid a lefty. See, that's where you can be better than them. Switch-hitting."

Mickey can't imagine being anywhere near as good as the great Joe DiMaggio. Mutt can. Maybe better.

"What about that catcher? Niedson?" Mutt asks.

"A switch-hitting catcher."

Mutt has taught Mickey well.

Chapter 11

There is war in Europe. Germany has invaded Czechoslovakia and Poland, and annexed Austria. England and France have committed to stopping the German onslaught. The United States is staying neutral. Stories in the papers suggest President Franklin Roosevelt is talking like he thinks the war is threatening American security.

"It ain't our war," is on most people's lips in the Tri-State district. "What happens in Europe don't have nothing to do with us."

The fighting might as well be on the moon. Folks around here are more concerned about other things. Like another possible miner strike or the damn dust and the failing farms.

Then the Japanese bomb Pearl Harbor, and the United States is at war after all.

"Where is that? Pearl Harbor?" Mickey asks.

"I don't know. Someplace in the Pacific, I guess," says Mutt. "What the paper says anyway."

"Are they gonna bomb us?"

"And damage our mines? I doubt it."

"But they could."

"I suppose, if they could get this far. That's one advantage to living in the middle of the country, so don't worry about it."

"Will you have to go and fight?"

"Me?"

"But you could? I mean you're a good shot and all."

"Squirrels, maybe. I don't know about Japs."

In the coming days, the Mantle family says little about the

war. That is somebody else's concern. When Mickey sees the local paper, he, like his father, heads for the sports page, but not before checking out the front-page stories. Despite his father's assurances, Mickey can't help being worried.

In a grim statement, directed to the people of Oklahoma, Governor Phillips declared, "Oklahoma is ready. Particular attention will be given to the protection of industrial plants, city water supplies, power plants, and the like." Taking the situation calmly, Phillips declared plans had been laid well and that "this is the time to put everybody on the keep-your-shirt-on committee."

The 45th Division is ready for war. This division, two-thirds of whose troops are from Oklahoma, is ready for any eventuality, according to a statement issued by Maj. Gen. William S. Key, commanding officer. "We are ready and will respond to any call that is made upon us," the general said. "We can move in less than 24 hours with our own transportation. We are in excellent physical condition, and the morale of the individual soldier is praiseworthy."

Turning to the sports page, Mickey sees that the Detroit Tigers slugger Hank Greenberg has been discharged from army service under the law that provides for release of draftees over 28 years of age. He has served six months.

On an early spring afternoon, Mickey, Nick, and LeRoy play fungo while waiting for Mutt to come home.

"Would you go?" LeRoy asks. "If you were old enough, would you?"

"Hell, yes," Mickey says.

"I would," Nick says.

"I'd join up right away," LeRoy says. "Fighting Japs. That would be cool."

"How old do you have to be to join up?"

"I don't know. Maybe 17."

"That all?"

"Maybe."

"I saw Billy Kink joined up," LeRoy says.

"That figures," says Nick.

"What's that supposed to mean?"

"He's the type. Always bragging about something. Thinks he's so hot. If he don't get killed first, he'll probably come home saying he won the war by his lonesome."

"My mother says we've all gotta buy war bonds," LeRoy says.

"What for?" Nick asks.

"I dunno. I guess we need the money to build more bombs or something."

"Well, they're gonna have to find it someplace else," Mickey says. "We ain't got enough for bombs."

"Yeah, we don't neither."

"How old is your dad?" Nick asks.

"I'm not sure," Mickey says.

"But he could go, couldn't he? I read they can draft men up to 45 years old. That's Mutt."

"Yeah, I think he's like 30 or maybe 29."

"Except they need the lead and tin and stuff from the mines, so they're probably not going to take miners. They'd rather have the lead."

"Maybe," Mickey says.

"Hey, you think they're gonna stop playing baseball because of the war?" Nick asks. "Major League baseball, I mean."

"Nah," Mickey says. "It's too American. They'll never stop it."

The others agree. There are some things so important to the country that no war in faraway Europe or Asia will ever stop it.

"Anyway, we don't have to worry," Nick says. "The war ain't coming to Commerce, and our baseball ain't gonna stop."

When a group of planes flies overhead dragging tails of white foam, the boys instinctively look up, uneasily.

―◦●◦―

Mutt has left for work. The rest of the Mantle household is eating breakfast.

"Mom, I'm going to ask Dad if I can join the peewee league over in Douthat," Mickey says between mouthfuls of cereal. "The other guys want to—Nick and LeRoy. You think he'll let me?"

"Maybe. I don't know. You know he's funny about your baseball training. Has his own ideas sometimes."

"Maybe you could tell him he should say 'yes.'"

"Nice try, Mickey."

"He'll listen to you more than me."

"You old enough? What's the age bracket?"

"Under 15."

"But as young as 10?"

"I think so."

"You sure you want to play against kids so much older? I mean they could be 13 or 14."

"I think I can play with them. Anyway, I'll have Nick and LeRoy, and they're my age."

Lovell doesn't say it, but she's thinking that Mickey is so small for his age. It would probably be better if he waited a year or two—at least until he got a little bigger. That wouldn't be such a problem for Nick and LeRoy. They are about average size for their age.

"I'm not afraid, Mom. I know how to play."

"I know you do."

"We can ride our bikes."

"To Douthat?"

"It's only four miles. I checked it on a map at school."

"Each way."

"Easy peasy."

"We'll see."

That night, while eating dinner, Mickey pops the question. Mutt not only agrees, he encourages it. Others will see the good work he has done with his son, and he doubts whether there will be any other players Mickey's age who are better.

"I ran into Elizabeth Halword in the market this morning," Lovell says after Mickey has gone to bed. "We got to talking, and she said she thought it was terrible the way you were pushing Mickey."

"I ain't pushing," Mutt says. "I'm leading, and anyway, that ain't none of her business."

"I know."

On Saturday, Mutt drives Mickey over to Douthat, where the season's peewee league is being organized.

"I could ride my bicycle faster," Mickey says.

"We'll be in plenty of time."

At the field, the boys are asked to play catch while the men who will be the coaches divide them into teams.

Mickey is about to have his first experience playing organized baseball. That night, he remains so excited, he barely sleeps.

Despite the war, Mutt's biggest concern is the peewee league. He talks to the manager of Mickey's team and insists Mickey be allowed to play catcher. When the manager says that he will decide where the boys play, Mutt tells him that Mickey will play catcher or won't play.

Mickey plays catcher.

The league supplies the equipment. Mutt proudly shows Mickey how to put on and adjust the catcher's chest protector and shin guards. He shows him how to get into and out of the catcher's squat with the equipment on.

The peewee league baseball games are played on Saturday mornings. Since there aren't a lot of other weekend social events in and around Commerce, the games usually attract handfuls of spectators. Some of the older boys, the 13- and 14-year-olds, are pretty good, making many of the games truly engaging.

Nick and LeRoy are on Mickey's team, and although the three friends are the youngest players, they get their chances to practice and sometimes play. On the afternoons of scheduled practices, they ride their bikes to and from the makeshift field, their baseball caps pulled low, their gloves hooked through handlebars. At first they race, but Mickey always wins, so after a few times, they stop competing.

When they play, Nick and LeRoy are usually in the outfield. Mickey is always the catcher. His small stature makes him almost disappear. When he squats down behind the taller batters, his chest protector—clearly made for a larger player—is so big that Mickey's feet can't be seen. About all that is visible is the enormous chest protector with two arms sticking out from the sides and two little eyes peeping out from the top. Like a scared turtle peering out from its shell.

Mutt has spent a lot of time working with Mickey on his hitting, but much less on playing in the field. The first time Mutt sees Mickey in a game, he is as nervous as he can ever remember. He stands, shuffling his feet, lighting one cigarette after another. His riveted eyes, firm and assessing, seem to catch everything on the field.

Sometimes, Ox goes with Mutt to the games.

"Mutt, it's a peewee game, not the damned World Series," Ox tells him.

"Don't matter."

"What, you think he should play like Mickey Cochrane in his first ever game?"

"No, I think he should play better."

"Because you know how Cochrane played when he was that age."

"Shut up, Ox."

When Mickey is behind the plate, the spectators either think he looks ridiculous or cute. Not so when he has a bat in his hands. The bat, even though smaller than regulation size, still looks a little too heavy for the youngster, but he knows how to wield it, even when he fails to make contact. In his first few games Mickey doesn't manage to hit the ball out of the infield, and behind the plate more than a few balls get by him.

"That little squirt catcher's gonna get himself hurt back there," Mutt and Lovell overhear a spectator remark.

"Keep your lousy opinions to yourself," Lovell snaps at him loud enough for everyone to hear.

Mutt might boil at the spectator's remark, but he would never respond like his wife does. She may not be as zealous as Mutt when it comes to Mickey's baseball capabilities, but she is far more bellicose in his defense.

"It ain't a lousy opinion if it's right, and believe me, it's right," the spectator says.

"What do you know?"

"I know a kid who's too damn little to be back there."

"Oh, your kid's some kind of giant?"

"Compared to him, yeah."

"Well, bully for you."

In his first games, Mickey continues to show signs of nervousness. He makes mistakes both he and Mutt know he shouldn't. Starting on the Fridays before scheduled Saturday games, he feels his stomach beginning to knot up. It isn't that he doesn't want to play the next day; it's more that he doesn't want to disappoint his father. He also understands that people think he looks ridiculous in his catcher's gear.

"Maybe I could play someplace else," he says to his father.

"You're a catcher, son. It takes time to learn that position. It ain't like no place else on the diamond. It's much more tougher, but you'll get it. I guarantee that. You're gonna make a top-rate backstop. Top-rate, just like your namesake."

Mickey isn't convinced but knows there is no arguing with his headstrong father.

Mickey's team is one of the stronger ones in the league, and as the summer games continue Mickey shows signs of improvement. When he manages to get a hit, Lovell cheers as if he were the team's star. Mutt shows little emotion. With all the work they have put in together, he expects Mickey to hit well. When Mickey makes mistakes, Mutt makes mental notes to work on their causes during their weekday sessions.

When Mickey hits a ball far enough that it rolls between the outfielders, Mutt doesn't see a young kid scampering around the diamond; he sees a full-fledged Major Leaguer sprinting between the bases. Even now, despite his stature, little Mickey runs with a speed that amazes everyone.

"Look at that little kid go. By golly, he can run!"

By the end of the summer, Mickey's team is winning most of its games. It takes the league championship. Mickey, Nick, and LeRoy whoop it up. They are champions, but Mickey is secretly glad the season is over. There will be no more stressful days leading up to each Saturday.

In the fall, Mutt continues to work with Mickey, but now spends more time on fielding basics, running the bases, and adopting the thinking necessary to become a good catcher. Though Mickey certainly hadn't excelled in the peewee league, he held his own against the other boys, most of whom were older – some by as many as four years.

Mutt feels justified. Mickey is on the way to confirming what Mutt has dared to dream. Mickey can escape the colorless world of northeast Oklahoma.

No one else Mutt knows sees what he sees. They see a flat and shriveled land. Chat piles. Square and simple little houses. It is all they expect, now and forever. But Mutt sees potential blowing through the dusty Oklahoma air. It is a gift he is passing on to his oldest son. Someday, Mickey will understand that.

Chapter 12

Mutt is on the weedy baseball field in Picher talking with Ed Gantner, coach of the Picher Junior Cardinal League team. Mutt is familiar with him from the mine where Ed works with the mules.

"Ed, I'm telling you, he can play at this level."

"He's 11, Mutt. Gotta be at least 12."

"You seen him play peewee, didn't you? You know what I'm talking about. He's already better than the other 11-year-olds."

"You're his father, Mutt. You don't—"

"I know baseball, and I know—"

"Yeah, and you never stop talking about it down in the—"

"He can help you."

"But we got rules we gotta follow, and they say kids under 12 don't play."

"You seen him, though. You know."

"I'm sorry, there's nothing I can do," Gantner says as he walks away.

Mutt follows him. "He ain't gonna get better unless he plays with players who are better. That's how he's gonna grow—playing against older kids."

"Yeah, next year, he can play with us. There will still be lots of kids older than him, and frankly, Mutt, better."

"You want the best team, don't you? He'll make you a better team, I promise you that."

"Maybe, but—"

"So, you could ask, couldn't you? You could ask the league if they could let him in. Couldn't hurt."

"Well, I suppose—"

"As a favor."

"OK, I guess as a favor."

The next week, Mutt gets the word. Mickey can play in the league at 11—as a favor to Mutt.

Mickey begins practicing with the team. He's not only the youngest player, he's also the smallest and lightest. Not more than 80 or 90 pounds. Squatting down in his catcher's gear, he looks out of place among the older boys and takes some ribbing about it. But he's holding his own. With a bat in his hands, he looks as if he won't be in over his head when they begin playing for real. And he can run.

"For such a little guy, he can really motor," Gantner says. "Gets around the bases real good."

He suggests to Mickey that maybe it would be better if he played another position, someplace he could utilize his speed.

"You mean, don't catch?" Mickey says.

"Well, maybe you could sometimes, but mostly you should play in the field."

"My father wouldn't like that at all. Have you asked him?"

"Son, I don't have to get his permission. I'm the coach."

"But I'm a catcher. I don't know anything about playing someplace else. I'm always the catcher. Don't you think I can play catcher?"

"Oh, you can play it, but you can learn another position, too."

"Like what?"

"I was thinking second base. We could use you at second. We don't really have a good second baseman now. We could use you there."

Gantner has two objectives in mind. He thinks Mickey's foot speed is being wasted behind the plate, but he also wants one of his bigger players back there. Mickey looks a little ridiculous, overwhelmed as he is by the gear, and he might get hurt if he were run over by a big runner while protecting the plate.

When Mutt shows up at a practice and sees Mickey at second, he immediately confronts Gantner.

"What's this? Why isn't Mickey catching?"

After Gantner explains his reasoning, Mutt reluctantly agrees to let Mickey play second—as a trial—but insists that if Mickey isn't good there, Gantner return him to catcher, or Mutt will pull him from the team.

Despite his protestations, Mutt realizes the coach is right. At second, Mickey can better showcase his talents. Still, he is a little disappointed. His dream always had Mickey behind the plate. From Mickey Cochrane to Mickey Mantle seemed right to him. A catcher is like the quarterback of the team: he sees everything, he controls play, he is the team's heart and soul. Mutt had long considered this Mickey's baseball destiny. Now he'll have to edit his dream.

Reluctantly, Mutt works with Mickey on the fundamentals of infield play. Mickey takes hundreds of ground balls from Mutt and occasionally from Charlie.

"Keep your butt down," Mutt repeats so often, that after a while Mickey barely hears it. "Keep it down, keep it low."

Mutt hasn't given up on Mickey as a catcher, so they work on that also. He's convinced that when Mickey grows a little, he'll be back behind the plate.

"What's wrong with a fast catcher?" Mutt asks Charlie.

"Not a thing, but I see the coach's point. Why waste that speed?"

"So, he'll be really fast running the bases. Mickey, keep your butt down."

Mickey, too, is a little disappointed. He had never thought of a baseball future at any position other than behind the plate. Even his name, coming as it does from a catcher, always seemed to cement that as his position. Still, playing second is fun too. He gets to run more and there is less pressure than being involved with every pitch as a catcher must do.

He quickly finds his footing in the Junior League Cardinals games. He bobbles grounders from time to time and makes a few wayward throws to first, but he hits well and soon becomes a favorite of the spectators. A scrappy little player. Even at his age, he shows promise.

At school, when his teacher hears him bragging about his hitting at a recent game, she suggests maybe he's getting a case of a swelled head.

"Pay a little more attention to your studies and a little less attention to baseball, and you'll be better in the long run. Someday, you'll be glad you did because you'll need to find a paying job. Unless you want to follow your father into the mines, you're going to need a good education."

"I could make money playing baseball, maybe," Mickey says.

"I wouldn't count on that."

"Do you know how much money Joe DiMaggio makes?'

"Mickey, I don't even know who Joe Maggio is."

Later, he tells Mosley, "I thought teachers were supposed to be real smart. How smart can you be if you don't know the most famous baseball player in the world?"

"She must lead a very sheltered life."

Where earlier Mickey was uncomfortable playing in front of anybody other than his friends, now he is beginning to appreciate the attention of the spectators, and there are a lot of spectators. On Saturday morning game days, so many spectators turn up to watch the kids that the games hardly look like amateur contests. The players range from 12 to 18. Only the little second baseman from the Cardinals is younger.

At game time, dozens of cars drive out to the field, the rising dust and honking horns heralding their arrival. They form a circle around the field. Some spectators sit on top of their cars; others spread out blankets or sit on egg crates. Picnic baskets are opened, and plenty of whiskey flasks stashed not-so-secretly in back pockets—Mutt's among them. People holler and cheer during the games. They are generally so respectful and attentive to the games that Lovell comments, "You'd think these kids were playing their way into the World Series."

Mickey draws particular attention for his switch-hitting.

"Ever see a kid that young switch-hitting like that?"

MUTT'S DREAM: MAKING THE MICK

"I ain't seen many grownups switch-hit like that."

Mutt is always at the games from the very first to the final pitch ... except once. He is at the hospital when Lovell is delivering another son. Mickey comes to bat in the eighth inning against a tall, skinny, curve-balling right-hander. As per Mutt's insistence, Mickey would normally hit from the left side, but on this day, with Mutt absent, he stands in right-handed. He strikes out on three pitches.

Before he gets back to the bench, he hears Mutt yelling out with a booming voice full of "you're-in-for-it now," ordering Mickey to go straight home. "And don't you ever put on that uniform again until you switch-hit like I taught you."

Mutt startles not only Mickey but also everybody else watching the game.

With spectators and players staring at him, Mickey feels punished. Humiliated. He is close to tears as he leaves the field. He finds his bicycle. He rides home shaken by the unexpected outburst from his father.

Thinking it's too early for Mickey to be home and seeing how upset he is, Charlie asks him what is wrong.

"He sent me home because I batted right-handed," he says as he throws his baseball cap across the kitchen.

"Against a righty pitcher?"

"I didn't think he was there. I didn't think Dad would know."

"Oh, I wouldn't worry too much. By supper, he'll forget all about it."

"Grandpa, I can't do this anymore," Mickey says as he stubs his toe trying to kick a bat across the floor.

"What? You can't play baseball?"

"Not the way he wants. It's always got to be the way he wants. I can't ever do what I want."

"He just wants what's best for you, and he's pretty damn sure that means switch-hitting."

"He yelled at me in front of all those people, made me look like an idiot, just because just one time I didn't hit from the side he wanted."

Charlie laughs, "Then next time, don't do it."

"Maybe there won't be a next time. Maybe I'll just quit playing. Then he won't have anybody to yell at."

"You know you ain't gonna do that."

"Oh yeah, that's what you think."

When Mutt walks in the door, he announces that the family now includes another boy—Larry—making a complete Mantle infield. Then he adds, "Probably grow up to be a switch-hitter."

———•●•———

Mickey, Nick, and LeRoy are waiting out a windstorm. They are sitting on the ground, leaning back against an abandoned house badly punished by the sun. A partially sand-buried fence, now rusted into a splotchy reddish-brown running next to the house, leans like a tree in the wind. In front of them the forlorn landscape is filled with dust and sand. And chat. Yet it is somehow empty. This is the only scenery they've ever known.

"This is it, isn't it?" Nick says wistfully.

"What's it?" LeRoy asks.

"Our world."

"What do you mean?"

"Wind, and sand in your eyes, and crummy houses, and alkali field, and chat mountains."

"Don't forget falling-down rusty fences."

"And falling-down rusty fences."

"Let's get out of here," Nick says.

"Go to the movies or something?" Mickey asks. "I got to be home when—"

"Not the damn movies, the damned mining area."

"My bike's got a flat," Mickey says.

"Nah, I mean like getting out of here when we're grown up."

"Oh, yeah. That's what I'm planning."

"You think baseball—?"

"I dunno, maybe."

"You're pretty good."

Mickey shakes his head. "You guys are, too. You're just as good."

"Yeah?" Nick says.

"Except you don't got fathers teaching you all the time like I do."

"Yeah, well, he teaches us too, in case you didn't notice."

"I know, but—"

"Anyway, that's just a dream, you know. We ain't never going to get out of here by playing baseball. It's just a stupid dream."

"Could be, but it's the only one I got."

"I know that's what your father—"

"He knows what he's talking about."

"Sure, he does."

After a long pause while the boys duck their heads against the wind coming whipping around the side of the house, Mickey continues, "I'm worried about him, though. He's coughing a lot more."

"They all cough. All the miners do."

"Except he's doing it more and more lately. Coughing like crazy, like his lungs are coming up or something."

"I know," says LeRoy.

Mickey picks up a stone and throws it across the yard.

"Every day down in the mine, he breathes in dust and damp stuff and foul air, but he never sees a doctor. He just says 'So, what the hell? Live like you can,' and then he lights up another cigarette like he's making his point real clear."

Mickey often muses about losing his father to silicosis or tuberculosis or cancer. It makes him nervous every time he thinks about it, but he can't make the thoughts go away. So many men around here are dying young. There's no reason to think Mutt won't be among them. Then what? How would they get by?

Every time his father criticizes Mickey for something he thinks Mickey is doing wrong, Mickey is hurt, and it makes him anxious because he is so often reminded that he may not have a father much longer. Perceived guilt is always with him.

"We gotta get out of here," Nick says more firmly than before.

Mickey and Mosley walk downtown to the Lyric Theatre.

The placard in the window reads: "The James Boys Ride Again in a Great Double Feature Program." Both films, *Jesse James*, "the picture recognized as Darryl F. Zanuck's greatest production," and *The Return of Frank James* "to avenge the murder of Jesse," star Henry Fonda. Both in glorious Technicolor.

For 20 cents, they could sit in the orchestra section, but they buy the 10-cent tickets for the balcony. In the first film, railroad agents forcibly evict the James family from their farm, so Jesse (played by Tyrone Power) and Frank (played by Fonda) turn to banditry for revenge. The second film has Frank avoiding arrest to take revenge on the Ford brothers for the murder of his brother Jesse. Exciting stuff for the boys. However, it is a section in the newsreel that really grabs their attention.

After clips of American soldiers in action in the Pacific, a clip shows a young outfielder who hopes one day to play in the Major Leagues. Pete Gray is an outfielder with only one arm. The newsreel explains that he is a miner's son who lost his right arm at the age of six, when he fell off a farmer's wagon and caught his arm in the spokes. The arm had to be amputated. Yet, there he is on film, swinging the bat one-handed and playing in the field. The film shows him wearing a glove without padding. When the ball is hit to him, he holds the glove out about shoulder height. When the ball hits the glove, he rolls it across his chest with his glove pinned under his right stump. He then makes strong throws with his left arm. To handle grounders, he lets the ball bounce off his glove, then drops the glove to snatch the ball while it is still in the air. At bat, he chokes up about six inches, but still has a perfect swing. When demonstrating bunting, he plants the knob of the bat against his side, slides his hand farther up the bat, and deftly pushes the ball into fair territory.

Mickey and Mosley are engrossed by what they are seeing.

"I don't believe that," Mosley says. "That's amazing."

"I bet he can't switch-hit," Mickey says.

While walking home, they don't say one word about Jesse or

MUTT'S DREAM: MAKING THE MICK

Frank James, or about Henry Fonda or Tyrone Power.

"He has to be lightning quick to pick that ball out of the air like that," Mosley says.

"You don't think it's trick photography or something, do you?"

"Nah, that was real."

When they get to Mickey's yard, they try to duplicate Gray's feats. After a few tries, Mickey is able to catch and throw a few balls using one arm.

"You could do that if you had to. You actually could," says the impressed Mosley.

Mickey breaks out into laughter, "Man, can you imagine what my dad would do if I did that in a game?"

"He'd have a conniption fit."

"What if he'd lost a leg? Think he'd hop around on one?" Mickey says while demonstrating.

"He'd have to."

"Shows you, though, what a handicapped guy can do if he really wants to."

This is not the last time Mickey's thoughts turn to the idea of a severely handicapped athlete. The next time, though, it will be personal.

Mickey shows up at a tryout for a Douthat team in the Gabby Street League. Nick and LeRoy are also trying out. The league is named after the catcher who played for five different Major League teams from 1904 to 1912 and then went on to manage, coach, and do radio broadcasts. Known as "The Old Sarge," he became famous for catching a baseball dropped from the top of the Washington Monument—on his thirteenth attempt. As a manager he won two National League pennants with the St. Louis Cardinals, and the World Series in 1931.

Street himself had come to the Tri-State district to explain how the league was to operate, after which the Joplin Lions Club voted to sponsor the league.

Mickey's Douthat team is managed by Red Lovelace. Boys from 10 to 18 are eligible to play in the league. Tryouts are at the high school in Miami. It doesn't take Lovelace long to select all three boys for his team. Games are scheduled from July 9th through September 5th. He sits his players down and tells them he expects them to come to all the practices and games. They'll need to supply their own gloves. At the end of the season, the championship team will be awarded jackets or sweaters. He isn't sure which.

Mutt is initially concerned that he won't be able to make the games, but after Mickey explains that the games start at six o'clock each evening, except on Tuesdays, when they start at five o'clock, he is relieved. He does not want Mickey playing organized baseball if he can't be there to take mental notes about how he is playing. He also wants to make sure the coach is using Mickey properly. Mutt knows the game; he's not so sure about Lovelace, but he is willing to give him the benefit of the doubt.

Before the first practice, Mutt grills Mickey. "He say where you're supposed to play, your coach?"

"He hasn't said anything about that."

"You tell him you're gonna switch-hit?"

"No."

"Well, you'd better, because I don't want him telling you nothing different."

"Yeah, I'll tell him."

"And to let you hit high in the order, so you'll get more at-bats."

"OK."

"Did he say anything about the lineup?"

"He didn't say anything, no."

"Or about how he's gonna manage? Anything like that?"

Lovell, who has heard the interrogation, calls from the kitchen. "For Pete's sake, hon, they haven't even started practicing yet. Stop with the third degree, will you?"

Mutt isn't home from the mine in time to catch most practices, so he always checks with Mickey to see how they're going. Mostly he gets "fine" for an answer.

Having seen Mickey play in the peewee league, Lovelace already has an idea how Mickey will do at second. Frequently, second basemen are the smaller, quicker players. Mickey is certainly that. So that is where Mickey mostly plays, although he still catches occasionally. Mickey doesn't want to give up catching altogether, but the more he plays the infield, the more he is enjoying it. He uses his speed to get under pop flies down the line and out into the outfield. He's pretty sure he gets to some that none of his teammates could have reached.

The games are mostly played on reclaimed waste sites washed flat by flooding—baked hard, and topped with swirling alkali dust.

"It a miracle we don't all have tuberculosis," LeRoy observes when the wind kicks up. But like all the others, all he does is complain and then beat the dust off his clothes.

All the games are in small mining towns like Picher and Douthat, so the large crowds are almost all miners, usually still in their dirty work coveralls and mining helmets. Often their families join them, with mothers towing little children and carrying babies. There are always beer kegs for the winning team's supporters. The crowds are loud and supportive of the players from their towns. The games make for enjoyable summer-evening diversions from the drudgery of mine work.

One of the players on the Douthat team is the son of the coach. Delbert Lovelace is the only player on the team from outside Commerce. The local spectators ride him mercilessly. One ginger-headed girl always stands up when he comes to bat and screams in a high-pitched voice, "Lovelady, Lovelady, Lovelady, you swing like a girl." The spectators get a kick out of her antics, and she becomes a popular regular at the games.

"I think she's about as much fun as the games themselves," Lovell observes.

"Speak for yourself," Mutt says.

In a mid-August Tuesday night game, Douthat is playing the team from Treece, another mining town just across the Kansas state line. The team is using a pitcher considerably taller than the other boys. They call him "Long John" Blair.

"That overgrown oaf can really smoke the ball," Nick says to Mickey as they watch him warm up.

"Looks like."

"Hope he don't throw at my head. I kinda like it like it is."

"Might make an improvement."

"And I like my teeth right where they are."

"He's probably just trying to scare us."

"If he is, he's doing a helluva good job of it."

Long John, who is also older than most of the others, completely dominates the game. Through the first seven innings, he is perfect. None of the Douthat players have reached base. Mickey, like most of his teammates, has already struck out three times. When Mickey comes to bat again in the ninth, he figures the only way he is going to get on is to use his legs. He strides to the plate, purposely looking as confident as he can by adopting an exaggerated swagger. Before he steps into the batter's box, he swings his bat a few times with all the force he can muster, then digs in forcefully with his back foot as he settles into his usual stance. His face shows his determination and intention. He's going to drive the ball as hard and far as he can. In the field, both the first and second basemen move back a few steps. Mickey might not be the biggest player in the game, but they know he can drive the ball pretty well.

Long John cranks up disdainfully and whistles a screamer toward the plate. Mickey takes a step out to meet the ball while jamming the end of the bat against his side and sliding his left hand up the bat, a la Pete Gray. He connects with the ball on the fat part of the bat, tapping it gently in the direction of the second baseman. He has judged it perfectly. The ball bounces along to Long John's left. He runs out after it but all he can do is wave his glove at it, while Mickey sprints toward first. The first baseman, who had also started for the ball, picks it up, reverses his direction and tries to beat Mickey to the bag. He doesn't. Mickey is safe, and the perfect game is gone.

Standing on the base, Mickey looks toward his father. Mutt is smiling.

Douthat loses the game, but Mickey has shown he is a smart little player. Driving home, Mutt doesn't say a word about that play. He doesn't have to. Mickey knows he has made his father proud, and that is easily the best thing about this day.

Chapter 13

As the war drags on, so do the deaths of area boys. Every week, the local papers list the dead and missing in action. Each week, Lovell says she will no longer look at the page with the lists, but she does and often finds names she recognizes—Jewell Spriggs, Ira Hawthorn, Homer Davis, Duke Kingfisher. And the list grows. She always looks first under the "Rs" to see if there are any Richardsons. Her large family includes several nephews she hasn't seen in years. One, Stephen, is listed as missing in action.

Over breakfast, Lovell is reading from the *Miami Daily News Record*. "Pfc. Walter O'Brien of Commerce is being held as a prisoner of war in Osaka, Japan. James Earl Douthit is missing in action. He was a Motor Machinist's Mate Second Class on the USS Frederick C. Davis destroyer escort that was sunk in the Atlantic ... You knew him, didn't you, Mickey? You know him, I mean."

"Yeah, from baseball."

"A shame about him missing and all."

"Yep," he says without looking up from the sports page, where there is a story about Stan Musial.

"Are sports the only thing you read in the papers?" Lovell says.

"Nope. I also read Joe Palooka, Alley Oop, and Red Ryder."

"Cartoons."

"Yeah, but good ones."

"Gotta pay a little attention to what's going on in the world, you know."

"The World Series."

"I give up."

"Four years," Lovell says quietly. "How much longer is it going to go on, the war?"

Mutt lights another cigarette. His third of the morning, and it's not even light yet.

"I dunno."

"Why don't you know?"

"Hitler didn't tell me."

"I can't imagine why not, seeing as how you're so interested in what's going on. What if the war is still in full swing when Mickey is old enough to be drafted?"

"It won't be."

"Oh, so now you know. Get a telegram recently from Hitler?"

Mutt takes a last sip of coffee. "I've got to get to work."

"Yeah, you do that."

Mickey continues to play in the Gabby Street League and play well. The more he plays, the more comfortable he becomes on the field—in everything except hitting left-handed. If Mutt isn't at the game, he always hits from the right side. When Mickey is at bat hitting from the right side against a right-handed pitcher, Nick and LeRoy are his lookouts. If they see Mutt coming, they call out "here he comes," and Mickey immediately jumps around to the left. Many spectators get a kick out of Mickey's ploy, but no one ever tells Mutt. They would rather protect the high-spirited kid than the hard-hearted father.

During one July afternoon game in which Douthat is running away in the late innings, Mutt arrives unnoticed by Mickey's sentries and sees Mickey hitting from the "wrong side." He doesn't say a word to Mickey. Rather, he goes up to Coach Lovelace and says, "Mickey's going home."

"Mutt, he's at bat."

"Not now, he isn't."

"Look, if you're trying to convince me that—"

"I'm not trying to convince you; I'm telling you."

Mutt's action speaks for itself. He doesn't say any more to Mickey about it. Mickey, the dutiful son, doesn't apologize. It's his singular small act of self-expression.

Mutt is like a surrogate father to both Nick and LeRoy. Neither have fathers in their lives, so Mutt always includes both boys in the baseball activities.

On most days, they arrive at the Mantle house early in the morning. Lovell always opens a fresh box of Wheaties. The boys enjoy the cereal's connection with sports figures.

When the slugger Hank Greenberg is on the front of the box, they spend much of the morning arguing about which is his best nickname—Hammerin' Hank, Hankus Pankus, or The Hebrew Hammer.

Other boxes bring other opinions.

With Mickey, Nick, LeRoy, Ray, Roy, Larry, and Barbara all sharing the wheat and bran breakfast, the box is always emptied down to the last flake.

As soon as breakfast is over, the boys go outside to play baseball. Sometimes football. Occasionally basketball. They will be at it all day until either they have a Gabby Street League game or batting practice when Mutt gets home.

When Nick and LeRoy and sometimes Mosley are there at dinnertime, they all sit around the kitchen table as Lovell puts out a big pot of beans, corn bread, and quartered onions. Maybe a big pot roast. It is an animated atmosphere, full of laughter, robust exchanges about baseball and other sports, corny jokes, and occasional outbursts from the younger kids. But almost never about the war or other current events. Lovell loves it.

Mickey, Nick, and LeRoy walk to the Lyric Theater for the Saturday matinee. They watch *False Colors* with William Boyd as Hopalong Cassidy and the 10th chapter of *Batman*. After the show, the boys stop at Ott Chandler's Drugstore, where LeRoy picks up a headache remedy for his mother, and then it's down the street to the Black Cat Café, where they take seats at the counter.

Sophie, the perky little waitress, knows the boys. "Three blue plate specials?" she asks with a knowing grin.

"Yep," Mickey says, "with all the trimmings."

"Why do you call it the blue plate?" Nick asks.

"Because that's what it is," Sophie says matter-of-factly.

"The plates are white."

"You think we should paint them?"

"Or you could call it the white plate special."

"I'll pass your idea on to Solly."

"Anyway, what's so special about it?"

"Beats me."

"It never changes—a hamburger, a bowl of chili, and a soda pop."

"Maybe it's the price. The price is special."

"Twenty-five cents don't sound so special to me."

"OK, I'll charge you thirty."

"I only have a quarter."

"I'll take two tablespoons of chili out of your bowl."

"Or maybe skip the pickle on the burger."

Sophie puts on an exaggerated smile. "You boys like breaking my chops?"

"Nah, just teasing," Nick says, returning the smile.

Since the war began, sugar has been under government control. For some unexplained reason, Mountain Dew always seems sweet enough, so that's what the boys drink. LeRoy explains that it had been intended as a chaser for moonshine and whiskey.

"Only you would know that," Nick says.

"You would too, if you ever read a book," LeRoy says.

"I read *Batman*."

"I don't mean comics."

"Ever hear of *Classics Illustrated*, smarty pants? I've read *Les Misérables*. Have you?"

"No."

MUTT'S DREAM: MAKING THE MICK

"It's French."

"Do tell."

"And *The Three Musketeers,* except there are really four. That's French, too."

"You could read the real books, you know, instead of the comic book versions."

"Why? Does the story change or something?"

"Oh, never mind."

The jukebox seems to be stuck on songs from Bob Wills and the Texas Playboys.

...And Rose, my Rose of San Antone.
Deep within my heart lies a melody
A song of old San Antone
Where in dreams I live with a memory
Beneath the stars all alone
It was there I found beside the Alamo
Enchantment strange as the blue up above...

When Sophie returns with the specials, she asks Mickey, "You ever take that off, your baseball cap?"

"Not unless I have to."

"Like taking a bath?"

"He don't take baths," Nick says.

"Or when you go to sleep?" Sophie asks as she plops the chili down.

"Not unless my mother makes me."

Mickey loves his baseball cap. He has worked hard getting it just the way he wants it by working the visor into a curve, similar to the ones he saw on the players in the minor league game in Joplin. He thinks it makes him look like an old hand at the game.

"Those Hoppies are pretty cool," Nick says, referring to the popular name for the Hopalong Cassidy films. "The way he rides and everything."

"I'd like to have a horse," Mickey says. "Maybe become a cowboy."

"Your father would probably make you ride left-handed ... or maybe switch-handed," Nick says.

"I'm having a hard time picturing you as a cowboy," LeRoy says.

"Yeah," says Nick. "You're too small. You gotta be big enough to rope them steers."

"No, you don't," Mickey says. "You just gotta be smarter."

"Who ain't smarter than a cow? Everybody's smarter than a cow."

Where's that gal with the red dress on?
Some folks called her Dinah
Stole my heart away from me
Way down in Louisiana...

While downing their burgers and chili, the boys engage in a lively debate about who is the best cowboy. Hopalong Cassidy or Roy Rogers, whose new film, *King of the Cowboys,* is expected to be at the Lyric soon. They also debate the merits of the superheroes they see in the comics. Batman, Captain Marvel, Captain America. Superman could beat any of them. No argument there.

"Don't forget Wonder Woman," Sophie adds as she clears away the dishes.

"Against Superman, are you kidding?" Nick says. "No way. Not against any of them, really."

"You don't know what you're talking about. The Greek gods gave her superhuman powers."

"The Greek gods?"

"Yeah, she's the daughter of Zeus and Hippolyta."

"Whoever they are."

"And she's armed with a pair of indestructible bracelets."

"Oh, wow! Bracelets," says Nick. "Captain America would make mincemeat of her, and Superman wouldn't even waste his time on her."

"Have you ever looked at a Wonder Woman comic?"

"I wouldn't be caught dead reading one of them."

"Why? Too many big words for you or because she's a woman?"

Mickey and LeRoy are breaking up listening to Nick do verbal battle with Sophie.

"That's right, and they can't, you know—"

"Little do you know," Sophie says adamantly. "Batman even called her the best melee fighter in the world."

"Well, Batman don't fight melees, whatever they are."

"And she could press 15,000 pounds even before she received her super bracelets. Then she lifted a 50,000-pound boulder over her head to inspire her followers."

"I'll tell you who the best real hero is," Mickey says. "Joe DiMaggio. He hit in 56 straight games. Wonder Woman probably couldn't even get down a bunt hit."

"Joe who?" Sophie says as she goes back into the kitchen.

"She's just putting you on," LeRoy says. "Everybody knows who Joe DiMaggio is."

Thoughts of righteous cowboys taking on the bad guys, virtuous superheroes fighting the forces of evil, and baseball idols performing seemingly impossible feats allow the boys to imagine themselves in more exciting circumstances. Away from the mundane world of mines, and dust, and wind, and fields of alkali. Escapist fantasies are seldom far from their thoughts.

Chapter 14

The day begins like most school days do; it ends as a day Mickey will never forget.

He has to be shaken awake by his mother. He eats breakfast, then rides his bike to school. His attention to the teacher is, as usual, broken by intermittent episodes of daydreaming. After school he rides home, changes his clothes, puts on his well-worn baseball cap pulled low. His mother asks him how his day in school went. He says it went fine. His grandfather asks him the same thing and gets the same answer. He downs a glass of milk and eats two chocolate chip cookies. In the yard, he plays catch with his eight-year-old brothers, Ray and Roy. Barbara joins them for a while but soon loses interest.

At a few minutes after four o'clock, he walks down to the road to meet his father. In a minute, Mutt arrives, dirty and unshaven and tired, but eager to work with Mickey. Mickey takes Mutt's lunch pail as they walk together up to the house. Mutt exchanges his steel-toed safety shoes for the leather cleats he always uses when practicing or playing baseball.

Charlie comes into the yard with the extra balls they will be using.

"Missed your game yesterday," he says.

"You didn't miss much. Nine nothing for the good guys."

"How'd you do?"

"Couple of hits, that's all."

"In the field?"

"Not much. I didn't get many chances. Kinda boring, really."

As they always do while waiting for Mutt, they warm up by playing catch. Mickey throws a few knucklers that his grandfather has trouble catching. "You're getting pretty good with that thing," Charlie says.

Mickey throws another one that gets completely away from Charlie.

"My goodness, you can really make that thing dip and dive."

"Yeah, when I get the grip right."

"Especially since you don't got the biggest hands."

"Nick's and LeRoy's hands are bigger, but they can't get it to dance at all."

"Maybe you're gonna be a pitcher someday. Ever pitch in a game now?"

"Nah."

"You probably could though."

"I guess."

As they always do, when Mutt joins them, he and Charlie alternate throwing to Mickey, so that he is continually switching from the left and right sides of the plate. For a change of pace, they spend a few minutes working on double plays. Mutt plays short, Mickey second, Charlie first.

"Getting two outs on one pitch can make a huge difference," Mutt reminds Mickey. "You always want to get to the bag and square up to the shortstop, even if he is behind the second base bag."

"Yeah, I know."

"On account of you gotta get the first out before you get the second one, so square up and give me a good target."

They practice this several times. Slowly, deliberately.

"Timing. You got to pay attention to the timing. When you catch the ball, you want your right foot to touch the ground the same moment you catch the ball. Got it?"

Mickey is impressed that his catcher father knows these details about playing second. Mutt, knowing Mickey is mostly playing there, has been paying particular attention to second-base play on his mine team.

After some ten minutes of fielding, they return to batting practice.

MUTT'S DREAM: MAKING THE MICK

Mutt knows good fielding is important, but good hitting will always take a player further. Hitting well is the key to Mickey's future.

They are at it for about an hour when Mutt goes after a ball that rolls off to the right. Mickey, hearing the disquieting throbbing of planes overhead, instinctively looks up. He can't see the planes. They must be above the wispy clouds.

When he looks down, he sees his grandfather slumped on the ground.

"Dad!" Mutt screams.

Mickey and Mutt rush to Charlie, who is struggling for breath.

Mutt kneels next to his father. "Stay there," Mutt says. "Don't try to get up."

Looking down at his grandfather, Mickey sees his own face looking back at him. It is truly frightening.

When Charlie's breathing evens out, they help him get back into the house.

"I'm OK now," Charlie says. "I'll be all right. Just gotta rest a little. I don't know what happened. I just ... I'm fine."

But he isn't, and they all know it.

Seemingly overnight, Charlie has become feeble. It is not long before Mutt has to help him out of bed. He stops pitching to Mickey, always saying that he will throw the next day. When he moves about, it is on wobbly legs that used to stride around town with such vigor.

A shadow has come over the Mantle home, and no one is enveloped by it more than Mickey.

The calendar says it is spring, but instead of a crisp morning the day dawns sultry.

Mutt tells Mickey, "Keep your eyes on the little ones, will you? I'm going to go out with your mom for a short while. Grandpa is taking a nap, so don't bother him, and try to keep the twins quiet."

Mutt and Lovell walk down to the river and then along a narrow dirt trail that runs along the bank. Lovell assumes Mutt must have something on his mind, since he almost never is interested in going on long walks. When he doesn't say anything for some time, Lovell finally asks, "What's going on?"

Mutt lights a Camel. "Why do you think something's going on?"

"You'd rather hit yourself in the head with your pickax than go for a walk with me."

"My ax is broken."

"OK, let's have it."

"I was thinking we should move."

"You mean to California? Haven't we been all through that already?"

"Not California. That ain't what everybody thinks it is, anyway, California."

"Then what?"

"Away from here. Out in the country."

"That's not something we can—"

"Away from the mines."

"And do what?"

"Farm."

"We tried that, remember?"

"Yeah, but—"

"It's so hard now and—"

"It's possible to sharecrop with all the—"

"Don't you see how many farmers—?"

"It ain't the same now as it was then, when we were on the farm," Mutt says unconvincingly. "It's different. It's better. Farmers are making money again. The war helps. I hate to say that, but it's true. With so many men away, there's more need for people to grow the food and all the—"

"The mine gives us a check every week. We can't gamble that we'll make enough to keep things going as they are. In case you haven't noticed, we have five kids and your father and—"

"We got to get away from the mine. Especially for Dad. Out in the country where the air is better."

"Is it, though?"

"Dad needs it, fresh air. He'd have a better chance of … you know, fighting what he's got."

"He hasn't even been in a mine for years."

"But he used to be, and that … those things don't go away so easy."

"No, of course they don't, but—"

"And me, too. I could get out of there, and we could live on a farm. You liked that before, didn't you? You liked it when we were on that farm."

"Except we damn near starved to death."

"Well, this time will be different. The Wormington place—"

Lovell suddenly stops walking and grabs Mutt by the elbow. "Mutt you didn't—"

"Yeah, I did. You'll love it."

"Doctor Wormington's farm?"

"It's only about five miles away, but it's far enough to … get away from—"

"How did you—?"

"I swapped our house for a few cows, a horse, a tractor and the right to sharecrop 160 acres of his land."

"Oh, Mutt, no, no, no."

"One hundred and sixty acres! We can do a lot with that."

"You should have asked me, Mutt. You should have asked me."

"I knew you wouldn't like—"

"But you did it anyway. How could you do that to me?" She turns and storms back to the house on Quincy that they are about to leave for good.

Dr. Wormington is a highly respected physician, surgeon, and registered pharmacist. A graduate of the University of Arkansas and the University Medical School in Kansas City, he has been a prominent practicing physician and civic leader in the area since 1900.

The way Mutt has it figured, Dr. Wormington is a decent and honorable man. Not one who would likely take unfair advantage of a tenant. Not like the last time they tried sharecropping. Lovell had been angry when Mutt told her about the move and becomes even more so when she sees the house on the farm.

Their house on Quincy Street, while far from luxurious, is a palace compared to the old house they move into. Its only advantage is that it has two stories, but it is dilapidated and cold. No bathroom. The outhouse is set well away from the house, making for chilly trips in winter. The cracks in the floor are so bad that when the wind comes up parts of the linoleum stand up practically straight.

Lovell is disconsolate, but determined to make the most of it. She is a strong-willed mother who understands that she can't show her displeasure when her children are around, so she puts on a positive front.

"Plenty of space here to play ball," she says to Mickey. "Look at the size of that lawn."

"Yeah, it's pretty big."

"And guess who will have the pleasure of cutting it?"

"Dad?"

"Guess again."

"Maybe we could just let it grow."

"Maybe you could cut it."

"I don't know how."

"You take the lawnmower that's out back and you push it around until there's no tall grass left."

When they settle into life on the farm, everyone gets assigned chores. Mickey's are to keep the lawn mown and take out the garbage every evening to burn in a trash bin. They all share in taking care of the animals. They have four cows, five horses, a slew of chickens, and a particularly nasty rooster.

"That damn rooster is meaner than any dog I've ever seen," Mickey tells Mosley. "Every time I step outta the house, that dang rooster's right there. And, man, it jumps on me like it wants to eat me."

"Maybe he knows you want to eat him."

"No, I love that rooster."

"Bull."

"Yeah, I take my bat and chase him all over the place. It's great training, running like that, dodging this way and that. He's quick, but he's making me quicker."

"A real training partner."

As they settle into farm life, all the kids learn to milk the cows.

When Mutt announces they're going to pick up a calf from another farmer, they take the back seat out of the LaSalle and shove the animal in there.

Mutt loves working outdoors again. Loves being away from the dark and clammy mine. Loves being his own boss. Mickey loves it, too. He takes the twins fishing; he hunts with his father. He learns to ride horses.

"OK, this one's yours," Mutt says to Mickey, indicating a horse on which Mickey seems particularly comfortable. It isn't a very big horse. It isn't a very fast horse, but unlike the rooster it is a gentle animal.

Mickey names the horse Tony. "Can I ride him to school, Tony?"

"To school?" Lovell asks.

"Sure, other kids do. They tie them up outside. The teachers don't mind."

"It's five miles."

"It'll save my legs. The bicycle, it takes a lot out of my legs that I could use better for baseball."

"You really think I'll believe that?"

"You don't ride a bicycle, so you don't know how hard it is to pedal for a long time."

"After I'm sure you're good enough, yeah, OK."

Two days later, Mickey begins riding Tony to school. Some days, he's Hopalong Cassidy, some days Bob Steele, some Buster Crabbe. Tony loves to run with Mickey on his back and to graze around a fishing hole while Mickey fishes.

"He's a real understanding horse," Mickey tells LeRoy.

"Yeah, what does he understand?"

"He understands that he don't like school any better than me."

Mutt isn't making much sharecropping, but with the kids getting bigger and Mickey's friends often eating meals with them, they need more food than before, and the farm offers them that. More importantly for Mutt, it offers better air for his father. Even so, Charlie isn't up to doing much around the farm. Most days, he sits at the kitchen table or in a wicker chair in the living room. He reads the paper and listens to the radio a lot, often falling asleep in the midst of a Cardinals game. He never used to do that.

Mutt is worried.

It is a sultry Sunday morning in August. Lovell looks up from reading *The Daily Oklahoman*. "I see they're hiring over at the DuPont place in Oklahoma City. The paper says they're looking for men to work on something they're calling the Pacific Northwest Construction Project."

"That so," says Mutt dismissively.

Lovell reads, "Top wages—now working 54 hours—time and a half for more than 40 hours. Must be a citizen of the USA. Workers now employed at their highest skill in essential industry need not apply."

"Not interested."

"Looks like it pays well."

"Except it's in Oregon or Washington or someplace like that, and I ain't going out there. I don't care how much it pays."

"War work ain't going to be around forever."

"We're doing just fine here on the farm."

"We're barely getting by, you mean."

"We got food on the table, don't we? Every day we got food. Three meals every day. That's good enough."

"Yeah," Lovell says with a deep breath of resignation.

"I see Musial has got his average up to .363."

"Great."

Mutt reads, "Oklahoma's sport front shifts to New York City, where Howard Raines, the all-Oklahoma baseball player, is shown the big city in company with other youthful players who'll take part in the East-West All-Star Game at the Polo Grounds. Raines hopes to get the starting call on the West team, which will be coached by Mel Ott."

"That's a big jump, from a small town in Oklahoma to New York City."

"Not too big if you're good enough."

"It won't work," Lovell insists. "New York will chew him up and spit him out. That's no place for a nice boy from around here."

"Give him a chance."

"I'll wager he'll be home within a month."

"Maybe. Maybe not."

"Who'd want to live and play ball in New York anyway?"

Mutt pushes back from the table. "I'm going up to see if Dad is awake and wants to come down for breakfast."

When Mutt tries to wake Charlie, he can't. Charles Edwin Mantle is dead at 62.

Although he hadn't worked in the mines for years, Charlie suffered the consequences. Hodgkin's disease attacks the lymphatic system, which plays a pivotal role in the body's defense system. Because the lymphatic system consists of channels that run through the body like blood vessels, it gives cancer a convenient route to all the organs and tissues. The farm's fresh air, which Mutt had hoped would give his father more time, had no role to play in the course of the disease.

Not for the last time, Mickey sees a Mantle man dying before his time. This will remain a theme of his adult life. He too is likely to die young, so he might as well enjoy life while he can.

With his grandfather gone, Mickey is enveloped in a cloud of memories. It seems like only yesterday that his grandfather showed off the power in his arms by taking one swing to split a hog's head open. He remembers, too, the awful stench that ran through the house after the dead hog was scalded and dried. He remembers his grandfather's curve ball and high hard one. What he can't remember is anyone ever saying anything mean about him. He had been a genuinely nice man.

Charlie is laid out on a table that takes up most of the front room. Throughout the day, family members stop by to pay their obligatory but heartfelt respect. Mickey will forever remember standing beside the casket with Ray and Roy, the three of them looking down as Mutt whispers, "Say goodbye to Grandpa."

Is that a tear Mickey sees his father wipe away? If so, it is the first time Mickey has ever seen his father cry. And it takes him aback. Even when Mutt is at his most excited, like at dramatic moments in a baseball game, he seldom shows his feelings. He is a restrained man, a man expressing few exclamation marks. When Mutt thanks the people who come, he does so in a voice the boys have never heard. It is a choky voice, as if something is caught in his throat.

Although they are not churchgoers, Mutt and Tunney agree to a funeral service at the Adair Methodist Church with Reverend Fisher officiating. Their other brother, Emmett, is with the Marines at Parris Island in South Carolina, and so is unable to come. After the service, Charlie is buried next to his wife Mae in the Adair Cemetery.

Mickey is struggling with thoughts of death. He is frequently anxious, unusually keyed-up, often on edge. When he sees men older than his grandfather, he thinks it isn't fair that such a good man is dead, while others carry on with their lives. People tell him that someday he will meet his grandfather again in heaven. Mickey would like to believe that but doesn't really.

Mutt tells Mickey he knows what he is feeling. He says he has experienced losing family. He was not yet eight when he lost his mother to pneumonia. Charlie felt that he had enough on his hands raising his three oldest children, so he took the baby to an aunt and uncle to raise as their own. Mutt, as the oldest, had to take charge of his brother Tunney and his sister Thelma, while Charlie went to work every day as a butcher in Spavinaw. So, in effect, Mutt sacrificed his own childhood to help his father raise their family.

"Maybe," Ox tells him over beers at the Black Cat, "that's why you're so damn stubborn about making Mickey into a baseball player. You had a relationship with your father centering around baseball, and so now with him gone, you—"

"You don't have any idea what you're talking about."

"And you don't see it."

"See what?"

"You're putting so much pressure on the kid that ... I don't know, you want him to live your dream because you never had a chance to. I know you had to be caretaker to your brother and sister. That wasn't fair; I understand that. But here's what you're missing. What if Mickey don't? What then? What if he don't ever become what you see him as?"

"Then he'll do something else, I guess."

"And if he does, he'll always feel like a failure. You're setting him up to be a failure—"

"No, I'm not. I'm making it possible for him to be a success."

"Mutt, you stubborn SOB. There's no reasoning with you because you won't listen to common sense."

"He'll be OK. He'll be just fine."

Some who see how the overbearing Mutt treats Mickey, along with the apparent detachment of Lovell, believe that Mickey, as he grows older, may well be traumatized by his upbringing. They see the potential for significant psychological damage. But they also understand that nothing they can say or do will help. Mutt doesn't seem to possess the emotional maturity to look at the situation realistically, and Lovell doesn't do anything to change that.

Any thoughts that things will change with Charlie out of the picture are quickly put to rest. Mutt seems even more determined. It's what Charlie would want, he reasons.

Chapter 15

To take their minds off Charlie's passing, Mutt works with Mickey to fashion an infield in the yard behind their house. Mickey cuts the grass. They lay baselines down with lime, fashion bases out of dried cow dung, find an old metal sign for home plate.

Mutt is still regularly throwing batting practice, but without Charlie throwing left-handed, Mickey isn't swinging as much from the right side. To at least compensate a little, Mutt plays pepper games with Mickey always batting right-handed.

Nick, LeRoy, and sometimes Mosley bike out to the farm for games on the makeshift diamond. When others occasionally join them, they can play full-team baseball. If you are a youngster in the Commerce area who wants to play ball, the Mantle farm is the place to go. Ray and Roy are now old enough that sometimes they also join. Even Barbara plays occasionally. Mostly they play baseball, but they also play football. Usually Mickey and Barbara against Ray and Roy.

"I've come up with a new game," Mickey tells his brothers and sister one summer morning while waiting for others to join them. "Here's what we're gonna do. Say I throw the ball over the house, and Ray catches it on the other side. As soon as you catch it, Ray, you take off running around the house, and I'll turn tail and start running in the opposite direction. You try to smack me with the ball."

"Throw it at you?" Ray asks.

"If you're fast enough."

"How will I know which way you're running?"

"You won't. Maybe you'll get lucky."

They create other ball-related games. Sometimes Mickey stuffs two pairs of socks with several other socks, and Barbara faces off against Ray or Roy boxing as Joe Lewis and Billy Conn.

"Come on, Roy, you can't let a girl beat you up," Mickey will say. He enjoys teasing Barbara. For the most part, she takes it well. Once though, the teasing gets to her and she runs off. Mickey runs after her. "I didn't mean it, Barbara, I didn't mean it."

When she comes back, Mickey lets her box against Ray barehanded.

"Hey, that ain't fair," Ray protests.

"You afraid of a girl?"

"She's got sharp knuckles."

"Then you'd better duck."

Life on the farm is fun, even if they miss their grandfather.

Once Mutt adjusts to life without his father, he comes to enjoy living on the farm. He still gets up as early as he did when he was working in the mine, but spending the day outdoors rather than underground is a joy. In spring he plants oats, wheat, and a small field of corn. After he milks the cows, he gives the full buckets to Lovell, who separates the milk from the cream and then sells what they don't need to the man who stops by regularly in the milk truck. The extra money for groceries is welcome.

One chore Mickey particularly enjoys is taking out the garbage and burning it in a trash bin behind the house. More than once, he proclaims that he might grow up to be a fireman. One day sparks from the burning garbage jump the bin and set the nearby dry grass on fire. Mickey races for a bucket and fills it with water as the fire races alarmingly toward the outside privy. By the time he gets to the flames, there are only a few drops of water left in the leaky bucket. Mutt, seeing the fire, rushes out of the house, beats the flames down with his jacket, then warms Mickey's britches.

Mickey finds all sorts of fun things to do on a farm.

One day he ties himself to a calf to pretend he is a rodeo rider.

The calf has other ideas and takes off like a shot out the barn door. Mickey slides off in a heap. The twins and Barbara break up laughing.

When she sees how Mutt and the kids relish living on the farm, Lovell comes to accept life away from town. She is patient when her children run wild in the house or invite their friends over for meals. She likes the fun, the energy, the lively atmosphere.

This is an idyllic time for the Mantles. Despite missing his father, Mutt enjoys spending his time in the outdoors. Lovell is happy her husband is away from the dangers of the mine. Mickey is having fun hunting, fishing, horseback riding, playing all sorts of outdoor games. And, of course, working with his father on their makeshift diamond.

As a family, they have never been more contented ... until the rains come. And come.

It starts with a drizzle that doesn't let up for days. The drizzle turns into light rain. Then a heavy downpour.

Mutt stands in the doorway, looking out at his soggy fields. "Three days. It's gotta stop soon. I gotta tend to the fields, but all I'm doing is sinking into mud."

"The paper says the river is rising an inch an hour," Lovell tells him. "Highway patrol is blocking most of the roads."

"It's gotta stop soon," Mutt repeats.

Lovell reads from the *Miami Daily News Record*, "Savage spring floods, swelled by incessant rains that have been falling since Thursday, were today inundating large sections of Oklahoma, and thousands have been forced to flee from their lowland homes."

Two days later, Mutt inspects his fields. They are all under water. The Neosho is still rising. The rain continues.

The paper says there is no end in sight.

The Mantles hold out as long as they can. Mutt is stubborn that way. His crops are finished. He knows that. So does Dr. Wormington.

"Maybe they'll come back," Lovell says with more hope than conviction.

Mutt shakes his head. "They won't."

The yard is a quagmire. Water is seeping into the house, and still it rains.

Mutt finds a house—not much more than a shack really—in a little area known as Whitebird, a small group of meager residences that has sprung up around the Commerce Mining & Royalty power plant. It is a mile west of Cardin.

It takes four trips in their farm wagon to move their furniture and belongings to Whitebird. Mutt drives the wagon, jaws clenched, eyes just staring at the road. Soon he will return to spending his days underground. The thought is dispiriting.

Their house on the farm had been shabby. Their house in Whitebird is worse. All seven of them will be crammed into the tiny house, with no inside plumbing and only a wood-burning cooking stove to keep them warm.

It is a bleak winter, made more uncomfortable by the frequent north wind that comes howling across the plain. In the frigid mornings, they have to cross the frost-covered ground on their way to the privy.

Upon awakening, Mickey's first task is to brace himself and start the fire in the stove. Mutt is usually already off to the mine by the time the rest of the family gathers around the stove trying to keep warm.

In summer, when the Oklahoma sun is burning into the land, Lovell has to wield a towel to chase the flies that swarm though the holes in the screens. Frequently a losing battle.

Mickey sleeps in the room with his parents and sister. His three brothers sleep in the adjacent room. He fantasizes about living in the old rusted barn next to the house on South Quincy Street.

This is truly a comedown from their life on the farm. Losing Charlie and then their house is depressing enough, but with little prospect of getting away from the mine, their situation is made even worse.

"Maybe we can get out to the farm again, someday," Mickey says to Mutt while playing pepper on a frosty Sunday morning.

"I don't know. Maybe that's just not in the cards," Mutt says.

"I liked it out there."

"I know. We all did. The important thing is to not get distracted. We can practice here as well as we always have."

"What about the cow dung bases?"

"Maybe I can go out and get some."

Lovell, who has heard this says, "Don't even think about it."

The dilapidated house sits about 100 yards off the highway, down a gravel road that leads from the mailbox. Most afternoons, after playing ball with his friends, Mickey waits by that mailbox for his father. He always takes Mutt's lunch pail from him as they walk back to the house. Sometimes, they race. Mutt in steel-toed safety shoes. Mickey in sneakers.

One day, Mutt takes off his shoes. "You can't take me now," he says.

"In your bare feet?"

"In my bare feet."

"On a gravel road?"

"On a gravel road."

"You're on."

They assume a sprinter's start position. Then on Mutt's "ready, set, go," they race toward the house, side by side. Mickey beats him by a stride.

"If I'd had shoes—"

"Excuses, excuses."

Mickey knows a few years earlier his father would have let him win. But now he's treating him like an adult. Mickey welcomes that.

Mutt doesn't brag. Not about Mickey. No one ever hears him say Mickey is going to be great. Never even hears him say Mickey is good. Mutt isn't about fuss or fanfare. He does what he believes he must do without talking about it. He is a humble, stoical man.

For that matter, Mickey doesn't brag either. He is Mutt's son. Just as stoical. Just as shy. Maybe more gullible and naïve than most kids his age. He is a farm boy with all the simple qualities that suggests. Once Mutt tells Mickey to clear out the area around some telephone poles. Mickey balks. Why bother?

"When you have a prairie fire," Mutt explains, "if you don't clear out a 10-yard spot around a telephone pole, it will burn down."

That is typical of Mutt. Straight to the point. Just the facts. No elaboration needed.

Some writers would later suggest that Mutt was a better ballplayer than his son. That's probably not true, because he never had Mickey's speed or grace, but he is one tough player. Mickey is lithe and agile, Mutt iron strong and wiry. A Ty Cobb, I'll-spike-the-first-guy-who-gets-in-my-way type of player who plays hard. Never gripes. Does whatever it takes to win a game.

That's what he wants his oldest son to learn.

Chapter 16

The morning paper carries the welcome message:
Millions lifted their hearts and voices today to hail the dawn of peace. There were tears, laughter, hysteria, and prayers throughout the Allied world as Japan, last undefeated aggressor nation, announced it had surrendered.

Lovell takes a deep breath, as if she's just come up from under water. "Thank goodness for that," she says to the empty house. In the back of her mind, she always thought that Mickey and his friends could be called to duty if the war dragged on long enough.

When Mutt gets paid each Saturday, Lovell goes into Commerce to do the week's grocery shopping. When he can, Mickey likes to go along. The cheery-cheeked grocer, who appreciates that Lovell never asks for credit, always lets him choose a bag of candy or an all-day sucker. Occasionally, bubble gum with baseball cards.

"You still playing baseball all the time? I hear you're pretty good."

Mickey likes to hear that people think he's a good player, but he's always hesitant to accept the praise. His shyness always comes to the fore in such situations, particularly when talking to adults.

"You gonna be a professional someday?"

"I hope."

"You can be anything you set your mind to, you know. That's what's so great about this country."

"Yeah."

"You don't want to be a miner, do you? That's not what a young lad like you should aim for."

"Maybe," says Mickey. Since that's what his father does, he doesn't like it when people say bad things about mining.

"I've heard too many sirens in the night."

"Losing too many customers?" Lovell says.

"Far too many. I only went down there once," the grocer says. "In a mine. I can tell you it was terrible—damp and dark and dirty. That ain't no way to live. The miners, they come in here. They're so filthy, sometimes I can't even recognize them. I mean, customers I've known for years, and I don't even know who they are. You want that?"

"I don't know," says Mickey.

"So, work hard at something else, even if you don't get no place with baseball. Most boys don't, you know. School, that's the thing you gotta pay attention to. Get a good education, and you'll have what you need in this world."

"Yeah."

"You good in school?"

"I'm OK."

"Because that's the key. That's more important than baseball."

"See you next week, Mrs. Mantle," he says as he hands the bag of groceries to Mickey. "I'll have more boxes of your cereal by then. Don't know how you go through so many every week."

Mickey carries two bags of groceries as he and his mother walk home.

"So, how many days did you ditch school this year?"

"I don't know."

"How many times did you get your tail tanned for it?"

"Too many."

"When are you going to learn your lesson?"

"I just don't … it's so boring sometimes. The teacher, she can go on about something that I just don't care about, that nobody cares about but her. It's so boring."

"So what? Pay attention anyway."

MUTT'S DREAM: MAKING THE MICK

"If she was talking about baseball—"

"You know there's more to life than—"

"She don't even know who Stan Musial is."

"You're a good student when you put your mind to it. You're not stupid. You can't just play games all the time."

"Why not?"

"What if every time you ditched school, you had to stay in your room for a week ... after school?"

"Then we could do batting practice in the house."

"Don't be a jerk."

Mutt has little to say about Mickey's occasional truancy. He gets more exacerbated when Mickey bats from the "wrong" side of the plate than he does when Mickey goes missing from school.

Mickey is anything but a rebellious teenager and seldom needs punishing, but when he does, it is dished out by Lovell, not Mutt.

One unexpectedly warm early spring day, Mickey goes out with Mosley and LeRoy near the Blue Goose Mine, to a cave-in hole that has partially filled with water after several days of steady rain. The result is a muddy pond. How deep is anybody's guess, but it is said anything that falls in will be sucked down to the bottom by a whirlpool action.

"You believe that?" LeRoy asks.

"Everybody says so," Mosley says.

"Well, I don't. There's no reason there should be a whirlpool."

Mosley gives LeRoy a mock punch in the arm. "Really, genius, why is that?"

"Because whirlpools happen when two opposing currents meet. This causes the water to spin around really fast."

"Well, maybe there are currents down there," Mickey says.

"It's rainwater, for Chrissake. Where the hell would currents come from?" LeRoy asks.

"I dunno."

Leaning over the edge and looking down into the newly-formed pond, LeRoy says, "Well I do. There can't be currents. You see any currents?"

"I don't see any currents," Mickey says.

"I'll prove it," LeRoy says as he pulls off his shirt and jumps into the water. Mickey and Mosley peer down. They don't see LeRoy. Mickey and Mosley exchange tentative glances.

"Goodbye, LeRoy, nice knowing you," Mosley says.

"He's pranking us, right?" Mickey says.

"Sure he is."

After what seems like maybe too much time for LeRoy to be holding his breath in the murky water, Mickey and Mosley exchange seriously nervous glances.

Mickey says, "Maybe you should—"

"You kidding? I'm not—"

"Yeah, me neither."

Finally, Leroy's head pops up through the surface. "You won't believe it. There's a mermaid down there."

Relieved, Mosley jumps in. "You weren't thinking of keeping her for yourself, were you?"

"First in gets the mermaid. It's in the rule book."

"What rule book?"

"The first-in-the-mine-cave-in-pool rule book."

"Never seen it."

"You wouldn't if it didn't have pictures."

Mosley and LeRoy horse around in the pool while Mickey watches from the edge. The swimmers purposely splash enough water up on Mickey that he becomes thoroughly soaked.

They are all surprised when Lovell shows up and sees how wet Mickey is.

"What the hell are you doing?" she demands.

"Mama, I'm just watching. I didn't go in, honest."

"What if you'd slipped? Look how muddy it is. Mickey, I might not be the smartest woman in the world, but I know one thing for certain, and it's you can't swim a lick."

She sees Mosley and LeRoy snickering. "What are you two morons laughing at? It ain't funny."

Lovell pulls Mickey up and grabs him by the collar. "Get up. You're going right home, young man. Let's go."

Mosley and LeRoy climb out. "How'd she even know we were here?" LeRoy asks.

"Some fink must've seen us."

"I hate finks."

Lovell lets Mickey have it on the backside.

By this time, Mickey's appetite for baseball has become all-encompassing. For most of his waking hours, when he isn't playing actual baseball, he's playing variations of ball games. Sometimes he'll go out to one of the local fields and shag stray baseballs. If it is raining or snowing or if it is too cold, he reads about baseball or listens to games on the radio.

He knows the names and batting averages of the top players in both the National and American Leagues. From looking at the newspaper sports page, he recognizes the faces of many players.

Ray and Roy, while not as obsessed with baseball as Mickey, still enjoy the game. Ray bats left-handed, Roy right-handed. Mickey uses them to pitch batting practice to him and chase the balls he hits when their father isn't around. Occasionally, when they balk at what Mickey sees as their family responsibilities, he complains to his mother.

"Tell them they need to pitch to me."

"Mickey, they ain't your private caddies."

Barbara, although she will sometimes join in the boys' activities, often becomes bored watching her father play when forced to sit all Sunday afternoon on the hard bleacher seats. Force fed sports the way she is, she develops an aversion to them.

Mickey enjoys a privileged position in the Mantle family. He is "The Promised One." None of the other children receives the attention Mickey does from either their father or mother. None of the others is being groomed to be successful in the way Mickey is. He is the chosen one.

Whitebird isn't large enough to have its own high school, so Mickey attends Commerce High, where athletics—baseball, basketball, and football—are central student activities.

"I'd like to go out for football," he tells Mutt after his first day at the school.

"You can forget that right now. You ain't playing football."

"Why? I'm fast. I could be a good fullback."

"I'll give you three reasons why you're not going to play football. One, you're too small. Two, you could get injured, which would screw up your baseball playing. Three, because I said so."

"A lot of the guys are going out for—"

"Conversation over."

A few days later, Mickey asks if he can go out for the basketball team.

"You're too short."

"I could be a guard. They don't have to be tall."

"You could get hurt."

"I could get hurt crossing the street."

"Especially if you're bouncing a basketball."

"Mosley is already on the team, and he's real good."

"And he's tall."

After numerous entreaties of a similar kind, Mutt gives in. Mickey can play basketball. Absolutely no football.

Frank Bruce, the Commerce High basketball coach, welcomes any boy who wants to try out for his squad.

"I have one goal for this team," the coach tells the boys trying out, "and only one goal—to win the Lucky Seven Conference crown. If you have any other ideas, you're in the wrong place."

He puts the boys through shooting, passing, and running drills that end with a squad of 10 players, Mickey among them. There is no question who the best player on the team is. Bill Mosley will be the center, the player to whom they will turn for the bulk of their scoring. He has a hook shot that is hard for anyone to stop.

Mickey has grown some recently, but he is still smaller than most of the other boys in his class, so naturally he will play guard. LeRoy will be a forward.

Coach Bruce explains that they will play differently than the other teams in the league. Most teams play by passing the ball around the perimeter, until a player is open enough to get off a set shot. Usually a two-hander. A relatively static game.

"We ain't doing none of that," the coach tells them. "We're gonna scramble, we're gonna run every time we get the ball. On defense, we're gonna guard the man. Forget the zone. Every man is going to guard another man. It's man-on-man. Most importantly, though, we're gonna be the first fast-break team anybody around here has ever seen. So that means we're gonna run a lot in practice, and you're gonna get in shape or drop dead trying."

Mickey is excited when the coach gives him a uniform with the number 22 on the front.

Although Mickey hasn't played the game before, Coach Bruce immediately sees that the little guy has athletic skills and can get down the court in a real hurry. Mickey is told to practice set shots until his arms fall off. Then he'll need to learn to drive to the basket.

"I'm going to be a guard," he announces to his parents. "Mostly, I've got to get the ball to Mosley. That'll be my job."

"But you can shoot too," Lovell says. "You'll be able to score."

"You bet I will."

After several weeks of practice, they play their first game against the team from down in Pryor. Mickey is on the bench when the game begins. He watches as Mosley in the first half scores six points, leading to an 18–18 tie at halftime. Mickey is anxious the entire time. He wants to get in the game, but he doesn't want to get in and screw up.

The players circle around their coach during halftime.

"We can win this game," Coach Bruce says. "We will win this game. We need to be more careful with our passes. We had too many damn passes get away. Move the ball. Move it, move it, move it, until you get an opening to get it in to Mose."

By midway through the third quarter, Pryor is up 26–20. Coach Bruce wants to change the tempo of the game. "Mantle, get ready. You're going in for Ballard. I want you to run, got it?"

"Run, yeah," says Mickey, his heart now pounding hard.

"We need to run them off the court."

Mickey's first minutes on the court are tentative. He runs hard up and down the court, but once he dribbles the ball off his foot. Later, he throws the ball over Mosley's head and into the stands.

"Settle down, Mickey, settle down," the coach calls out to him.

Late in the game, Mosley pulls down a rebound, turns, passes it off to Mickey. Mickey races down the right side of the court. He finds himself alone when he gets about 10 feet from the basket. Unsure of whether he should wait for Mosley or the others to catch up, keep dribbling, or shoot, he puts up a tentative-looking two-handed set shot. The ball hits the backboard then drops down and rattles through the net. Mickey has his first points in an organized basketball game. Mickey tries unsuccessfully to stifle a smile.

The game remains close until the final seconds, when Mosley passes the ball to Charles Childress, who swishes it through the net on a one-hander. Commerce has won 33–32. Mosley ends up the team's high scorer with 12 points. Jack Brower added eight. Still, Mickey is thrilled. He has played and scored in a high school basketball game. That was fun.

Basketball will be a fun way to spend the winter months when he can't play baseball.

As the season moves on, Mickey gets more and more playing time. His confidence grows. He gets more accurate with his set shots, learns to slash his way to the basket for a close-in shot when he sees an opening, and is beginning to become a leader. When double-teamed while driving to the basket, he progresses at dropping the ball off to Mosley. Mostly, though, he is becoming a proficient outside shooter. People call him and Mosley "Mister Inside and Mister Outside."

Mutt comes to accept Mickey playing basketball as an "intermission" in his baseball training. He attends many of Mickey's games. Lovell becomes one of Commerce's most steadfast cheerleaders—and certainly the loudest critic of the referees. When Mickey is whistled for a dubious, or semi-dubious, foul, Lovell will jump up and scream.

"Are you blind, ref? That weren't no foul. Open your eyes, you damned bum."

"What the hell are you looking at, ref? It sure ain't the same game I'm watching."

"Where's your white cane, you blind SOB?"

Her outbursts become a fixture at the games. Listening to her, one might assume Mickey never commits a foul in any game ever.

Mutt, not nearly as demonstrative, becomes embarrassed at his wife's profanity-laced flare-ups. When she begins screaming, he moves to a seat as far from her as he can get.

To Mutt's way of thinking, basketball, while fun, shouldn't be taken seriously. It's a harmless wintertime diversion. Nothing more. There is no professional future in the game as there is in baseball. Anyway, as good as Mickey is on the hardwood, he doesn't have the physical attributes to compete on a higher level. Maybe if he were as tall as Mosley ...

Chapter 17

The sun has not yet risen on what will be a bright, clear day. Larry is the first to wake for a sneak peek at what Santa has left under the tree. Mickey isn't far behind. They understand that there isn't much money for Christmas presents, but they always get something. Lovell and Mutt see to that. When Mickey spies his present, his eyes well up just short of tears. He will later tell Mosley that seeing that present took his breath away.

To Mickey, there is nothing in this world that compares to a new baseball glove. The feel of the sumptuous leather, the beautiful bronze color, the elegant smell. But this is not any glove; this is a Marty Marion signature glove. Mickey knows all about "Mister Shortstop," the great Cardinal infielder. Mickey picks the glove up as if he were cradling a newborn baby. A Rawlings G600 deep well model with Marion's signature running up the fielding heel. It even says "Mister Shortstop."

There's a card next to it from Rawlings: *You're in The Big League with Rawlings' Marty Marion. Here's a real Major League Glove that Marty Marion, ace infielder of the St. Louis Cardinals, helped design. With one of these gloves, you'll pick off the hot ones, the high flies, and the grounders easy as catching 'em in a basket. You'll be the envy of all the other fellows on the team!*

Boy, when you own a Marty Marion made by Rawlings, you've got the best!

When Mutt comes in, he sees Mickey breaking the glove in by throwing a ball hard into the pocket over and over again. Mickey looks up with a smile as wide as his face. Mutt simply nods. Message sent.

"Man, oh man, thanks, Dad," Mickey says. "This is great."

"Why are you thanking him?" Larry asks. "It's from Santa, ain't it?"

"Yeah, sure it is. It's from Santa, all right."

"Gosh, a Marty Marion model. I mean, he's the best there is. This is so great. Wanna go out and play catch, Dad?"

"Sure, in a few minutes, when everybody else gets their presents."

"I'll be outside," Mickey says as he bolts for the door.

"I think he likes it," says Lovell.

"What gives you that idea?"

When Mutt gets outside, he finds Mickey catching the ball in his new prized possession as it bounces back to him off the side of the house.

"I'm going to show you how to keep it lubricated proper. Keep it nice and flexible like you need for playing the infield."

"With what?"

"Well, Vaseline works great. Some oils will work, too."

"I've seen you use shaving cream."

"That's probably the easiest."

Mickey is eager to use and show off his new treasure. When Nick arrives later in the morning, Mickey is in the yard throwing a ball as high in the air as he can, then catching it in his new glove. It's a good way to break it in.

"Take a gander, my friend," Mickey says to Nick as he throws him his glove.

"Man, this looks good."

"It's better than good."

"I'll say."

"Man, this glove is really built. They only use the best flexible tan leather."

"Yeah, it looks like it," Nick says, examining the glove closely.

"See that deep well pocket?"

"Yeah."

"It's inner-greased."

"Really?"

"What they say. It makes it real flexible. See, all the edges are rolled and bound in leather, and it's lined with glove leather on the inside. It's even got an adjustable solid ball trap!"

"Man, that's swell."

"I bet I never bobble another ground ball."

"I'll take that bet."

Mickey appreciates what the glove represents. It's more than just an implement to catch a baseball. It represents a sacrifice. He knows the glove costs $25 because he saw it advertised in a magazine. About a third of his father's monthly salary. Throughout the winter, Mickey caresses and cares for the glove as if it were a holy relic. He fully realizes what it says about his father's love for him and about his pride in his son's ability.

Although there is no organized baseball in the winter months, the mild Oklahoma weather allows for plenty of outside play.

When there aren't enough boys to put together two complete teams, they often play a game they call "scrub." There's only one base. The batter hits the ball and then has to get to the base and back home again. If he does this safely, he gets to hit again. When he makes an out, he goes into right field. When the next batter makes an out, he moves to center, and after another out, to left. He eventually makes it to the infield, pitcher, catcher. Finally, he gets to bat again.

If there are enough players, they choose up sides in the time-honored manner. Two boys are chosen as captains. One of the captains throws the bat to the other captain, who catches it one-handed. Then the other captain puts one hand directly on top of the first captain's hand. They continue alternating hands on the bat until there is no longer any room for a full set of fingers. Then, if the captain whose turn it is to grip the bat can grasp it with the tips of his fingers firmly enough to swing it around, he gets the first choice of whom he wants on his team.

They improvise as needed to be able to play. Sometimes they play out in the alkali with dung bases baked hard by the Oklahoma sun. Sometimes they use folded-up feed bags nailed into the ground for bases.

One day they are playing scrub. Mickey is catching with Bobby Lancaster at the plate and a runner on first. When the pitcher throws a pitch higher than Bobby's head, Mickey instinctively leaps up to snag the errant delivery. Bobby, never the most selective of batters, swings. Rather than hitting ball, he hits skull, catching Mickey squarely in the back of his head. Mickey drops to the ground. He is woozy. It takes him a few seconds to focus.

"Mickey, talk to me," says LeRoy. "Do you know where you are?"

"No, do you?"

LeRoy laughs. "Do you know your name?"

"Stan Musial."

"Thank goodness. I thought you might be hurt, Stan."

For some time, Mickey remains light-headed, a little unsteady, and slightly nauseous. He does his best to conceal the effects of the beaning from his parents. This is the first time he has been seriously injured playing sports. It won't be the last. The next time will be much more serious.

On the Commerce High baseball team Mickey struggles with his fielding. Usually playing shortstop, he learns to charge ground balls reasonably well. If he gets a good angle on a grounder, he generally fields it cleanly and gets off a fast throw. But when it comes straight at him, he is often undone. He continues to have problems judging the speed and bounce of these balls. He understands he shouldn't step back, but his instincts usually take over and he lets the ball play him. Or he turns his head as the ball reaches him and lets it skip by or bounce into his face, resulting in numerous fat lips. The more often he gets hit, the more he shies away from hard-hit balls. When he does field a ball cleanly, he is in the habit of just letting it fly toward first without setting himself properly, resulting in balls sailing untouched into the stands.

At the same time, Mickey's hitting gets better, and his speed on drag bunts allows him to pull himself out of slumps. "I can pretty much get a hit that way anytime I need to," he says.

At the plate he dotes on fastballs. He hit curves too, but he gets bigger hits on fastballs. When a pitcher falls behind in the count, Mickey knows he will likely come back with a fastball, and he is ready to "bust it into small pieces," as he says.

Mutt has always emphasized hitting. Big hitters earn big dollars. Still, he is troubled by Mickey's sloppy fielding. Is it bad enough to keep him out of professional baseball? Maybe not if he hits well enough. Ted Williams isn't much of a fielder either, but look at his career. Some baseball men who have taken note of Mickey's power and speed aren't convinced. He's a hitter, but is he a complete baseball player? Not now. Will he ever be? That's always the question when evaluating young talent. Still, it's hard not to pay attention to the strong hitter from Commerce High.

With the high school baseball season over, Mickey, Nick, and LeRoy turn to playing summer ball in the Gabby Street League.

In their biggest game, the coach gives the ball to Mickey. "You're pitching," he says. "LeRoy will be your catcher. Go warm up."

Mickey likes to pitch. He's got the arm for it and can uncork a real knuckler once in a while.

Their first game pits Commerce against the Whites in a Thursday afternoon game at Jaycee Park in Picher. Mickey sets the Whites down in order in the first, then doubles in the second as part of a five-run outburst. He is pitching well but in the fourth surrenders three runs, losing his shutout bid. The final score is Commerce 9, Whites 3. Mickey gave up only three hits and struck out seven.

"Not bad for an infielder," LeRoy says, "but if you'd have paid more attention to my signs you would have had your shutout."

"If I'd paid more attention to your signs, I wouldn't have made it out of the first inning."

Mickey continues to pitch and play short for his team. Some people opine he might have a future as a full-time pitcher.

Mutt won't hear of it. "Major League pitchers play what, every fourth day? Or fifth. You'd waste what you do best. Pitch now if you want, if you have fun doing it, but concentrate on your hitting."

Mickey and Mosley are sitting at the counter in the crowded and smoky Black Cat Café, wolfing down their usual Saturday lunch of a hamburger and chili. Bob Wills and the Texas Playboys are on the jukebox.

Take me back to Tulsa, I'm too young to marry
Take me back to Tulsa, I'm too young to marry
We travel all over this country wide
Playing music by the hour
Always wear this great big smile
We never do look sour

"I could be a musician," Mickey says. "You know how I love music—Tex Ritter, Al Dexter, Ernest Tubb."

"You can't be a musician, Mickey."

"Yeah, why not?"

"You can't play music."

"Other than that?"

"You're gonna be a baseball player."

"I am a baseball player."

"A professional baseball player."

"I know."

Mosley scoops up the last of his chili. "You should go out for football. In the fall, you should try out for the team."

"Nah, I can't."

Mosley is already the regular quarterback on the Commerce High Tigers. "We could really use your speed. You'd be a quick little scatback, and I could throw to you and—"

"C'mon, Mose, you know I can't."

"Because of your dad."

"If I didn't get killed by some fat slob linemen first, he'd do it for them."

"Think about it."

"I'm thinking."

When the Yanks raised
The Stars and Stripes on Iwo Jima Isle
Thru' the blood and tears they won thru'
Bless the heart of each Yankee
There on Iwo Jima Isle

"While you're playing football, I'll learn to accompany myself on the guitar."

Mosley rolls his eyes. "Yeah."

The next time Mickey hits fungoes with his father, he broaches the issue of playing football. "I'd like to go out for football in the fall. Mose is the quarterback, and he thinks I could really help out on account of how I'm a fast runner and all."

Mutt glowers at him and holds his gaze for several uncomfortable seconds. Then he takes a full swing and hits the ball hard at Mickey's feet. He goes into the house without saying a word.

Chapter 18

Mickey and Mosley are spending more and more time together. Mosley lives with his mother in a small house not far from their school. His father had been a dynamite man in Blue Goose Number One. One night, after everyone else had left, he set off a charge but didn't make it out in time.

Since it's a long walk from the school in Commerce to Whitebird, on days when Mickey misses the school bus his parents let him stay overnight at Mosley's. Many nights they stay up late talking about sports. Of course, they will keep in touch all their lives. Of course, they will always be friends. Maybe Mosley will be a two-sport star—a basketball center and a football quarterback; Mickey will be an all-star shortstop on the world champion Cardinals.

One day after school, a girl in Mosley's class, Patty McCall, asks Mosley if he would like to come over to her house. She's having a small get-together.

"Mom's made some punch and cookies," she says coyly.

"Your house?" Mosley asks.

"Ruth and Suzy Anne are coming, too."

"I don't know. Mickey's coming over to my place and—"

"Bring him along. The more, the merrier."

"He's kind of … you know … shy around—"

"Ask him anyway."

When he finds Mickey, he puts the idea to him.

"You like Patty?" Mickey asks.

"Yeah, well, I like her all right."

"I dunno, maybe I should get on home."

"You've already missed the bus."

"I could use the walk."

"C'mon, we'll go over for a while, and then we can come back to my house and shoot some hoops."

"You know where she lives?"

"Yeah, St. Louis."

"What?"

"Someplace in town. I dunno, we'll find out."

"I could use the hoop practice. Maybe we should just—"

"What are you afraid of?"

"I'm not afraid."

"Good, then let's go."

It turns out to be a fun afternoon after all. Four girls show up along with Mickey and Mosley and another boy from Mosley's English class. The punch is sweet, the chocolate chip cookies gooey. The girls are giggly.

After a while, the boys begin purposely dropping things, so the girls have to bend over to pick them up while the boys steal a look up their skirts.

"For athletes, you boys sure are clumsy," Patty observes with a chuckle.

"I know," Mosley says. "I guess we need more practice."

"I'll say."

The next day at school, Mickey and Mosley are summoned to the principal's office.

The tall, raw-boned principal, who has eyes that remind Mickey of Bunsen burners, tells them he has heard from Patty's parents. "Patty told them what you were up to at her house yesterday."

"What?" says Mosley. "We were just drinking some—"

"It's bad enough what you did, but lying about it only makes it worse, so my advice is to keep your mouths shut and take the punishment like … like mature young men, which you are obviously not. You know, there's such a thing as civility, and it's about time you developed some."

MUTT'S DREAM: MAKING THE MICK

Both boys get paddled by the principal, who seems to get as much enjoyment out of it as the boys had from their looking-up-the-skirts episode. "You think I should tell your folks?"

"Definitely not," Mosley says.

Mickey knows that Mutt might pass it off as a just-being-boys thing. But his mother wouldn't, and that would result in yet another licking.

"If I hear of one more stupid incident from you two clowns, I will contact your parents. Oh, and you'll be off the basketball team faster than you can get off a shot. Understand me?"

"Yeah," says Mosley. "We've learned our lesson; you can be sure of that."

"Now get out of here and get back to your classes."

As the boys are walking down the hall to their classes, Mickey asks, "I didn't even know the girls saw us … what we were doing."

"You kidding me? They knew, and they liked it."

"Then why would she tell her parents?"

"Girls are like that. Can't trust 'em."

Other than local sports, Commerce offers little in the way of divertissements for active teenagers. The main drag has a city hall, the volunteer fire department, the Black Cat Café, a bank, the movie house, a handful of small stores, a motel, and four churches, none of which the Mantles attend.

Mutt has said on more than one occasion, "Religion doesn't necessarily make you good. As long as your heart is in the right place and you don't hurt no one, I think you're going to heaven … if there is one."

LeRoy's devout mother insists that he regularly attend Sunday services and Sunday Bible study classes. LeRoy occasionally talks Mickey into keeping him company. His oft-repeated joke is, "The Bible's really a baseball book. Doesn't it start with, 'In the big inning?'"

When Mickey does go with him, he sits in the church, invariably daydreaming about playing with the St. Louis Cardinals. As he tells it, "That's as close as I come to believing in saints."

Commerce also has a pool room. It's typical of many small-town pool joints. Smoky, grimy, dim, bereft of any decoration other than beer signs and a calendar showing off scantily clad women in various pool-shooting tableaus.

On many rainy afternoons Mickey and his friends spend hours shooting pool. Standard eight-ball, mostly. None of them is particularly good at the game, and none has any money to gamble. They play and horse around on a back table while the more serious shooters play and wager on the front tables.

One afternoon Mickey lingers after his friends have gone home. In the windowless hall, he fails to notice the sun has set. Mickey doesn't like walking home in the dark. Doesn't like walking beyond the old Eagle-Picher Mining offices. They are always lit up at night, but once he passes the offices the rest of the route is pitch dark. No streetlights. No lighted windows or signs. Blackbirds suddenly fly up, startling him with flapping wings. His imagination runs wild. He fantasizes about the macabre tales he has heard. About murders in the mines. About bodies being dumped down abandoned shafts. Everybody knows these stories. It's a perfect place to commit murder and hide the bodies. The fact that no bodies have ever been found only goes to prove the point. As soon as he reaches the mine, Mickey always runs the rest of the way home. Although he always denies it, he is scared of the dark.

In the pool hall on this day, he asks around about a ride home. No takers. Seeing the phone on the wall next to the cigarette machine, he gets an idea. He calls the fire station down the street.

"There's a fire in Whitebird."

"Whitebird, you say?"

"Yeah, a garage, I think. Anyway, I see smoke."

Mickey goes outside. As the fire engine roars out of the station, Mickey jumps on the back of the truck for the speedy ride out to Whitebird. Whitebird is small enough that the firemen quickly determine there is no fire. Mickey jumps off about a hundred yards from home.

"You're a bit late, aren't you?" Lovell says as he walks in the door.

"Sorry, time sort of got away from me. I didn't mean to stay so late."

"How'd you get home."

"Oh, I caught a ride."

With rain clouds looming on the horizon, the umpire pushes the teams to cut short their warmups and begin the game a few minutes early. It is a Gabby Street contest between Commerce and the Miami Blues. Clifford Littlejohn will be on the mound for Miami. Mickey will pitch for Commerce. Mosley will catch.

"He's as tough as they come," Mosley says. "Got a blazing fastball and can break off a wicked curve from time to time."

"Yeah, well, so do I," says Mickey "and I can throw in the butterfly once in a while."

"OK, one finger for the heater, two for the curve, three for the floater."

"You got it."

Miami, the visiting team, comes to bat first. They score three runs off Mickey in the first inning. In the bottom of the inning, Mickey strikes out.

"It can't get a lot worse," he mumbles to Mosley as he flings his bat away.

But it does. The Blues score seven more runs off him in the next two innings, and he strikes out again. LeRoy replaces him on the mound. Mickey goes to short. The first ball that comes to him is a sharply hit grounder. He slides to his left, sweeps his gloved hand down, rises, and throws the ball about five feet over Nick's head at first. Later, he makes two more errors—one on a bobbled ball and one on a dropped popup. The game ends with Mickey striking out for the fourth time. It is Littlejohn's 17th K. The Blues win the game 10–3.

Mickey is furious. Embarrassed. The worst player on the field. He hurls his bat across the diamond like an Olympic javelin thrower.

He starts to throw his cherished cap but then thinks better of it and heaves another bat instead.

Mutt, who has seen his son's temper display, comes out of the stands and quickly grabs him by the elbow. "What do you think you're doing?"

"I can't play this game. I'm the worst—"

"I don't want to hear that from you. Not now, not never. You listen to me—"

"I'm quitting baseball and—"

"Like hell you are."

"Doing something else like—"

"You're coming back in the next game and you'll—"

"Becoming a farmer or a musician or—"

"Play like you know how."

"Something. Anything else. I'm never going to be as good as Mose or—"

"Who the hell do you think you are? Everybody has bad games. You think Stan Musial never has a bad game? Last night, he went 0 for 4 with three strikeouts. This game is hard. It's supposed to be hard. If it was easy, everybody would hit 1.000. But it ain't; that's the point. And having a bad game, it's good for you once in a while. Shows you what you need to work on. So stop acting like a spoiled brat and go pick up your bat … if you can find it. It went farther than any ball you've hit in a while."

As Mickey goes after his bat, he shouts, "Musial did not go 0 for 4 last night."

"I must have misread that in the paper."

"Probably never has in his life."

On a muggy Saturday morning, Lovell tells Mickey to take an early bath. He knows what this means. His father has told him that he had saved up enough money that one Saturday he would take Mickey to St. Louis to see a Cardinals game. This would be that glorious day.

As Mickey will come to understand, some things in life are not a

MUTT'S DREAM: MAKING THE MICK

matter of choice. One does not choose a team to root for, just as one does not choose where to be born. They are confirmed upon you. Mickey is a Cardinals fan because he could not be anything else.

Mickey's bath in the metal tub lasts all of two minutes. He quickly puts on clean blue jeans and a clean t-shirt, carefully works the curve on the bill of his baseball cap, and is standing next to the front door by the time Lovell hands him an apple for the drive to St. Louis.

"Looking at you, I might think you were eager to get going," Lovell says.

"Whatever gave you that idea?"

"Damned if I know."

Mutt has the LaSalle gassed up, so after a quick stop to pick up Ox, they are on the road, albeit slowly. Mutt's overcautious driving tests Mickey's patience.

"By the time we get there, Dad, the game's gonna be over."

"But at least we'll get there in one piece."

"Could you step on it a little, please?"

"Relax. There's plenty of time. Anyway, we're gonna get to see three games. The one today and then the doubleheader tomorrow."

"If we ever get there."

The 300-mile journey takes them on U.S. Route 66 through Joplin, then Springfield, where they stop briefly so Mutt can "stretch his legs." Then it's a straight shot all the way to St. Louis, which sits on the wide Mississippi and is easily the largest city Mickey has ever visited.

The wide-eyed Mickey sits in the back. Excited expectation consumes him. In the front seat Mutt and Ox chat idly about their work in the mine and other things, to which Mickey pays no attention. He stares out the window at the passing scenery. When everything is new, everything is interesting, even the advertising signs.

IF YOU
DON'T KNOW
WHOSE SIGNS

THESE ARE
YOU CAN'T HAVE
DRIVEN VERY FAR
BURMA-SHAVE

They stop at the Wagon Wheel Motel, Café, and Station in Cuba, Missouri, where the overly cautious Mutt has his tank filled again.

"Where you off to?" asks the attendant, as he sticks his head under the hood to check the oil.

"St. Louis. To see the Cards."

"Nobody's beating the Cards this year, I can tell you that."

"Hope you're right."

"Them Red Sox is pretty good, but they ain't the Cards, know what I mean?"

"They ain't the Cards, no."

"Should've won it all last year, you know, but with so many players in the service, what are you going to do, right?"

"That's right, yeah."

The attendant sees Mickey leaning against the station drinking a bottle of Coca-Cola. "That your son? Taking him to the game?"

"Yeah."

"He play baseball, your son?"

"Yeah, and he's good enough to play for the Cards someday."

"You know, I hear so many people say that about their kids, but that don't happen most of the time—that they're good enough to get paid. You shouldn't get his hopes up. Know what I mean? You don't want him to think about that. He'll only get disappointed. And I know what I'm talking about. My boy, I thought he was good enough, too. That's all he ever wanted to do. But then he went to one of them tryout days and guess what? Everybody there was better than he was. So, what does he do? He comes back and works even harder at baseball, but then one day, him and his friends are horsing around, and he gets his damn leg broke. Busted into two pieces. That's it for baseball. Now he's … I don't know what he is. A bum, I guess. Oil's good, you don't need no more."

"Good."

"Well, enjoy the game but make sure—"

"Yeah."

"Your boy learns to do something—"

"OK."

"That can make a good living for him."

"Thanks for the advice."

"That's free, but the gas is gonna cost you $2.45."

Back on the road, the LaSalle slowly makes its way to St. Louis. Not knowing how to find the ballpark, they stop at a corner, where Ox gets out to ask a pedestrian for directions. It's on the northwest corner of Grand Boulevard and Dodier Street, on the north side of the city, he is told. Soon enough, they pick out a ring of light stanchions.

Sportsman's Park.

The car radio crackles. Deliberately, almost lazily, they approach the park.

All around the stadium, eager fans exchange hopes, expectations, predictions. Businessmen, shop clerks, grease monkeys. Believers, doubters, cynics, drunks. Followers of every game. The devotees. The board. The faithful.

Some hurry to the gates. Some tell themselves there is no rush. Some linger to buy a scorecard or a souvenir or a bag of peanuts.

"Wow," Mickey says. "That's really big."

"That's what Major League ballparks look like; they're big. Someday, Mickey, someday."

Mutt is annoyed that he has to pay a kid 25 cents to park in a dusty lot.

"There are two types of baseball fans," Ox observes. "Those that come to batting practice, and all the others."

"We'll see it, though, right?" asks Mickey, looking at his father.

Mutt, who is going to do anything he can to please his son at his first Major League game, smiles. "You bet we will."

They buy tickets and then go to their seats in the left-field bleachers. The park is nearly empty. "See, only the real fans are here," says Ox.

These days, Musial often plays first base, but during batting practice he shags fly balls in left, close to where they are sitting in the bleachers. Enos Slaughter and Harry Walker exchange banter with Stan nearby. Great players on a great team. Almost close enough to touch.

"We lucked out," Ox says about their proximity. "Or maybe it's part of God's plan, what do you think?"

"I'm not even going to respond to that," Mutt mumbles.

Mickey, straining to identify the players as he scans the field, downs the first of what will be several hot dogs on the day.

"There's Musial," Mickey says when he spots his idol. "That's him!"

"In the flesh."

What a team these Cardinals have. Stan Musial, Red Schoendienst, Enos Slaughter, Whitey Kurowski, Marty Marion. Truly great players all.

Mutt fills out the scorecard. He wants Mickey to keep it as a reminder of this day. Schoendienst will lead off, followed by Walker, Musial, Slaughter, Kurowski, Terry Moore, Joe Garagiola, Marion, and Ted Wilks, the pitcher.

Mickey has never seen any place as green as this. As beautiful as this. As perfect as this. He takes in every detail. The big scoreboard in left-center with the scores of games for both leagues, surrounded by ads for razor blades, cigarettes, and Falstaff Beer. The patriotic war chest sign. The giant flagpole standing in center. An ad from the local newspaper, *The Globe-Democrat*, on the right-centerfield wall identifies the star of the previous game: Enos Slaughter.

The Cardinals' opponents for this game are the New York Giants, 14.5 games out of first but with a lineup that features former St. Louis stars Johnny Mize and Walker Cooper. The Cardinals begin the day 3.5 games behind first-place Brooklyn, whose game against the Cubs Mickey will closely follow on the scoreboard. With the Dodgers in town for Sunday's doubleheader, the Cardinals have a chance to tighten up the race this weekend.

Two rows in front, a woman sits with four children, the youngest of whom can't be more than three years old. Someday, muses Mickey, she will tell her grandchildren that she saw the great Stan Musial play, as will he.

With a little help from Mutt and Ox, Mickey identifies each of the players.

"That's Marty Marion," Mickey says. "He looks skinny."

"He's quick as a whip, though," says Mutt.

"And look at Slaughter next to Dick Sisler. Man, he looks a lot smaller than I thought he would."

"The scorecard says five feet nine inches."

"Where does he get that power?"

"Watch him closely when he comes to bat. Probably has great wrist action."

When the teams clear the field after warming up, it's time for another hot dog. Coming back to his seat, Mickey's attention is on the field when a man bumps into him, sending a splotch of mustard onto Mickey's shirt.

"Oh, really sorry," Mickey says. "I didn't see you, I—"

"Well, watch where you're going next time."

"Sorry."

"This is not some playground where you can run around willy-nilly."

"Yeah … I mean, no … no it's not. Sorry."

Mutt, who has seen the end of the exchange says, "Mickey, you don't have to apologize to that guy. It was his fault."

"I know, but—"

"You've got to stand up for yourself."

"I know."

"Act more confident."

"Yeah."

As Mutt has observed, on a baseball field Mickey has developed the ease and self-assurance he is yet to know off the field. He's going to need that when he gets to the Major Leagues, an issue of some concern to Mutt.

"Ladies and gentlemen, please rise for our National Anthem."

Most men in the crowd are wearing ties, jackets, and hats, which they remove. Mickey can't help noticing that Mutt and Ox are not dressed like most of the other men. It makes him a little self-conscious. He takes off his baseball cap and holds it over his heart, while a fat man steps to the microphone behind home plate to lead the crowd in "The Star-Spangled Banner."

The park is filling up. The building buzz of expectation. The cries of peanut salesmen.

"How many people are here, do you think?" Mickey asks.

"I'd guess about 6,000," Ox says.

The righty Ted Wilks is throwing for the Cards. He hasn't lost a game all season but struggles in the first, when Cooper hits a three-run homer that scores Mize and St. Louis native Buddy Blattner.

"Those St. Louis guys really came back to haunt us that inning," says Mutt dejectedly, as Sid Gordon flies out to end the Giants' first.

Musial is third in the batting order, so he comes up in the bottom of the first inning with runners on second and third. He's facing the rookie right-hander Mike Budnick, just back from service in the Pacific Theater for the U.S. Navy. Musial settles in at the left side of the plate, standing motionless. Just a hint of tense readiness.

"Now, watch his swing carefully," says Mutt. "It's kind of a peek-a-boo stance, and he lunges a little, but he does what all the good ones do; he keeps his hands back."

"Yeah."

"It's a good lesson for you, watching the great ones. Now, what I want you to pay particular attention to are the details. That's what baseball is, really. It's the little details that make all the difference—how an outfielder shades his eyes from the sun, how a batter adjusts in the batter's box according to how the pitcher is throwing, how the shortstop moves a foot or two depending on how the pitcher is throwing to a particular batter. It's the details that make the greatest players. Most fans, they don't see none of that, but we're not most fans because we see those kinds of things. Know what I mean?"

"Yeah, sure."

"Look at these people sitting around us; they'll never notice the little stuff that we do."

Mutt sits back and closes his eyes against the warming sun. All at once, he is back in Spavinaw, a young man again, playing catch with his father. Now he sees Mickey down on the field with Musial and Marion and Slaughter. Mutt feels the bond among the three generations—Charlie, Mutt, Mickey—united by the timelessness of baseball. Time is standing still.

Musial pops out to third.

"Don't worry," says Ox. "Next time, he'll murder the ball."

The crowd rises as one every time the ball is hit deep. In the second inning, Mickey sees a ball hit straight toward him. As it rises, Mickey's eyes are instinctively glued on its flight. As it starts to descend, there is Walker, gliding to the exact spot where it comes down to nestle into his glove. That is not an easy catch, but he makes it look ordinary. Everything looks like it comes easy to players like Musial and Walker. Like they never have to seriously exert themselves.

"I'll never be able to do that," Mickey says.

"Catch a deep fly ball?" Mutt says.

"Not like that."

"You could if you played in the outfield, but you don't."

"He's so … smooth, the way he moves and all."

"If you shagged as many deep balls as he has, you'd get smooth, too."

"I doubt it."

The Cardinals fall behind 6-1 after three innings, but they rally to tie the game with two in the fourth and three in the sixth. All five runs are driven home by Walker and Musial. It's Stan's two-run single to right that ties it up.

Mickey glows.

"He's as good in person as on the radio!"

The game moves into the eighth with the score tied, but a single by Mize, a bunt by Cooper, and a single by Goody Rosen push across a run to give the Giants a 7-6 lead. The Cardinals put a runner on second with one out in the ninth, but Marion flies to center, and pinch-hitter Erv Dusak pops out to end the game.

Musial goes 2 for 5 with three runs batted in, but Mutt can't stop thinking about that pop out in the first. And the Dodgers have defeated the Cubs, to increase their lead over the Cards to 4.5 games in the standings.

Ox rips up his ticket and throws it into the air. "Tomorrow's another day."

"That's baseball," Mutt says. "No matter how bad things might seem, there's always better days ahead—or at least that's the hope."

"We'll get them tomorrow," Mickey says.

"You bet we will."

An older man in a business suit watches Mickey and thinks the young man cares, really cares, about the game. His unbridled joy of watching the game with his father is on full display. Why should anyone care so much about something that seems trivial, maybe even foolish, in comparison with all the issues in the world? Never mind. Perhaps the youthful passion that sends a boy into such a state of elation over the arbitrary flight of a distant fly ball is but a small price to pay for such a gift, for surely it is that.

They collect their car and drive to a motel on the edge of the city, where they find a room to share. Mutt and Ox stay up late, sharing Mutt's flask of whiskey and talking about Musial, Slaughter, Marion, and the Cards' chances of making the World Series.

Mickey nods off to sleep, dreaming of making that impossible catch. He can still hear the sounds of the game. The umpire's call of "play ball." The ballpark announcer's stentorian voice. The unmistakable crack of the bat as it hits the ball. The delirious cheering.

In the morning, they drive to the Fairgrounds Hotel, where

MUTT'S DREAM: MAKING THE MICK

Mutt has learned the Cardinal players are staying. They order breakfast in the dining room as they observe the players trickling in. Here they are, bigger than they ever look on the field, bronzed and animated.

Mickey is too shy to ask for an autograph anyway, but Mutt insists that they don't intrude on the players' privacy. Even when they see Musial on an elevator.

Mickey sits and gazes in awe while his griddle cakes go cold. A cold breakfast is a small price to pay to be in the presence of such greatness.

On Sunday, with a crowd of more than 32,000 on hand, they watch the doubleheader against the Dodgers. Both games are won by the Cardinals to tighten up the National League race. In the second game Stan is The Man, hitting a lead-off homer in the 12th inning for a 2-1 win.

The guys lunch again on hot dogs, then drive home through the twilight as happy as obsessed fans can possibly be. Mickey is asleep by the time they reach Whitebird.

Memories of these days will hold him in thrall all of his life.

Chapter 19

Oklahoma has long been a battleground, with the "Wets" and the "Drys" clashing over the state's liquor laws. In 1907, when the Oklahoma Territory became the nation's 46th state, it did so as a dry state. For years Oklahoma ran a "dispensary," or liquor agency, to sell liquor for "medicinal" purposes, which led to a statewide illness epidemic and a boom in prescriptions for the alcoholic medicine. When Prohibition came and went, Oklahoma retained its dry status. Then the pro-beer Wets, led by a group called the Beer for Oklahoma League, argued that beer sales would boost revenue for the state, which had been hit hard by the Great Depression. The Prohibition Thousand organization argued that "suds" would mean more crime and more jails. Oklahomans, knowing their state needed the money, passed a referendum allowing beer sales, though the Drys continue to fight off determined efforts to legalize liquor.

Dry state or not, the miners are not going to settle for beer limited by law to 3.2 percent alcohol, so trips to the local bars to drink the harder stuff have become opportunities to relax, "shoot the bull," share stories, tell jokes, laugh, and talk about things that interest them. Strike rumors, the pennant races, mine management, the weather. There are a number of bars in and around Commerce, all of which are shabby, but in which the miners can easily get real liquor. Everybody knows the routine. If a raid is imminent, police will notify them in plenty of time to stash the booze, make the joint look acceptable. The sheriff or a deputy will come in, look around perfunctorily, smile broadly, and say something akin to "Looks good. Enjoy your beer, boys." He'll leave expecting his regular payment to be made on time.

Mutt enjoys his times drinking with his buddies. So long as it doesn't interfere with his baseball activities, he's a willing imbiber. He'll sometimes buy a pint, and when he comes home from the mine, he'll take it out of the icebox and have a nip or two.

Lovell's brothers and children from her first marriage are all heavy drinkers. Probably alcoholics all. Lovell always casts a wary eye toward Mutt when he drinks too much.

"Don't set a bad example for your kids," she warns.

"A few drinks don't hurt nobody. Anyway, if they turn to drink, you ain't gonna stop them."

"I know what it can do, heavy drinking. I seen it."

Mutt turns toward Mickey. "Don't you ever drink," he says with an exaggerated wink. "It ain't good for you. Your mother knows."

"Wouldn't think of it."

Still, whether he admits it or not, Mickey is surrounded by addictive behavior, a condition which he will someday adopt with disastrous results.

The entire Mantle clan plus Nick pile into the old LaSalle to visit Lovell's family in Spavinaw. While the others are visiting, Mutt goes off to play cards in the room at the back of the town's hardware store. He's gone for several hours when Lovell tells Mickey and Nick to go down and get him. "And tell him 'now.' We're getting ready to head home."

The boys, happy to know they'll be heading home soon, find Mutt still playing cards.

"I ain't leaving in the middle of a game," Mutt grunts

"Mom says she's ready to go home," Mickey says.

"Well, she'll just have to wait. You have any cigarettes?"

"You know I don't."

"I'm almost out."

The player sitting across from Mutt slides him a mostly empty pack of Luckies.

"Thanks, I'll pay you back."

"No, you won't, but keep those. They're on the house."

When the boys return with the news, Lovell asks if Mutt is drinking. They tell her he is.

"Well, let the darn fool be then."

Two hours later, frustrated that Mutt hasn't yet shown up, she sends the boys back again. They find Mutt still at the card table, but now he's in a real stupor.

Mickey taps his father on the shoulder. "Dad, Mom says you've got to come now."

Mutt's slurred voice manages to get out what Mickey thinks is "Or what?"

"C'mon, Dad, let's go."

Mutt's head drops down hard on the table. "I can't. I've been drugged. Somebody drugged me."

Mickey and Nick exchange quizzical glances. "You say, drugged?"

"Drugged, stole all my money."

"You're not drugged, Dad. You've had a little too much to drink, that's all."

"No more money."

"Well, maybe more than a little."

Mickey finds this amusing. His father is not often a heavy drinker, but when he does occasionally drink too much, his typical reticence gives way to an air of ebullience that seems so un-Mutt-like. So out of character. So … funny.

"You gotta get up and go," Mickey tells him.

Nick is cracking up. "I don't think that's gonna happen, Mickey."

"OK, Dad," Mickey says while trying unsuccessfully to stifle his own laughter, "you stay and have another drink. We'll go get Mom."

"Your father's hysterical when he's blotto," Nick says as the boys are running back to the house.

"You telling me?"

"Have you ever seen him like that before?"

"Once or twice."

"Who woulda thought?"

"I know, it's funny, right?"

"It's like there's a different man hiding inside that comes out when he's drinking. A happier man, maybe."

"Ah, it's good for him once in a while. Lets off steam."

"Doubt if your mother's gonna see it that way."

"She damn well won't."

As predicted, Lovell is not amused. She says she's going to drive the LaSalle downtown, and together they're going to put Mutt in the car and drive him home.

"Mom, you don't know how to drive," Mickey says, finding that thought also hilarious.

"How hard can it be?"

"Plenty."

"Everybody, in the car. And I mean now!"

They all load in the LaSalle—Mickey, Nick, the twins, Barbara, Larry. Lovell slides in where she has never sat before—the driver's seat.

"Try not to hit anybody," Mickey says.

"I don't want to hear nothing out of any of you. Sit down and shut up."

Lovell has watched Mutt drive enough that she knows how to start the car, release the hand brake, depress the clutch, put it in first gear, and accelerate, albeit slowly like Mutt. After several jerky starts accompanied by considerable merriment on the part of her passengers, she manages to make it downtown.

"OK, you clowns," she says to the other (and only slightly less inebriated) card players. "Let's drag his sorry-ass carcass into the car."

People tend to see Mutt as a serious man. A determined man, a quiet man, a respectable man. Not particularly a fun-loving man. But Mickey, who has always looked up to and followed his father's leads, sees in episodes like this that maybe it's OK to drink too much once in a while. It certainly doesn't seem to hurt his father any. He never misses a day of work because of it. He doesn't turn nasty. He doesn't hurt anyone. Besides, it's funny. Even Lovell, for all her insistence otherwise, can't help thinking, yeah, a staggering-drunk Mutt is actually rather funny.

They all manage to pile the semi-comatose Mutt into the back seat as they might a bag of feed. Mickey and Nick squeeze into the front passenger's seat. The young kids have no choice but to sit on top of their father.

"Don't worry," says Lovell. "He'll never know. Anyway, by the time he wakes up, he won't even remember he'd been drinking."

They set off for Whitebird ... in first gear. Everyone is in stitches.

Mickey is laughing so hard he can hardly speak, but eventually he manages, "Hey, Ma, put 'er in second, put 'er in second."

Lovell keeps the car in first all the way. The laughter is so infectious that Mickey and Nick can't stop until they are home.

They leave Mutt in the car to sober up.

Mutt's brother Tunney watches a Commerce High baseball game in which Mickey pitches a complete game. After the game, he offers congratulations to his nephew and then asks him if he would like to join the Scouts.

"The Boy Scouts?" Mickey asks.

"I'm chairman of the Scout board, did you know that?"

"No."

"Well, I am, and I think it would be good for you to ... you know, have some activities other than baseball."

"I play basketball."

"Activities other than sports, I mean."

"I don't think that's—"

"Because your father won't let you?"

"I don't know."

"Don't get me wrong, I love sports, particularly baseball, but there's more to life than playing games. And what happens when you can't play anymore? Ever think of that? The day will come when you can't, even if you don't think of those things now. Scouting is great. It would give you other skills and interests you'll need if baseball … anyway, you should think about it."

"Yeah, OK."

"Look at me. I spent years in the mines, but I had other things I could do, too—Scouting, and I'm also a councilman from Ward 4. I was elected last year. Your father tell you that?"

"No."

"You could do that someday, be on the city council, or even something bigger, but you gotta do something other than play games all the time."

"That's what I like to do, Uncle Tunney."

"You can't always do only what you like. There's more to life than—"

"Yeah."

"Just having fun."

"Sorry, but I gotta run. Some of the guys are waiting for me."

"Think about the Scouts."

"For sure."

On a particularly breezy Sunday, Mutt loads the family in the car to watch him play for Spavinaw in a game against Salina. Barbara puts up a fuss about losing a Sunday afternoon when she could have put it to better purpose—and any purpose would have been better.

When they arrive at the field, Mutt tells Mickey that today he gets to play shortstop.

"For real? Mickey asks.

"Yeah. I'm gonna pitch. Uncle Tunney will be at first. You'll be all right."

"Shortstop?"

"You know where that is, right? Between second and third—"

"I think I can figure that out, but I don't know if I can—"

"You can what?"

"You know, with adults and all …"

"I don't want to hear it."

The game, like all the sandlot games in the area, attracts lots of spectators. These may be amateur contests outside any organized league, but there is no less desire to win. The infield is rough, and the grass in parts of the outfield is deep enough to lose a baseball.

Mickey is as nervous as he can ever remember being. If he screws up with everybody watching and his father and uncle in the game, it will be the end of life as he knows it. Or so the anxious young man imagines. He can picture balls rolling between his legs, striking out on pitches over his head. It's one thing to play with boys his own age in high school, because he knows he's a good high school player, but with men his father's age ...

Mickey also understands that he has reached the age where his father has stopped making allowances for his youth. He will have to perform at the level of mature, experienced players. He has to be a real player. No excuses for a bad play based on his age.

As the home team, they take the field first. While warming up, Mickey throws a ball to first well above his uncle's head. Tunney leaps up and barely manages to snag it before it goes into the stands. Tunney signals with his hands for Mickey to calm down.

When the game begins, Mickey's only thought is *"Please don't hit the ball to me."* No one does.

In the bottom of the inning, Mutt pays no more attention to Mickey than he does to the other players on the bench. Mickey is relieved. He doesn't want his father singling him out for attention. He's just one of the guys.

As the game progresses, Mickey is called on to make a couple of routine plays at short. He bobbles one, but still manages to snatch it out of the air. With his strong arm, he gets it to Tunney in time to nab the not particularly fast runner by a step. At the plate he manages only a squirrely ground ball to the first baseman and a pop-up to the second baseman in his first two at-bats. Then in the bottom of the seventh inning, he gets a fastball right down the middle of the plate. He turns on it, driving it into deep right-center. When the center fielder and right fielder both shy off for fear of running into each other, the ball gets between them. With his blazing speed Mickey rounds the bases and makes it all the way home. He gets handshakes from some of his teammates, including Mutt.

In the ninth, he lets a ground ball go through his legs.

On the drive home, Mutt tells him for the umpteenth time to keep his butt down when fielding ground balls. He never mentions the home run.

⸻

Mickey wants to play football for his high school. Mosley wants him to play. LeRoy wants him to play. Coach Allan Woolard wants him to play. Mutt doesn't.

"You know why," Mutt says every time Mickey brings up the subject.

"I'll be careful."

"Don't be stupid. You can't be careful in football. It's a violent sport. It's meant to be violent, and players get hurt all the time. Is that what you want? You want to break a leg or something? You want to kiss goodbye to baseball?"

"Of course not. But lots of boys play, and they don't get hurt. Mosley plays, and he's the quarterback. Everybody's always after the quarterback, and he don't get hurt. And LeRoy runs the ball, and he's never been hurt. And—"

"Ain't it enough you play basketball in the winter? You don't need football, too."

"But football around here is all everybody—"

"Conversation's over. I don't want to hear about football no more."

Mickey comes to hate football season during his freshman year. His friends are playing. They are at practice after school all week, and then on Fridays or Saturdays they play games. Most students and many of the townsfolk show up to watch. During the games, Mickey sits in the stands feeling left out. Football players are looked up to in ways baseball players are not. The best players are always popular in school.

Perhaps the most valuable social currency in Commerce is school sports, and football is the most valuable of them. The term "gridiron heroes" is in wide use; "baseball heroes" isn't.

Before the 1946 season gets underway, Coach Woolard makes the trip to Whitebird to talk with Mutt.

MUTT'S DREAM: MAKING THE MICK

"C'mon, Mutt. This is Oklahoma. You know football is king around here."

"It ain't king in this house."

"I gotta be honest with you, Mutt, people are … you know, they're talking, saying maybe Mickey don't got the … you know, guts to play football."

"That's absurd."

"Because they know he's a good athlete. I mean they seen him on the diamond and on the court, and they know he's real athletic. They know he can run as fast, probably faster, than anyone in these parts. Nobody could catch him once he got past the line. Nobody."

"I don't doubt that."

"And he's got good hands too. Look at how he handles a basketball. He's a gifted kid."

"Football's for big kids. Mickey ain't that."

"His speed would make the difference. He'd run around guys, not through them."

"You want him to be a back?"

"We could sure use him. I mean, we got some good boys who can run the ball—the Williams kid, Bennett. But you know damn well Mickey's a better athlete than anyone we got back there now."

"Yeah, he's a good athlete."

"Because of you. You've trained him, worked with him, and—"

"He'd be good on any account. He's a natural."

"Here's the thing, Mutt. Seeing as how this is football country, well, some people look at it like Mickey's got a responsibility to the school … the town, really, and he's … letting everybody down by not playing. They think that since he's such a good athlete that he owes it to Commerce to play football."

"Owes it? He don't owe nobody nothing."

"I'm just saying that's what some people think."

"What do you think? Do you think that?"

"I think it would be best for everybody if he played—particularly for Mickey. These high school kids, they have their own social … ideas.

I know sometimes Mickey feels like an outsider, and well … playing on the football team would help him … socialize a little more. He's basically a shy kid, and football players are looked up to in a way that others aren't. So, it would help him if he played, and as I said, the whole town … well, he'd be more popular all around."

"You telling me he has a duty to play football."

"I wouldn't put it quite that way."

"I think you just did," Mutt says, practically snorting.

Finally, Mutt tells the coach that if he can be assured that Mickey will be home every day with at least two hours of daylight left so that he can work on his baseball, he will let Mickey play. Reluctantly.

The coach is ecstatic, but his frozen face holds firm, offering no window to his sudden joy. What he tells Mutt is that he will give Mickey a fair chance to make the team and, if he works hard, maybe he will. He emphasizes the "maybe." Says it several times. What he really thinks is that with Mickey running the ball he can win the league, and because of that he can move on to a bigger school in a bigger town.

"I appreciate your loyalty," he tells Mutt. "I really do."

Mickey, who has listened to the conversation through the window, waits until the coach has left before he comes into the house.

"I suppose you put him up to that?" Mutt says.

"Me? No."

"What did Coach say?" Mosley asks Mickey the next morning before school.

"I think he said it was my duty to play."

"And?"

"Dad said he absolutely hated the idea, but … he finally agreed—reluctantly."

"Boy, that's great."

"Yeah, I can't wait."

Mickey is now a three-sport player in his high school. He may not be the best athlete—Mosley is generally considered that—but sports will now consume most of Mickey's days. Baseball, basketball, and football during the school year. Baseball all summer.

Chapter 20

Mickey turns out for the football team in September. Coach Woolard has no qualms about putting Mickey right into the action. He's too athletic not to play. Mickey has a lot to learn. His father would never have taught him football fundamentals even if he had known them himself. But Mickey has his friends from whom he can learn. Mose is unquestionably the star of the team. He's a powerful and quick runner and has a strong arm. LeRoy is a halfback with good acceleration and the instincts to follow his blockers until holes open up.

"You're gonna work with the backs," the coach tells him on the first day of practice.

This is what Mickey wants to hear. He wants to carry and catch the ball, not spend the game trying to knock down big linemen.

The Commerce High Tigers are a team of 40 boys. At 130 pounds Mickey is one of the smallest, but as they begin practicing it is evident that he is going to be a real asset to the team. He quickly confirms Coach Woolard's expectations. He is easily the fastest player on the team and has good hands; in the coach's words, "that kid gots guts."

Woolard runs a straightforward T-formation offense with Mosley as the quarterback and Mickey behind him as one of three running backs—usually in the position considered the fullback. LeRoy is one of the halfbacks, Tommy Williams the other. Mickey is the smallest back, but when he gets past the line of scrimmage nobody catches him. Since the boys all play both ways, the coach has Mickey play deep when they practice defense, where his speed allows him to close fast on receivers. He shows he's a willing tackler too, although bigger players sometimes get the better of him.

"Man, you're really gonna help a lot this year," Mosley says to him as they walk off the field after a sweaty practice. "You and me, we're gonna show this league a thing or two."

"I hope so."

"There's no chance your dad's gonna pull you, is there? You know, if you get banged up or something?"

"Who knows? I sure hope he don't, though. I love it. This is fun."

"Fun? Wait until some 200-pound slob decks you. You may change your mind and pull yourself out."

"That ain't gonna happen."

"I know."

When he gets home from practice, Mutt looks him over like he's a surgeon, examining him for broken bones. Mickey is limping slightly.

"You hurt already? You ain't even played a game yet."

"I'm not hurt. Just a little stiff."

"Maybe you should—"

"No."

This is the first time Mickey has gone against his father's will. A small act of rebellion. Perhaps if his friends weren't playing, he might not have had any interest in football, but since they are …

Mutt hopes Mickey will get nicked up a little. Just enough to convince him football isn't something he really wants to do. Or maybe the coach will work the boys so hard that Mickey will decide it isn't worth it. The fact is, however, that Mickey is acting like he enjoys the practices. This makes Mutt uneasy. He would like to put his foot down and forbid Mickey from ever touching a football again, but he can't bring himself to do it.

Although Mickey would prefer his father show approval, he is in some ways free from the pressure Mutt puts on him when he plays baseball. On the gridiron Mickey seems looser, more spontaneous—than he does on the diamond or even the hardwood. He jokes around with Mosley, LeRoy, and the others he knows from his classes. He is, as he says, having fun … until a brisk afternoon in early October. Under Woolard's watchful eye, the team is running offensive plays when the coach calls out, "Mickey, take a few snaps. Give Mose a break for a while."

Assuming he doesn't get injured, Mosley will be the quarterback all season. Everybody understands that. But it won't hurt to have somebody ready as a backup should the situation call for it. Mickey's short stature might make it difficult for him to see over taller defensive linemen, but he's quick enough to get out of trouble, and he'll always be a threat to run. The coach considers him the second-string quarterback, so occasionally he practices taking snaps.

On this day, which turns out to be so momentous in the life of Mickey Mantle, he settles in behind Johnson, the plug-squat center. Mickey calls the running play. Johnson snaps the ball. Mickey takes several steps back and pivots to hand the ball off to Joe Mountford, who is in Mickey's usual fullback position. But the timing between the two players, who are not in their familiar places, goes wrong, and Mickey is kicked in the shin as the ball bounces away.

The coach blows his whistle to stop the play and goes to check on Mickey, who is on the ground, rubbing the shin.

"Well, that was a real foul-up," he says. "You OK?"

"Yeah, fine."

Woolard reaches down to help Mickey get up, but when Mickey gets to his feet, he realizes he can't put any pressure on the injured leg.

"Here, help him to the sidelines," the coach says to LeRoy.

While LeRoy and Montford help him off the field, the coach tells him, "You'll be OK. Maybe put some ice on it later. Yeah, put some ice on it. Keep the swelling down. You're fine. Gonna be a little black and blue, that's all."

Mickey nods between grimaces.

"Mose, get back in there. Same play. Sweep right and try not to bump into your backs. Let's go."

Mickey, assuming the pain in his leg will soon subside, watches practice from the sidelines. It doesn't. Max, the team's manager, looks at the leg. It's ugly. Black and blue and red and swollen. "Can you put weight on it?" he asks.

"Not really," Mickey says as he gets up and tries to take a step.

"OK, sit back down. Best not to test it anymore."

More than the injury, Mickey is concerned about what his father will say. But it's just a kick in the shin, he rationalizes. It's not a serious injury. It's a bruise. Bruises heal. Bruises are not long-lasting injuries. A bruised shin is nothing compared to a real football injury like a broken bone or a busted knee. He'll be fine in the morning.

At the end of practice, Max suggests that Mickey spend the night at his house, as it's less than a block from the school. LeRoy says he'll go out to Whitebird and tell Lovell and Mutt that Mickey will spend the night at Max's.

"Make sure you tell Dad it ain't nothing. Just a little bruise."

"Don't worry."

"I don't want him to think—"

"Mickey, I know the situation. I'll take care of it."

"Tell him I'll be fine in the morning."

"I'll tell him you're fine now, just staying with Max to talk football."

"Talking football, yeah."

Mickey hobbles to Max's house where Max sets him up on the couch. Max's mother makes him tea and tells him it will make his leg feel better. But with or without the warm drink his leg throbs, keeping him awake most of the night.

When Mickey doesn't show up at school the next day, Coach Woolard becomes concerned. Mickey has been known to ditch classes from time to time, but it's not like him to miss a day when a game or practice is scheduled.

When the coach goes to Max's house, he finds Mickey on the couch with his leg propped up on a pillow. It is as red as a beet and even more swollen than it was the day before.

"My God!" the coach says. "That doesn't look so good, Mickey."

"Just needs a little more time."

Max's mother tells the coach she checked his temperature, and it was 103.5 degrees.

"That's it," says Woolard. "You gotta get that checked out."

Mickey does a poor job of acting blasé. "We don't need to do that," he says.

The coach shakes his head. "Better be safe than sorry. They can probably give you something at the hospital to take that swelling down. They got all sorts of medicines these days to do things like that."

"I don't know."

"You got an infection or something. That's what making your temperature so high. They got pills to kill infections, and you need to get them because infections, they can be big trouble."

"From a little kick in the leg?"

"Looks like it. Your folks know you're here, don't they?"

"LeRoy told them."

"They'll need to take you over to the Eagle-Picher Mine hospital. Your dad works there, right? At the mine."

"Yeah."

"They'll take care of you—the hospital. Prescribe some medicine."

Although Mickey doesn't want his father to see that he's been hurt, he is becoming frightened. The leg isn't getting better on its own, that's for sure. It's painful, ugly.

While Mickey waits apprehensively, the coach goes to the mine to get a message to Mutt that Mickey needs to be taken to their hospital. Mickey is apprehensive about what his father will say when he sees how discolored and swollen the leg is. Of course, he won't say it out loud, but his I-told-you-so look will shout loudly enough.

When Mutt arrives, he looks at Mickey with eyes that bore into him, but doesn't express either anger or concern. He helps Mickey into the old LaSalle and drives him to the hospital.

"It's a good hospital. Everybody says it is," Mutt says more for himself than for his son. "There are other hospitals, of course. But they cost more, and besides, this is a good hospital. Everybody says it is."

This is the type of injury Mutt has dreaded all along. Both father and son understand that, but if Mickey is expecting a dressing-down, he doesn't get it.

A doctor at the hospital greets them brightly. Much too brightly for a doctor, Lovell thinks.

"Well, let's see what you got here," Dr. Connell says as he pulls Mickey's pant leg up.

Dr. Connell, a respected physician who also owns a drugstore, has seen and treated his share of athletic injuries. Immediately, he knows Mickey has a dangerously severe infection from what he calls "a bone disease."

"What's that mean?" Mutt asks.

"An infection? Well, that's caused by some kind of bacteria—tiny little organisms—that do things like cause ... well, you see that for yourselves here in the leg."

"But you can treat it?"

"We'll do what we can, but infections can be ... stubborn."

Mickey's mood swings among fear, embarrassment, and guilt. He has no experience with hospitals. He only knows the stories of the miners hurt in the mines and taken to the hospital in the white ambulance. So many of them die.

Confusing thoughts are running through his head. What if my leg doesn't heal? What then? What if I can't play sports again? What is Dad thinking? What will he do? But no. It's a bang on the leg, that's all. OK, the doctor says it's infected, but they can treat it. Stubborn means it might take more time. Of course, Dad didn't want me to play football in the first place, but you can hurt your leg doing all sorts of things—falling off a bicycle or a horse, tripping on a step, getting caught in a fence—all kinds of things. Heck, you could get hurt playing baseball too. Mickey Cochrane knows that all too well. Lots of players have gotten hurt playing ball.

"We're going to find a room for you," the doctor says.

"A room?" Mickey asks with a shy smile. "No, I can get back home OK. I don't need—"

"Son, you have a high temperature, and that's dangerous if it's not taken care of. We're going to keep you tonight and work on getting that temperature down."

"So, he can go home in the morning?" Mutt says.

"We'll see."

The doctor writes on Mickey's chart: "Infection of the lower end of the tibia on the left leg."

"We're going to find a bed for you, and then I'm going to lance that ankle so we can see if we can drain that infection right out of you. And I'm going to order a regimen of a new ... well, a relatively new drug called penicillin."

This is the first time Mickey, Mutt or Lovell has heard that word—penicillin—but it is far from the last. Mickey learns he is to be administered 300,000 units a day.

"That sounds like a lot," Mickey says.

"You are lucky we even have that much," Dr. Connell says as he writes the order on the chart. "If you had been injured even as recently as last year, we wouldn't have that much on hand. Nobody around here would have. You can probably thank the war for that. The medics found out it was a miracle drug for treating infections, so we started making a lot more of it, and you, young Mickey, you're going to get the benefit of it."

Producing usable penicillin from the Penicillium mold is difficult. It takes 2,000 liters of mold culture fluid to produce enough pure penicillin to treat a single case of infection. In the build-up to the D-Day invasion, medics pushed to make it in larger quantities. When researchers determined that not all the penicillin given to a person is broken down, they were able to reuse penicillin extracted from a patient's urine.

More than 20 American companies answered the call and began working around the clock to meet the demand. At least 100,000 soldiers benefitted from penicillin treatment in Europe following D-Day, and thousands more lives were saved during the bloody combat in the Pacific.

"It really seems to be a miracle drug," Dr. Connell says. "I've also read where some people have claimed that penicillin won the war. That may be an exaggeration, but it certainly helped with wound infections … and the rampant syphilis infections, too, for that matter."

"What's—?"

"Never mind, Mickey," Mutt says.

"Anyway, we're going to give it to you, and you should thank your lucky stars that we can."

"How do you—?"

"In the butt or the thigh."

"With needles?"

"Unless you know some other way I don't."

"Pills."

"We need to inject it. Fifty-thousand units every three hours around the clock."

"Even during the night?"

"We'll wake you up."

"You'll be OK, Mickey," Mutt says with uncertain conviction. "Just hang in there and do what the doctors say. That stuff they got, that'll take care of it in a jiffy."

"Yeah."

They put Mickey in a room with three other disabled children. They have all been there for weeks and mildly resent the intrusion of an outsider. Mickey doesn't ask what is wrong with any of them. His leg pulses with what the nurse calls "discomfort." He is sweaty from the fever. Exhausted, anxious, confused. This is the first night he has ever spent alone away from home. He has always been surrounded by brothers and sisters and often by friends.

A pill makes him groggy even before his parents leave. After they are gone, in an effort to take his mind off his situation, he tries to picture the Cardinals players. They've all probably faced injuries at some time or other. They will understand what he is feeling. But any image he sees quickly vanishes.

They needn't have had plans to wake him for his injections.

Mickey sleeps little.

His wish for a short hospital stay is not realized. The treatment for what one nurse calls "cancer of the bone" has an immediate but limited effect. As the doctor had suggested, it is proving stubborn. In addition to the every-three-hour penicillin jabs, he is treated with sulfur, peroxide, hot and cold compresses, and a variety of smelly liniments. Nothing makes much difference. The swelling goes down some, and his temperature lessens somewhat, but it is evident that the infection isn't completely gone.

He is visited daily by different doctors who examine his leg, scan his chart, look concerned, then leave.

Mickey's inherent shyness prohibits him from being anything but a compliant, if constantly anxious, patient. Every day he asks when he can go home, and every day he is told the doctors don't know. They don't have a lot of experience with penicillin yet, but the reports that they have seen suggest positive results … in time.

Every day, Lovell walks the mile from Whitebird to catch the Northeast bus to the hospital in Picher. She remains through the day until Mutt arrives, and then she goes home to fix dinner for the kids. Mickey is always pleased to have her there, although he gets a little embarrassed when her feisty side aims a caustic comment at one of the nurses or doctors.

"That food ain't enough for a growing boy. See what else you can dig up."

"Do you really have any idea how much of that stuff you should be shooting into him? You need to get that figured out. Like now!"

On the other hand, Mutt, for all his worrying, appears calm. Mickey keeps expecting a lecture about how he was right. It never comes.

His friends stop by when they can. Nick and Mosley keep him updated on football activities, LeRoy on school assignments.

On their way out of the hospital after a visit that found Mickey particularly depressed, Nick says, "He doesn't know what's going on. That's the thing. I don't think the quack doctors do either."

"I know," Mosley says. "He ain't used to lying in bed all day—

Mickey, being as active as he always is. I think having to stay so still is bothering him more than the pain in the leg."

"You see how he looks?" Nick asks. "So pale and all. And he's so quiet."

"He's always quiet."

"Not that quiet."

"You think it's serious?"

"Serious? Hell yeah, it's serious."

"But not … you know … that serious."

"I don't know."

"What if he can't ever play sports again on account of the leg never heals all the way?"

"That ain't gonna happen."

"Nah."

"He's real sad, though, ain't he?"

"Who wouldn't be, stuck in that dump all the time?"

"Yeah."

The nights are the worst times for Mickey. He stares into the darkness, alone with his thoughts. Sleep may not come easily to him, but sweating spells do. In the mornings his sheets are wet with perspiration. Some nights he has anxiety-driven hallucinations. In one nightmare, he sees himself hit a home run, but when he tries to run, he can't. His leg is swollen to the size of a tree trunk.

This is the first time he has had to seriously question what lies ahead for him. Sure, there have been times when he thought he would never be good enough to fulfill Mutt's dream, but mostly he goes along with Mutt's dream without giving it much consideration. He plays sports. He talks about sports. He listens to Mutt. At his age he mostly thinks about the "now" in his life. There are few thoughts about tomorrow and no thoughts at all about endings. Still, lying in a hospital bed for days makes him think about these things, and he doesn't like what he is thinking. Maybe life is more comfortable when you don't have to make choices. Maybe Mutt making the choices for him is the easy way. What if he is left a cripple? Sports would be out. What else could he do? Could he even work in a mine?

Mutt's concern has never been about Mickey's athletic abilities but about his son's sometimes flagging self-confidence, something that is essential to fulfill his dreams … or Mutt's dreams.

One day, Mutt arrives with a small radio. "You don't want to miss the World Series," he says.

"Where'd you get that? The radio."

"Found it on sale at that little appliance shop over in Miami. Game Four is today, and the Cards are down 2-1. Red Munger is throwing for us today, Howie Pollet tomorrow. I don't know who the Sox are gonna throw."

"That would be good—listening to the games."

"While you're laid up, it's a good time to get some mental work in. Try to picture the games in your mind's eye and pay attention to the little things. See yourself as each player as he comes to bat. Watch the pitcher carefully. Can you pick up anything he's doing that might give away what pitch he's gonna throw? Do you need to adjust your position in the batter's box depending on what the pitcher is throwing? And the game situation, does that change how you're gonna hit? Can you pull the ball? Or is it better to try to go the other way? All these little things, and a lot more, that's what you gotta think about. Know what I mean?"

"Yeah, the little things."

"You got a good head on your shoulders, and you gotta use it to be a good ballplayer."

"I know."

Mickey may know that, but the reality is that when he is at bat he doesn't think about these things. He waits for the ball. If it looks like it's going to be a strike, he swings as hard as he can, trying to hit the ball out of sight. There isn't much thinking to it. He is pure "see ball, hit ball."

"When you get out of here, put it to use—what you learned listening."

"Yeah, OK."

He does listen to the games. Every inning of every game. With the score tied 3–3 in the eighth inning of Game Seven, Harry Walker strides to the plate with Enos Slaughter on first. Slaughter runs with the pitch, and Walker laces a liner to left center. The throw to the plate is too late, and Slaughter scores in what became known as the "Mad Dash". That's it. The Cards hang on to win the game and the Series. Alone in his room, Mickey is teary-eyed.

Garagiola, Kurowski, Slaughter, and Walker are the hitting stars of the Fall Classic. Musial hits four doubles but by his standards has a rather quiet offensive Series. Still, he ends up winning the National League's Most Valuable Player Award.

Listening to the World Series is great, but the doctor telling Mickey a few days later that he will be going home is even greater. The leg isn't completely healed, but it is better.

"You've got to take it easy now, Mickey," the doctor tells him. "Get plenty of rest, and whatever you do, don't stress that leg by trying to play football, or any other sport for that matter. Not yet. We've got the infection under control, and we want to keep it that way. Later, when it's completely gone, you can get back to your sports. OK? You understand that?"

"Sure."

"Now, don't let your father talk you into playing ball right away, and he probably will—try, that is—but unless you want to come right back here—"

"Don't worry. I hope I never see this place again."

"But you'll miss the cute nurses, right?"

"I guess."

"We're going to set you up with a pair of crutches. I want you to use them to keep the weight off that leg for a while."

"Crutches?"

"Just use them. It's OK to look like a gimp. The girls will feel sorry for you, and that's a good thing, don't you think?"

"Sure, yeah."

So, after a 12-night stay, Mutt takes Mickey home in the LaSalle.

Chapter 21

Mickey stays off the leg as best an active teenager can, but when he sees Dr. Connell for a check-up, he gets bad news.

"We need to readmit you."

Mickey nods knowingly. The leg has gotten worse. Not as bad as when he first injured it, but it is not healing as it should. It is still swollen, still red, still painful. Even without having it checked, Mickey knows his temperature is on the rise once more.

When Dr. Connell asks Mickey about the boils on his legs, Mickey tells him, "I've always had them. At least for as long as I can remember."

"This many?"

"Yeah. Sometimes more."

This leads the doctor to question whether Mickey might have had an earlier infection, or perhaps several infections. This could explain why he was underweight. Perhaps his latest injury reactivated and intensified previous infections. Maybe the infection is deep-seated and more pervasive than is apparent. He doesn't mention this to Mickey or his parents, but since the leg is not responding as he had anticipated, the suspicion lingers.

Mickey is put back on penicillin and given sulfur pills, many of which he throws out the window.

"They're god-awful," he tells Nick. "They'd gag a maggot. Want to try one?"

"I'll pass," Nick says.

"If you change your mind, there are plenty on the ground outside the window. Feel free to help yourself."

"Don't you think you should be swallowing them? If the doctor thinks they help—"

"Don't look to me like the doctor has any idea what helps."

"Does it hurt? The leg?"

"I can take it. So, what's going on with the team?"

"We're doing OK. Here, I cut out a few articles from the *News-Record*."

Mickey looks at one and reads out loud. "The local football wars will open at eight o'clock tonight when the Miami High School Wardogs take on the Commerce Tigers at Miami Field. The rough and experienced Wardog line, which averages 171 pounds per man, will outweigh the Commerce linemen, who average 162. Probably the big job of the Miami forward wall will be to stop Bill Mosley."

"They didn't stop him."

"Nah. Slowed him down a little, didn't stop him."

"Wait till I get back, then nobody is gonna slow us down," Mickey says without a lot of conviction.

"Do they tell you how long you're gonna be kept prisoner here?"

"They don't tell me nothing."

"It's getting better, though?"

"Yeah."

"Jeez Mickey, you gotta get back to action."

"You telling me?"

"'Cause this place is boring."

"Particularly at night. I don't sleep so good. Anyway, all they want to do is make a pin cushion outta me, and they don't stop at night either."

After Nick leaves, Mickey reads another article Nick has clipped for him.

Commerce's Tigers played inspired ball all the way as their injured halfback, Tommy Williams, lifted them to the heights with his Spartan effort. They sprang one of the biggest upsets of the 1946

Oklahoma high school football season last night, defeating the powerful Broken Arrow Tigers 18 to 13.

Quarterback Bill Mosley, who raced through and around the ends for sizeable gains and who turned in some remarkable passing, led the Commerce offensive. Yet the plucky Williams, with a severely bruised right shoulder, was the boy who drove his teammates on—once with a beautiful 74-yard quick kick and on other occasions, even though seriously hurt, with consistent advances on the ground.

Mickey thinks he should have been playing halfback that night. He could have been the hero of the game. He could have played hurt.

Self-pity is a trap into which Mickey has fallen. As much as his infection, it is his enemy, but despite the face he puts on, he can't shake it. He doesn't realize that feeling sorry for himself only makes his life worse.

Mary, a dour nurse who administers the injections during the early hours of the morning, sees the dark cloud that is enveloping her patient. For just such occasions, she has a ready list of sayings.

"The heart watered by tears of self-pity soon turns to stone; it is incapable of compassion," she tells Mickey while administering an injection. "You cannot separate the reasons you have for feeling sorry for yourself from the sorry way you feel."

Mickey appreciates that she means well, but he wishes she would stop with the corny aphorisms.

After three nights in the hospital they release him, but he is not sure if he is being sent home because they think the leg is getting better and will continue to do so, or because they think the leg will never completely heal and don't know what else to do.

―※―

Mutt and Ox are sitting at the bar at the Black Cat. They would have been playing a game in Miami had it not been pouring all day.

"Any better today?" Ox asks.

"I don't know. I don't think so. He don't complain much."

"Mickey kinda keeps things wrapped up, don't he?"

"Pretty much."

They sit and sip for several minutes. The rain pounding on the roof sounds like a herd of stampeding horses. The rain, the cancellation of their game, the gloomy day—all add to their melancholy feelings.

Ox pivots on his stool to look through the smudgy window at the rain. "Into every life, a little rain must fall."

"That so?" says Mutt without turning.

"It ain't all sunshine and roses, life."

"I guess not."

"So, here's my question, and I ask it as your friend. I am your friend, right?"

"You must be if I'm drinking with you."

"My question, and you know damn well what I'm talking about, is have you done right by him? Mickey."

"What are you talking about? Of course, I have."

"Except that you've forced him to set his mind in stone to become a professional baseball player and only a professional baseball player. Now it looks like maybe that ain't gonna happen. Not playing is one thing, but knowing he's letting you down, that's gonna tear him apart, Mutt. He's never gonna be the same person again; he's always gonna think of himself as a failure because you've … well, you've set him up that way. In some ways, you set him up to fail. And you have other kids too, Mutt. Ever think about them? They've gotta believe you don't care about them, all the attention you give to Mickey."

"Go to hell, Ox," Mutt says as he walks out into the pelting rain.

Mickey is back in the hospital.

Dr. Connell orders X-rays of the leg. His recent suspicions are confirmed when he, along with two other doctors, review the results. Mickey is suffering from osteomyelitis, a potentially serious infection in a bone. It means that the infection is in the bone itself, not the soft tissue as he had earlier thought. The deep wound he suffered on the football field either gave bacteria a route to enter the leg bone or reactivated an infection that had been there all along.

He meets with Lovell and Mutt to explain.

"If left untreated, the infection can become chronic."

"What the hell does that mean?" Lovell asks.

"Well, either lasting for a long time or constantly recurring."

"How long time?"

"Hard to say."

"Try."

"There's no way to know, really. If it is chronic, it can cause a loss of blood supply to the affected bone. If this happens, the bone itself will eventually die, but—"

"That doesn't sound—"

"It's much too early to think about that. Anyway, that may never happen. Probably won't."

"How did this happen? I thought you said you could control it."

"Osteomyelitis is caused by a bacterium, a tiny little organism much too small to see with the naked eye."

"Then how do you know they're there?"

"Well, they can be seen with a very powerful microscope. There are millions of them all over the place. Most aren't harmful. Most are beneficial to us, but a few, they can cause problems like the ones Mickey is dealing with."

"So now what?"

"Well, we're going to increase the penicillin and hope."

"Hope! That ain't good enough," Lovell says in a voice just short of a shout. "You gotta fix this. He's an athlete and—"

"We're doing our best."

"Maybe that ain't good enough, doc," she says as she yanks the door open and leaves the room.

"She's high-strung," Mutt says.

"She is that."

The next day, a surgeon operates on the injured leg. He opens the abscess, allowing it to drain. When Mickey's temperature doesn't go down in the next two weeks, it is an indication that the operation hasn't had the desired effect.

"There's something else we might try," Dr. Connell tells Mickey. "Now, don't overreact until you hear everything I have to say about it."

"OK."

"There have been some good reports on maggot therapy."

"Did you say maggots?"

"I did. I know what it sounds like, but maggot therapy is a controlled application to a wound that has provided rapid, precise, safe, and powerful debridement."

"I don't know what that means, whatever you just said. That word."

"Debridement. It's a word we use to describe the removal of dead, damaged, or infected tissue, so that the remaining tissue can heal itself. As I understand it, the wound-healing benefits of maggots—fly larvae, really—have been documented for centuries, and in this country, maggot therapy has been used for at least 100 years. The maggots remove the dead tissue quickly and stealthily without disturbing the host ... the patient."

Mickey has been depressed for some time, but when he hears the doctors want to treat him with bugs, his depression deepens. The only reason they would resort to something as primitive as this is because they are licked. They don't know what else to do. Hope for a full recovery seems impossible. For the first time, he questions whether he will ever play ball again. Maybe this is the end of ... everything. Maybe this could kill him, but they don't want to tell him that. Maybe his life will end because he insisted on playing football. Maybe his father was right all along.

He fends off these frightening feelings as best he can. It's absurd to think a knock on the leg could kill him, but thoughts of mortality keep returning.

"You have to be prepared to accept the fact that he may never play baseball again," the doctor says, as if it's of no consequence.

"Well, I ain't telling him that, and you ain't either," says Lovell, her icy stare locked on the doctor.

Throughout Mickey's ordeal, Mutt has remained quiet. Morose even. At the hospital, he says little other than, "We'll get through this."

When Mickey is rereleased, he has a large indentation in his left shin covered with a nasty raised scar. A keloid, the doctor calls it.

"Man, that's ugly," Mosley says. "That's as big as a—"

"Yeah, they scraped the bone pretty good."

"That gonna go away anytime soon?"

"I hope."

"That's it, then? They think they got it; the infection?"

"I dunno. They don't tell you a lot, these doctors. I don't think they know, really."

Mosley is too good a friend to bring up what both boys are thinking: will this mean the end of Mickey's baseball plans? They chat for an hour, skirting the subject like it's a forbidden topic. Mosley tells Mickey about the team's football games. They made the semifinals of the State Class B championships before losing to Fairview 37-6.

"We made some stupid mistakes," Mosley says. A fumble took us out of a long drive. We had a shot, though. We were only down by 19 when I was able to pick up 34 yards off-tackle down to the nine. Then on fourth down, I rifled a pass to Dick Stratton in the end zone. He wrestled the ball out of the hands of three Yellowjacket defenders for the six points, but the pass for conversion didn't work. That was it for our scoring."

"They must be pretty good, Fairfield."

"Yeah. It was a pretty good season, though. LeRoy did a good job at halfback, but he's no Mickey. Doesn't have your speed. Mostly Mountford was at full. He definitely isn't as good as you would have been, but he's getting the job done … sorta."

"Maybe next year …"

"For sure."

But he's not sure. Neither is Mickey.

"Can you put weight on that leg? Can you walk?"

"Not really. The doc says it's gonna take a while to heal, so I shouldn't even try."

"Because they're gonna put on a big banquet for us next week. Maybe you could come."

"Yeah, maybe."

Over the next few days, Mickey does his best not to use the leg. Lovell even has to carry him out to the outhouse, which embarrasses him, but Lovell insists. Once, when she catches him hobbling on his own, she smacks him with a towel. "Try that again, and you'll get a lot worse."

Mickey remains housebound. His friends stop by to try to cheer him up, but mostly he is bored and frightened. The leg isn't getting any better. Neither is his confidence.

Chapter 22

Everyone in the house is asleep except Lovell and Mutt. Despite the cool night air, they stand in the open doorway looking out at the moonlit night as if they are searching for … something.

"I took the bus into Oklahoma City today while you was at work."

"Why'd you do that?" Mutt asks while lighting a Camel.

"I met with a lawyer one of the gals I see in town once in a while told me about."

"What the hell you talking about? We don't need no lawyer."

"Except he knows about the doctors over there. They got bigger hospitals with more important doctors."

"That don't mean nothing."

"Look, this thing keeps dragging on, and … they don't seem to be doing nothing that's making a difference, and that's why she thinks the lawyer could get us to a better doctor."

"I don't understand. A lawyer?"

"To get us in."

"In where? Stop beating around the bush. What are you trying to say?"

"The Crippled Children's Hospital."

"The charity hospital?"

"Don't tell me you're too proud? Anyway, we gotta do something, don't we? You got a better idea?"

Mutt looks up at the starry night sky, takes a deep breath. "No."

"Good, because he's already made the arrangements, the lawyer. He's gonna do the paperwork and stuff to get us on public assistance, so they can take Mickey."

"How much is that gonna cost?"

"Nothing. He'll do it for free on account of he thinks football is important for towns like Commerce."

The next morning, they put Mickey in the backseat of the LaSalle for the 175-mile drive to Oklahoma City. Mickey sprawls full length across the seat, arm crooked over his eyes such that he won't be looking into the rearview mirror where he could see his father's stern stare. He has heard about the hospital where they accept sons of poor miners.

Sure, they are poor, but Mickey hates the thought that it has come to this: accepting charity. Maybe never playing baseball again. Maybe being handicapped the rest of his life.

The hospital smells of ether and sulfur. Mickey nearly faints.

Several doctors examine his leg. Their probing is painful, causing the patient to audibly wince.

Then Dr. Keck, a tall, brusque, humorless man who seems to be in charge, tells the Mantles that Mickey will receive increased treatments of sulfur drugs and penicillin. "Fifty shots every thirty hours."

They had hoped to hear something different. How many penicillin shots had he already received, with little or no effect? They didn't bring him all the way to Oklahoma City to do what already didn't work.

"Doctor," says Lovell with a clear edge to her voice. "He's already had I don't know how many penicillin shots. They don't work. You've got to try something different."

"Mrs. Mantle, why don't you just allow us to do our jobs? We'll give him the penicillin for a few days, and then if that doesn't work, we will have to take a more aggressive step."

Lovell is becoming more agitated by the moment. "Like what?"

"We will have to take the leg."

"What are you talking about, take the leg?"

"Amputation."

That word hits Lovell, Mutt, and Mickey like they have been shot.

Lovell takes a quick gasp of breath. "You ain't a-gonna take that leg off. I'll tell you right now."

"If we can't stop the infection—"

"Don't even think about it."

"—it could eventually kill your son."

"There ain't no place in the world for a one-legged man."

Mutt thumps the wall in frustration. "There's gotta be some other way."

"I only bring it up as a last resort."

Lovell looks hard at the doctor to make sure she holds his full attention. "You're not going to do that."

"We'll cross that bridge when we come to it."

"Well, we ain't coming to it. C'mon, Mutt, let's go. We're taking Mickey home now."

"You don't want to do that, Mrs. Mantle. Your son needs to be treated. If it comes to the possibility of amputation—"

"It won't."

"—you'll be informed. We can't do anything unless you and your husband give your permission."

"If we show up, and find that you've already—"

"Don't worry, that is not going to happen."

Mickey is taken to his room, where they begin immediately administering the increased doses of sulfur and penicillin. Naturally, he is shaken by the mention of amputation. He is frightened, but it is guilt that is uppermost in his mind, and he feels helpless to do anything about it. This is his fifth stay in a hospital, but it is the most difficult for him. Now he is really alone. When he was closer to home his friends and family could visit, but here he is 175 miles away. Other than Sunday visits from his parents, he feels isolated, alone, and fearful. Despite the pills they give him, he doesn't sleep much, so he is often tired. A young nurse, knowing his interest in baseball, brings him the sports pages from the *Daily Oklahoman*. Even though the professional season is over, there are still hot stove reports about club doings, but his capacity for concentration is thwarted by his high anxiety levels.

What if he does lose his leg? What could he still do? Maybe with an artificial leg he could play ... something. What? He thinks about Pete Gray playing without one arm. Missing an arm is one thing, missing a leg something else altogether. He tries to push these thoughts away, but they return often.

He has no appetite, no energy. He can't focus on anything for long. And still the leg throbs.

The next Sunday, Mutt arrives with more bad news. Mick's Uncle Tunney has died of cancer. He was 34. A few months earlier, Tunney was in the hospital for an expected appendectomy. During the operation, doctors discovered the cancer. It was too advanced to do anything about it, so they sewed him back up and sent him home. His weight quickly dropped from 215 pounds to 90. Now, just a few months later, he is gone.

That night, alone in his hospital room, Mickey cries. He has always believed he will die young. Doesn't death take all the Mantle men at a young age? It will be his fate, too. He is sure of it.

It has taken almost two months of hospital stays over a 13-month period, hundreds of shots of penicillin, and countless sulfur pills before his leg shows significant improvement.

Mickey is given crutches and sent home.

"This time for good, I hope," he says to the nurse helping him out to his father's waiting car.

"I don't think we'll be seeing you again anytime soon. Just watch out for those tacklers. Maybe run around them next time."

"I don't know that I'll be playing football again."

"Good idea."

The first thing he does when he gets home is tell his mother to burn the crutches.

"I'd rather limp than be seen with them."

"Oh my, aren't we proud."

Mickey goes back to school and struggles to catch up, but he is overjoyed to be back among his family and friends.

Over the course of the winter, the shin remains infected, but they are able to keep it reasonably under control by watching it carefully, keeping it clean, taking the sulfur pills and making occasional trips back to Oklahoma City for more penicillin. He will have flare-ups of the osteomyelitis all his life, but he has learned to treat them right away.

For years Mickey had experienced boils on his arms and legs, and occasionally on his eyelids. Whether due to the massive amounts of penicillin he has received, or the pills, or something else completely, his boils clear up and he begins putting on weight.

"Man, what did they give you in there?" LeRoy asks. "You've buffed up like ... I don't know what."

"Healthy living," Mickey says with a knowing smile.

"Healthy living, my ass. It has to be the drugs."

When he first went into the hospital, Mickey weighed 130 pounds; by the time his hospital stays were over, he was down to 100 pounds. Now he is up to 160 pounds, looking as if most of it is muscle.

"What did they feed you in there?" Nick asks.

"Drugs. Lots of them."

"Got any leftovers you don't want?"

"Yeah, bend over. I'll give you a shot in the ass."

"Is that how they—"

"Yeah."

"Never mind."

Chapter 23

By spring, Mickey has come a long way. The crutches are gone, and he's running again and regaining his strength.

As soon as Mickey is up to it, Mutt returns to practicing with him every afternoon. Working at a level of intensity like never before, Mutt is more driven than ever. So is Mickey. After experiencing the possibility of never playing again, Mutt's and Mickey's resolves have totally fused. Mutt's obsessive expectations are now entirely in line with Mickey's renewed desire to please him. The son is committed to be the baseball player his father wants him to be. His awareness that he almost lost the ability to play baseball drives him to become a better player. They are a team, Mutt and Mickey. Partners. Doing what they both want.

When Mickey is again able to run all out, Mutt sees to it that he is included in Sunday games. They both are playing for the Spavinaw team in games against towns like Salina and others in the area. Over Barbara's protests, Mutt takes the whole family along.

Mickey now gets to play shortstop, while the versatile Mutt plays outfield, catches, or pitches. Mickey shows focus and intensity beyond anything he had demonstrated before the injury. And he is bigger and stronger. People are taking note. Ironically, the injury is perhaps the best thing that has ever happened to his athletic ambitions.

The Sunday games, played with well-worn gloves and every type and size of bat imaginable, always attract crowds. The infields are pebble-strewn, the outfield grass tall and thick enough to hide a ball. Kids run wild in the outfield.

Straw-hatted umpires hustle to cover the calls on the bases. Merriment prevails, but never at the expense of serious competition. In the stands, flasks are passed around, and people howl encouragement and disparagement with equal fervor. The crowd often includes Indians from the reservations, who customarily drink enough to start throwing rocks at passing cars.

Mickey feels the pressure to play well enough so as not to let his father down. These are lively and fun afternoons. Mickey loves them. Loves playing with his father. Loves the feeling of camaraderie. These days will be among Mickey's happiest ever.

By now Mutt has stopped making allowances for Mickey's youth. He may be by far the youngest player on the team, but that does not excuse mistakes, either physical or mental. Nor does he ladle out the praise when Mickey makes an exceptional play. Mickey should expect to make those plays. Nevertheless, Mickey can sense the pride his father has in showing off his talented son to everyone. When Mickey hits a home run, Mutt, like the other teammates, applauds and shakes Mickey's hand when he returns to the bench, but that's all he shows. Afterwards Mutt won't mention the home run, but he will the errors.

"Twice, you lifted your head up on a ground ball. How many times do I have to tell you—"

"I know."

"Then do it."

"Mickey, I'd like you to meet Barney," Mutt tells him after a game in which they both played for Spavinaw.

"Your pop and I work together in the mines," Barney says.

"Yeah, I know, he's told me."

"I seen you play today, and I seen you play in the Gabby Street League. You're pretty good with that bat in your hands."

"Sometimes."

"How about playing for my Baxter Springs team?"

"The Whiz Kids?"

"Yep."

MUTT'S DREAM: MAKING THE MICK

"Really?"

"Really."

Mutt knows three things about his co-worker: he works hard, he knows the ins and outs of baseball as well as anyone in the area (probably better), and he's thought of as a "boy's best friend."

Who doesn't love Barney Barnett, a 275-pound bald Irishman with a perpetual grin on his face? He seems to get genuine joy out of helping young boys. He is a warm, cheery fellow. Nobody can remember him ever saying anything nasty about anyone … other than umpires. Even then, he always goes up to the umpires after games to apologize.

Every spare moment he has, he devotes to coaching and promoting youth baseball. He doesn't make more money than Mutt, but he finds enough to outfit the boys and buy the necessary equipment. He even manages to raise $3,500 to have the baseball field in Baxter Springs outfitted with lights, so "his" boys can play night games there.

Barney has become a baseball guru, advisor, and friend to the rambunctious boys to whom he teaches baseball tactics, fundamentals, and discipline. If they had the opportunity to vote for their good-natured coach for president, they likely would.

Mickey is thrilled to be asked to play on the Whiz Kids. He only manages to get into four games. Still, this is a big step for him. This is a serious team, known to everyone in the area. He feels he is on his way.

At the end of the season, Barney throws a big party for the boys at his house with Cokes and as many ice cream sandwiches as they can eat, and they can eat a lot. He unboxes the new uniforms—which he paid for—that they will wear the next season. On the back of the shirt in big red letters is "Whiz Kids," on the cap "BW."

Mickey sincerely loves playing for Barney, and later he'll say there should be a hall of fame for Barney and others like him, who share their love for the game and keep baseball alive in the small towns of rural America.

Mickey feels his dreams have come true.

During the summer, when he is not playing or practicing with the Whiz Kids, Mickey works a few hours each week digging graves in the cemetery—a job Mutt found for him. Mickey thinks his boss, Harry Wells, looks more like he should be working behind a mahogany desk at Banker's Trust than running a cemetery business. He has Mickey digging graves and hauling around tombstones. Good muscle-building activities that help develop strong shoulders and arms.

One day, he calls Mickey into a storeroom where he keeps the vaults.

"We'll be using this one to bury old Jonesy," he says, pointing to a vault in the corner.

"Harry, are you kidding? That's way too heavy for me to lift."

"It'll give you a stronger back."

"It'll break my back."

"I thought you wanted to get stronger."

"Yeah, but that's concrete and steel. Probably weighs a ton, maybe more."

"Just kidding," Harry says. "We got cables to lift and let it down."

When not working at the cemetery, Mickey hangs out with his friends, goes to the movies at the Coleman in Miami, plays lots of pool. Mickey is competitive to the point that he has honed his skill at eight-ball enough to hustle pocket money.

One afternoon after work, Mutt comes home and says he's going down to Finch's Bar. Mickey is on the couch reading a Superman comic.

"No friends today?" Mutt asks.

"I went to the movies with Mose, but we didn't stay for the second feature. Mose had to get home. Anyway, it seemed like a drippy movie called *The Other Love* or something like that with Barbara … somebody."

"I'm going down to have a drink. Want to come?"

"You mean for a drink?"

"Why not?"

"I'm not old enough to—"

"Ain't nobody gonna stop you."
"Except Mom."
"Nah."
"You sure about this?"
"Yeah. I want to relax a little after a bad day in the mine."
"Why, what happened?"
"We had a couple of accidents. One guy got it pretty bad."
"He gonna be OK?"
"I dunno. So, ready to go?"

This will be Mickey's first real taste of hard liquor. Sitting next to his father on a bar stool, sipping whiskey and talking like an adult, is pure joy. Every bar stool on which he ever perches will remind him of the happy times with Mutt. It is something Mickey will always remember.

―――⁓●⁓―――

They're on their way to St. Louis to see the Cardinals play the Dodgers. Mickey and Nick banter with Mutt, mostly about his slow driving, which if anything, only makes Mutt slow down more. Having left around midnight, they arrive at Sportsman's Park at eight on a beautiful Sunday morning. They are looking forward to the afternoon game with Howie Pollet going for the 23–28 Cards against the 27–24 Dodgers, who will throw Joe Hatten. Mickey is particularly eager to again see Stan Musial – the reigning National League Most Valuable Player.

When they arrive at the park, they see something they had not anticipated. There is a long line of fans stretching around the block. All Negroes. All waiting to get tickets to see the Dodgers' new first baseman, Jackie Robinson.

Robinson had been called up by the Dodgers six days before the start of the season. He made his debut on April 15 as a 28-year-old rookie. The first player since 1880 to openly break the Major League color barrier. His appearance on the field drew mixed reactions from the press and from players. Reports circulate that some players on the Dodgers said they would sit out rather than play alongside Robinson. However, team management came down firmly on the protestors.

The Dodgers' manager, Leo Durocher, has been suspended for the year by Commissioner Happy Chandler for "association with known gamblers," and is replaced by Burt Shotton. But prior to his suspension Durocher made it clear he would not tolerate any dissent among his players regarding Robinson. He was widely quoted as saying, "I do not care if the guy is yellow or black, or if he has stripes like a fuckin' zebra. I'm the manager of this team, and I say he plays. What's more, I say he can make us all rich. And if any of you cannot use the money, I will see that you are traded."

St. Louis is the southern-most Major League city, so Robinson's appearance here is met with considerable hostility. Still, there are more people waiting for tickets on this day than there are seats in the outfield pavilion, the only place the black fans will be permitted to sit.

From a passing car, a man shouts, "Coloreds ain't wanted here. Go back where you belong."

Neither Mutt nor the boys have any experience with Negroes. None live near them. Theirs is a white world in which they don't talk about or even think about integration. That is something happening in other parts of the country.

Mutt is clearly annoyed that he has to stand at the end of a long line to buy tickets.

"They ain't all gettin' in, anyway," he grouses, "so why the hell should we have to put up with this?"

Eventually he gets to the ticket window and buys tickets to the whites-only pavilion.

"Do you think it's right, letting Robinson play?" Mickey asks.

"No," says Mutt, "but that ain't up to us."

"I don't like it."

"I don't either, but there ain't nothing we can do about it, I'm afraid."

"It doesn't look right."

"It doesn't."

"They got their own Negro Leagues, right? Why do they have to play in ours?"

"I dunno."

"The Cards will never do that though, will they?" Mickey asks. "They're not gonna let any Negro play on their team."

"No. Not in St Louis. The people here would never put up with it."

Earlier in the season there were rumors that the Cardinals had threatened to strike if Robinson played, and to spread the walkout to every other team when they played the Dodgers. Enos "Country" Slaughter, a North Carolina tobacco farmer and fellow Southerner, reportedly led the strike proposition. The strike never came about, but among all the league's teams the Cardinals remained among the staunchest anti-integrationists.

"Let's just enjoy the game and forget all the other stuff," Mutt says.

"Absolutely," Nick says between bites of his hotdog. "Robinson is gonna get his."

Nick is right. Every time Robinson comes to bat, Cardinal players, standing on the top step of their dugout, shout epithets at him.

In the first inning, Robinson hits a weak grounder to second: "That the best you can do, boy?"

When he comes to bat in the sixth, "Warning, nigger at bat."

It is hard to tell who is doing all the shouting. Not everyone on the Cardinals is involved.

Many in the crowd sitting around Mutt and the boys clearly enjoy the insult-a-thon, while the black spectators appreciate Robinson responding with two of the only seven hits the Dodgers can manage against Pollett. Brooklyn is beaten 11–3, by a 17-hit Cardinal attack.

On the drive home they talk about the game before the boys fall asleep. Mickey will later claim that while he was initially opposed to blacks playing Major League ball, his feelings were never strong and didn't last long.

Mickey is shagging balls in the outfield for the Miami Owls, a Class D team in the Kansas-Oklahoma-Missouri League. It is a long late-morning batting practice session, and Mickey's speed is on display as he runs down balls no one else on the field can reach. Seeing the kid showing them up by making these plays does not go down well with everyone.

Jim Morris, an Owls player, goes to the outfield, and without saying anything yanks Mickey's glove off his hand, throws it over the outfield fence, and then walks back to the infield.

Mickey stands there for a minute, then goes to the fence where he finds a spot he can squeeze under. He retrieves his glove, finds his bike, and pedals home. There is a certain pleasure knowing that you're good enough to warrant such a response from older professional players.

The late July day is stiflingly hot, and the boys decide to go to their Neosho swimming hole.

"It's skinny-dipping weather," says Nick.

Leroy pulls his shirt over his head. "Is it ever!"

The boys all strip. Swimming in the buff is a good thing to do on a hot day.

As always, Mickey sticks close to the shore while the others dive into the deep spot. Soon, Nick pushes a log he finds on the bank into the river.

"Mickey, c'mon, hang on," he says. "I'll pull you out to the middle."

Mickey isn't too sure about the idea, but he already feels that they think he's a water wimp, and refusing the log ride would make him look even more so. He wraps his arms over the log, and Nick pulls him farther out. Meanwhile, LeRoy and Mosley drag a makeshift raft that is always available on the bank for anyone who wants to push it to the center of the swimming hole. Mickey is uncomfortable hanging onto the log, and so is somewhat relieved when he gets to the raft. Mosley helps pull him onto it. He sits on the edge, his legs dangling in the water.

"You coming to the team meeting?" Mosley asks him, referring to the season's first assembly of the football team.

"I'd sure like to."

"Do it."

"I don't know."

"Why, because of your leg or your father?"

"The leg's fine; it's just—"

"Your father then."

"I haven't even brought it up."

"He let you once, didn't he?"

"Yeah and look what happened."

"A freak accident. We sure could use you."

"Thanks a lot," says Nick, knowing that his chance to carry the ball will be diminished if Mickey is there as a running back.

"Hey, two good runners are better than one, aren't they," Mosley says.

Mickey instinctively rubs his leg. "Yeah, especially if one gets hurt and is lost for the season."

Mosley punches Mickey on the upper arm. "I know damn well you want to."

"Yeah."

Mickey fully understands it's football more than baseball or basketball that fires up the locals. People admire the football players in ways they don't look up to athletes in any other sport. And he wants to be with his friends, not left sitting on the sidelines like he is in swimming.

"I'll ask him," Mickey says, the "him" being obvious.

"Shit, there's a girl looking at us!" LeRoy yells.

The boys look to the bank on the far side of the river. Sure enough, a young girl is watching the naked boys. They immediately jump into the water. Without thinking, Mickey joins them. He goes under, then comes up thrashing and splashing and gasping for breath. In his panic he swallows water, which makes it even more difficult to breathe. He sinks back into the murky water, where the slow current begins drawing him downstream. He reaches up wildly, as if trying to grab something to pull himself up. Mickey's almost at the point of blacking out when a hand from above grabs his. It is Mosley's. Mosley and Nick drag Mickey onto the bank, where he spews out water while gasping for breath.

It is the last time Mickey will ever go swimming.

———•●•———

Barney Barnett knows everyone in the Tri-State district connected with baseball worth knowing. More importantly, they know him. Major League scouts know him, too. When traveling through, they often stop to see Barney and his young players. It is the first time that Mickey is noticed outside the immediate area.

Mickey is having one of those games. Everything is going right. The Baxter Springs Whiz Kids are smashing the Carl Junction team, 12–0. At short, Mickey is making every play he needs to make. Barney has moved him there, saying his strong arm was being wasted at second, but in previous games at shortstop Mickey had struggled, bobbling grounders and throwing wildly to first. Barney has kept him there despite the miscues because he likes Mickey's dogged attitude. He never quits on a ball, even after he misses it. He'll chase it down as if his life depends on it. Barney feels it is that tenacious attitude, as much as his athletic talent or Mutt-inspired work habits, that will take the kid a long way.

"He's a competitor," Barney is known to say. "Hates to fail. Hates to look bad."

His first time up in this game, Mickey launches a shot to right-center that carries well over the outfielder's head and bounces once before going into the stream that serves as the outfield boundary. The next time up, he smashes one even farther out to right-center.

He steps to the plate for his third at-bat, batting left-handed against a right-handed pitcher. Barney has previously told Mickey

MUTT'S DREAM: MAKING THE MICK

that it might be best if he sticks to one side of the plate. Probably the right side, as that is where Mickey shows the most power. However, he told Mickey this in confidence. He doesn't want Mutt to think he is meddling. Mickey still switch-hits in deference to his father's wishes.

Mickey has already impressed the 200 or so fans watching the game with his long home run drives, when he launches the longest one yet. A high arching drive that lands in the middle of the river.

Hysterical fans, applauding and yelling louder than Mickey has ever heard, jump to their feet. Mickey will later say it tightened the skin on his chest and neck. As he rounds third and heads home, he takes off his cap and waves it to the appreciative crowd. His teammates rush to the plate to congratulate him with pummeling backslaps and hair rustling.

The crowd is amazed at what they have just seen.

"Wow! Ain't never seen nothing like that."

"That's gotta be 500 feet. Maybe more."

"That kid's unbelievable."

Barney shakes his head in disbelief. "Did I say you should have been batting righty?"

The consensus among those who saw the blast is that it is the longest home run anyone has ever smacked on that field. No one has ever put one in the river on the fly before. People will talk about it for years.

One excited fan gets an idea. He will pass his straw hat around the stands and take up a collection for Mickey, as a tribute to his Ruthian feat. He has no trouble getting contributions.

After the last out in the lopsided game, he approaches Mickey and holds out his hat.

"What is that?" Mickey asks.

"It's for you."

"What do you mean?"

"It's from the fans. I took up a collection. It's for you."

"A collection?"

"For that homer. You earned it. Deserve it."

"Wow."

"Here, take it."

Mickey breaks out in an ear-to-ear smile. "Thank you. Thank you so much. I don't know what to say. Thank you."

"But I'd like my hat back," says the fan, obviously pleased that Mickey is pleased and that he could do something as a tribute to this amazingly powerful young player.

Mickey transfers the money to his cap, and when he gets home he dumps it on the kitchen table. Some of the coins bounce to the floor. His brothers scramble to collect them.

"Where'd you get all that?" Larry asks.

"At the game. My fans gave it to me."

Lovell makes a quizzical face. "So, you got fans now?"

"On account of my home runs. Well, the last one anyway. You should have seen it. I mean it was … real long, and it went all the way into the river. It was a shot, I'll tell you. Somebody said nobody ever reached the river like that before, but I sure did. I sure did."

"Well, don't let that head of yours get too big," Lovell says.

"Let's count it," Larry says.

"Yeah, OK," Mickey says, beginning to stack up the coins and flatten out the dollar bills. When they are done, Mickey announces proudly, "53 dollars and 75 cents."

That's roughly two weeks' wages for many miners.

Hadn't his father insisted there is money to be made in baseball? Hadn't his father told him he would be a great baseball player? Doesn't this prove he is?

When Mutt gets home, he hears about the game and Mickey's feats, and he sees the money. Mickey is concerned that Mutt might put limits on what he can do with his haul. Maybe he'll insist he share it with his brothers and sister. But Mutt doesn't.

"You earned it; you can spend it," he says. "On any ol' thing you want."

This is the first time Mickey has ever had this much real spending money of his own, and for a boy his age in rural Oklahoma, it is a lot of money. A lot more than he ever made digging graves. He is elated to have the money to spend on himself, but he is also a little ashamed. The price of lead and zinc is down enough that the mine is likely to cut back on salaries, and his family could sure use the extra money. Not ashamed enough, however, to offer to share it.

"When was the last time you had that much money in your hands at one time?" Mosley asks him.

"Never."

"So, what are you going to do with all that loot?"

"Well, first I'm gonna buy us both hamburgers and shakes."

"Sounds right to me."

For the remainder of the summer, Mickey continues to play shortstop for the Whiz Kids. He still makes his share of errors at short, but now he is something of a celebrity. People show up at games just to see him hit home runs. And he doesn't disappoint. He doesn't reach the river again, but he hits plenty of long balls.

"You're swinging for the fences a lot," Barney says. "You know, sometimes just hitting behind the runner or going to the opposite field with a single is the thing to do."

"Yeah, I know. I'll try to do those things when that's best."

But hitting singles doesn't bring hats full of money. Hitting singles doesn't bring the adulation of the fans. This is a lesson he will long remember.

With Mickey leading the way, the Baxter Springs Whiz Kids win the Ban Johnson League pennant. As a reward, Harry Wells offers to take Mickey and his teammates Billy Johnson, Buddy Ball, and Jim Canega to a Cardinals game at Sportsman's Park.

They leave the night before the game, and despite the chilly night persuade Harry to put the top down on his brand-new red Plymouth convertible. Harry shivers the whole way while the boys laugh their heads off. They're baseball champions enjoying the last days of summer vacation, and they're going to a Major League game.

Shortly before dawn, as they cruise along the narrow highway to St. Louis, Billy Johnson gets an idea. He stuffs a big wad of chewing gum into his mouth, chews it until it goes soft, then takes it from his mouth and throws it at the windshield of a car coming in the opposite direction.

"Dammit, I missed," he says. "Gotta try again."

Soon all the boys are following suit. The bubble gum goes flying, windshields are hit. Drivers curse. All the while, the boys are in hysterics.

Harry doesn't mind. He even stops off before he gets to St. Louis so the boys can restock bubble-gum missiles and pick up candy and soda pop.

This is all great summer fun, but they know it will soon come to an end, as school will begin again in a few days. Mickey has no inkling of the trouble that is about to come his way.

Chapter 24

Mickey walks down the hall of Commerce High, his shirt neatly pressed, his shoes shined as always for school. This first day of school brings some normal anxiety, but it also brings promise. Mutt has grudgingly agreed to let Mickey try football once more. He knows separating Mickey from his friends all fall would lead to an animosity that Mickey would hold against him. So Mickey can look forward to football, then basketball in winter and baseball in the spring. Yes, it promises to be a good year at school.

Mickey is saying hello to schoolmates he hasn't seen all summer when he hears, "Mickey Charles Mantle, the principal wants to see you."

It is the voice of Mrs. Miller, the longtime school secretary, who always calls the students by their full names.

He makes a quick U-turn and goes into the office.

"Mickey, I know you are a stalwart on our athletic teams," Principal Baker says before Mickey is even through the doorway, "but you need to know that you will no longer be able to participate in any athletic activities at this school, or for that matter in any other school."

Mickey feels as if all the air has been sucked out of him. "What do you mean?"

"It's a decision made by the Lucky Seven High School Conference."

"I can't play?"

"It seems you accepted money for playing this summer. You did, didn't you?"

"Somebody gave me some."

"Technically, that makes you a professional."

"This fan just passed the hat around."

"Mickey, I'm afraid once you accepted the money … well, there are rules … regulations that all the schools in the conference have to abide by."

"I'm no professional baseball player. I don't get paid to play. It was just a fan who gave me the money, not the league. Nobody on the Whiz Kids gets paid. We play for fun, that's all."

"That's not the letter of the law."

"This is crazy."

"I understand your feeling."

"I didn't know anything about—"

"Lack of knowledge of the law is not an excuse for breaking it."

"Nobody ever told me that—"

"I'd suggest you spend the school year concentrating on your studies, which I understand could use a little more concentration. Then later, after you graduate, you can play for all the money you can earn."

"There's gotta be something—"

"There's nothing that can be done, Mickey. It's out of my hands. Now, I suggest you get to your class."

A despondent Mickey has trouble paying attention to the teachers. It's not fair. He didn't know about the stupid rule. If somebody gives you a gift of money, what's wrong with that? He didn't get paid for playing. A spectator, a private person not connected with the team or the league, decided to give him a gift. So what? What is his father going to say? He knows Mickey isn't a professional. Someday, yeah, maybe, but not now. What are the coaches going to say? They'll be counting on Mickey for the football and basketball teams. So will Mosley. It's not right. It's not fair. It's a stupid rule in a stupid school with a stupid principal.

After school, he tells Mosley what the principal said.

"They can't do that," Mosley says.

"That's what I told him."

"There's got to be something—"

"He says there isn't."

"Let's talk to Coach Bruce. He'll know what to do."

But he doesn't. "There's an Oklahoma State Athletic Commission that regulates high school sports," he tells Mickey and Mosley. "And they're about as flexible as a flagpole. I think we're just going to have to move forward without you, Mickey. I'm sorry to have to say that, but maybe you can still practice with us. I'll check into that."

"I don't want to just practice."

"I'm not even sure they'll let you do that. We'll have to see."

When Mickey tells Mutt, his father is as angry as he is.

"That's an idiotic rule. They can't do that to you."

"That's what I said, but—"

"What if you gave the money back?"

"Except I already spent it."

"You could get another part-time job. Promise to pay it back a little at a time."

"You think they'd go for that?"

"Maybe."

"I could do some odd jobs around town."

"Why not?"

Mutt asks Lovell to go to the school the next day to talk to the principal about returning the money. He reaffirms there is nothing he can do, saying it is in the hands of the Athletic Commission in Oklahoma City.

"They could change their minds?" Lovell says.

"I wouldn't think so."

"But they could?"

"I suppose."

"Who's the boss? Who's in control?"

"A man named Walt Henderson."

"Is he a ... reasonable man?"

"I really couldn't say, but I wouldn't bet on it. The Commission is not known to be flexible. Their job is to enforce the rules, and that is precisely what they do."

When Lovell passes on this information to her husband, Mutt decides to go to Oklahoma City to press Mickey's case. After Mutt tells Henderson that Mickey didn't know he was breaking any rule by accepting a gift from fans, and is willing to pay it all back, he agrees to consider Mutt's appeal.

A week later, the principal tells Mickey he has heard from the commissioner and that his eligibility will be reinstated if he pays the money back. But he will have to return the entire amount first. Paying it back over time is not acceptable.

"Man, that's going to take me a long time," Mickey says. "I mean, I don't know how fast I can get that much working after school."

"So maybe you'll have to give up basketball this year—"

"And football."

Mutt thinks that is probably a good thing. "But you should be OK by baseball."

"I hope so."

The next day, Mickey meets with Barney.

"I'll tell you what," Barney says. "I'll see if they'll let me donate the money to charity in your name."

"What charity?"

"I don't know. I'll think of one they'll like."

"I think they want me to pay it back."

"Let me take care of that."

"You can't use your money to—"

With a big wink Barney says, "You can pay me back."

The commission agrees. Barney donates $54 to the Crippled Children's Hospital in Oklahoma City. Mickey is allowed to participate in high school sports and immediately rejoins the football team.

Mickey never pays Barney back.

On the morning of the season's first Commerce Tigers football game, Coach Woolard tells Mickey he will be a starter that afternoon against the Miami Wardogs at College Field in Miami. On offense, he will line up as the fullback behind Mosley, their experienced quarterback. He will be joined in the backfield by the equally experienced Jack Brower and Roy Mowrey.

Everyone understands that Mosley is the star of the team. One of the best backs in the district. Their vocal leader. In the game he doesn't disappoint, as he accounts for 89 of Commerce High's 124 rushing yards and their only touchdown in a 14–6 loss.

Despite the loss, Mickey is pleased his leg holds up. Mutt is too nervous to watch much of the game. Most of the time, he is behind the bleachers, smoking an entire pack of Luckies. After the game he doesn't say anything about the leg or the dangers of football. He doesn't have to. It is tacitly understood. Mickey is going to play through the season with the threat of injury no further away than the next play. Mutt has to admit, however, that Mickey is not a bad football player—but hopefully not so good that it will push the baseball dreams aside.

Like everyone on the team, Mickey plays on both offense and defense. It's not long into the season before he is involved in almost every play in every game. It soon becomes obvious that Mickey is a fine football player. Once through the line, his speed is difficult for defenses to deal with. He also shows good hands catching the ball out of the backfield. And somewhat surprisingly, when the team needs to pick up short yards for a first down or touchdown, he shows considerable strength, power, and will.

He and Mosley make a good backfield pair. The Miami paper declares: *When Mosley tires, Mantle can usually pick up a few yards with his hard drives from the fullback slot.*

As they walk off the field after a game against the Afton Eagles at Seymour Stadium in Commerce, Mosley drapes his arm over Mickey's shoulder.

"We make a pretty good team back there, don't we?"

"Yeah, we do."

"That was a great run, pal," Mosley says, referring to a second-quarter play when Mickey broke loose for 65 yards down to the one-yard line. On the next play, he plunged in for the score.

"It was fun."

"What's your dad saying these days about your football playing?"

"Not a whole lot."

"I'll bet he's proud, though."

"I dunno, but if he is, he's too stubborn to admit it."

"Ever think maybe football's in your future more than baseball?"

"I wouldn't dare."

"You can think it, though."

"I'm not big enough."

"But still growing."

"Dad would have a heart attack if I ever mentioned anything like that."

"He can see though what kind of a runner you are."

"I guess, but that's not his, you know—"

"Oh, I do know. Anyway, you and me, we're the only three-sport stars in Commerce."

"You think we're stars?"

"Hell yes."

After taking a knock on the head in the game against Afton, Mosley has to sit out against the Picher Gorillas. The Tigers will have to rely on Mickey's running. In the third quarter he breaks into the clear and scampers 65 yards to cross the goal line, only to have the play called back due to an offsides call. Commerce ends up losing 7–0.

The Tigers finally get their first win against the Chelsea Dragons, 20–0. In the third period, after a long punt return by Mosley, Mickey plunges over from the eight-yard line. Later in the game he scores again, when he intercepts a Chelsea pass and runs 14 yards into the end zone.

Mutt may be less than vocal about Mickey's football exploits, but Lovell isn't.

"Be careful. You're getting awfully good at this football stuff," she says.

"Be careful of what?"

"You know damn well what."

In this football-crazy part of the world, Mickey is getting more mention in the press now than he does playing baseball. Lovell cuts the articles out, but doesn't leave them around for Mutt to see.

Mickey Mantle Leads Commerce to Victory in Lucky Seven Contest

The Commerce Tigers, and a whirling dervish named Mickey Mantle in particular, rudely chilled the Quapaw Wildcats' homecoming celebration Friday night when they trounced the Wildcats 47–19 in a Lucky Seven Conference tilt.

Mantle accounted for four of the Tigers' seven touchdowns, scoring on long runs of 70, 25, and 45 yards, and snagging an 80-yard pass for the fourth six-pointer. Mantle's 70-yard run came on the very first play from scrimmage and gave the Tigers a lead they never relinquished.

Commerce racked up two touchdowns in the first quarter with Mantle handling the ball and two more in the second, scored only once in the third, and then made two more touchdowns in the fourth.

"I never thought of you as a whirling dervish," Lovell says, looking up from the paper.

"If it's in the papers, it must be true."

"Then why doesn't the whirling dervish do the dishes tonight for a change?"

"I'm a star, didn't you know? Stars don't do dishes," Mickey says with a knowing grin.

"They sure as hell do in this household. If you want dinner tomorrow night, you'll do the dishes tonight."

"Yes, ma'am."

Commerce visits the Wyandotte Bears, looking for a third straight Lucky Seven Conference victory. The start of the game is delayed while the field is dedicated to Robert Brewster, a former Wyandotte athlete killed during the war. Then early in the game, Mickey takes a handoff from Mosley. The timing of the play is a little off, and Mickey has to cut quickly to avoid a collision with his quarterback. While making the cut, he twists his left ankle and is immediately hit by a defensive lineman. When he gets up, he can barely put any pressure on the ankle. He limps to the sideline.

Memories come flooding back. The pain, the hospital, the shots. The thoughts of losing the leg. He makes it to the bench. With play on the field continuing, he is left alone to deal with the ankle. He takes off his shoe and sock. For sure, the ankle isn't broken and there is no blood. He isn't cut. Wasn't that how the osteomyelitis got started the last time he was injured? No, he's OK. It's a sprain, that's all.

Mutt comes down from the stands, shaking his head.

"Just sprained, that's all," Mickey says. He doesn't get back in the game, which Commerce wins 19–7.

The paper the next morning reports: *The win was a costly one for the Tigers, with Mickey Mantle, their star fullback, being forced out of the game with a seriously sprained left ankle. It is not known how seriously Mantle's ankle is injured nor how long he will be out of action. The high-scoring Tiger back has tallied ten touchdowns in Commerce's three conference games.*

At home Lovell has Mickey lie on the couch with his ankle elevated on pillows. "I'll get some ice," she says. "Ice, that's what you need."

"It's not bad, Mom, honest. I just need to stay off it for a while."

"Let's find your old crutches."

"I burned them, remember?"

"You play football long enough, we won't be able to afford all the crutches you'll need."

As with his previous injury, Mutt doesn't say, "I told you so." His look says it for him.

The next game is against the Nowata Ironmen in their homecoming game. Mickey, the leading scorer in the conference, is back with the team, although not starting. He is still favoring the ankle. The game ends in a 6–6 tie. The following week, the Tigers come from behind to nip the Grove Ridgerunners. Because of the still-tender ankle, Mickey is used sparingly. He gets in the game late and after taking a lateral, passes to Ivan Shouse in the end zone. The Tigers win 7–6.

At season's end, Commerce is fourth in the Lucky Seven Conference. Mosley is acknowledged as the most valuable player on his team. Mickey leads the league in scoring.

Mickey and Mutt sit in the LaSalle on their way to Oklahoma City to pick up some material Lovell has asked for. She wants to make new covers for pillows. As usual, Mutt is creeping along, annoying drivers who want to pass but can't find an opening on the curvy two-lane road.

"Well, you had enough yet?" Mutt asks.

"Of your driving?"

"Football."

"I don't know. It was fun."

"Mickey, that's not enough. It can't always be about fun. You've got to think about the future."

"I was pretty good. Maybe I could—"

"Baseball, that's your future. Football is ... as you say, fun. Look, I know it is, but you can be a professional baseball player someday, and you know it. Professional football? Who cares about that? Nobody cares about that. Baseball is our national game. Baseball is important. People pay attention to baseball, and baseball pays. Do you know what DiMaggio and Ted Williams make? Do you?"

"I don't know. A lot."

"$65,000 each. Yeah, that's a lot, and the papers say Joe is gonna get $100,000 next season. Think about that for a minute. $100,000 for playing a game."

"I'm no Joe DiMaggio."

"At his age? I don't know, maybe you are."

"Do you think I could drive?"

"What are you talking about?"

"It's about time I learned to drive the LaSalle. I mean, if I make $100,000, I'll want a car and—"

"With that money, you could pay for a driver."

"C'mon, Dad."

"OK."

Mutt finds a space to pull off the road so that he can switch seats with Mickey.

"Now, just take it slow."

"I've watched. Seen how you do it."

"Seeing and doing ain't the same thing."

When the relieved drivers behind them pass, Mickey eases the car into the road as Mutt injects instructions. After a few bucking episodes, as Mickey gets familiar with the clutch, his driving evens out, and before they reach Oklahoma City he has the car up to 45 mph.

Mutt squirms as if he were in mortal danger. "Slow down, son! You're airplanin' it."

"At least we'll get there sometime today."

Coach Woolard coaches both baseball and football.

"I thought you'd like to know Mickey made the all-district football team," he informs Mutt.

"Did he?"

"Mosley too. They both made it into the first-team backfield. And well deserved, I must say. Mickey's a helluva runner with the ol' pigskin in his hands."

"I saw."

"He could go someplace, you know. In football, he could go maybe to college on a scholarship. He's that good."

"Football is not … it's not where he's headed, you damn well know that."

"Mutt, I want to tell you something, and I hope you believe me. Yes, Mickey is a good baseball player. That's pretty obvious. But in my opinion, and I should know because I coach him in both sports, baseball is Mickey's second-best sport."

"That's ridiculous."

"He is the best football player I have ever seen."

"Mosley's better than Mickey has ever been."

"I don't think so. Oh, Mose is very good. Maybe he's a better athlete, I don't know. But Mickey has something you can't teach. He's blessed with blinding speed ... and he's strong, too. Put those two things together and you've got ... you've got a real football player."

"Except he ain't gonna go on with football. He's going on with baseball."

"Is that what he wants? Or is it what you want?"

Mutt looks at him sternly, then turns and walks away without saying another word.

A few days later in the locker room before a basketball practice, the coach finds Mickey changing into his practice clothes.

"Ever think of going to college ... to play football?"

"Not really."

"What if you had a scholarship? A full scholarship. Your folks wouldn't have to fork over any money."

"Good, because they don't have any."

"You know who Bud Wilkinson is?"

"The football coach?"

"Yeah, the Oklahoma Sooners coach. He's really building a big national program there. Anyway, one of his recruiters was here and saw how you ran, and was he ever impressed! He wants me to ask you if you'd like to go up to Norman for an official recruiting visit. I could drive you."

"I never thought about that. About playing more football."

"Well, you should, Mickey. You could get a great education without it costing you anything ... or at least not much. You know an education is the best way to ensure that you can make a good living when you leave school, and that time isn't far away. Oh, I know your dad is steering you towards baseball because he thinks that will make you tons of money, but that's a hard thing to count on. You gotta face it, you might not make a lot of money playing baseball. Or maybe you won't make any. You know how many kids playing baseball all over the country dream about having a Major League career? Thousands. And how many will make it? A handful. Baseball may be a dream, but a football scholarship would set you up good."

"You don't think I'm a good enough baseball player?"

"To have a Major League career? Who the hell knows? You're a good baseball player, no doubt about that, but I think you're a great football player. I've never seen better at your age."

"Wow, the University of Oklahoma. I don't think I could … college courses, I don't know if I could … I'm not crazy about studying and all the school stuff."

"I wouldn't worry too much about that. Those big school football programs, they look out for their athletes. They'd take care of you. Classes wouldn't be a problem. I can guarantee you that."

"I don't know."

"Think about it."

"OK, I'll think about it."

"Just know when all their scholarships are allotted, they can't offer any more, so if you want me to drive you up there, let me know soon, and I'll schedule it with them."

"What about Mose? Is he going?"

"They didn't ask me about him, only you."

"That's crazy."

"Is it?"

Chapter 25

Mickey shows he is a fast learner on the basketball team. He hadn't known much about the game when he first started playing. He was tentative and deferred to the other players, but the more he played, the more he lost his inherent reticence. Now he is proving valuable as a guard, bringing the ball up court, dishing off to Mosley, lofting his own set shots—which are becoming more accurate—and occasionally driving for layups.

Mosley solidifies his status as one of the best basketball players in the Lucky Seven, when he sets a conference single-game scoring record by sinking 36 points against Quapaw.

There is no question who are the biggest contributors to the basketball team. Mosley and Mickey lead the team in just about everything. Points, rebounds, assists. In the game against Chelsea, Mosley goes for 20 points, Mickey for 19. The rest of the team records a combined 13 points.

"Batman and Robin," Mickey suggests.

"You mean you want to be Robin to my Batman?"

"I'm thinking the other way around."

"You kidding me? Batman's little buddy is Robin, so you can be my little buddy."

"Maybe this was a bad suggestion."

"Oh, I don't know. I kinda like it."

"Maybe the Lone Ranger and Tonto."

"Same problem."

"The two musketeers?"

"Works better with three."

"Mr. Inside, Mr. Outside?"

"That's it, for sure."

In the next game, Mickey scores more than Mosley for the first time. He receives congratulations from the coach and his teammates but feels a little embarrassed by the attention. Although not as reticent as when he was younger, he is still more introverted than most students his age. With Mosley, though, he is much more outgoing. He will always have close friends to whom he opens up even when he is guarded around others.

"You taking my job away?" Mosley says jokingly as they're showering after the game.

"I can't help it if you can't shoot."

"Oh. Maybe you could give me some lessons."

"How much you want to pay me?"

"How about a kick in the ass?"

Lovell reads from the paper. "The Eagles' one big mistake was a defensive one. They put a close watch on Bill Mosley but left guard Mickey Mantle in the clear. Mantle then went wild, netting ten field goals and one free throw for 21 points. The game soon developed into a scoring duel between Afton's Tom Hudspeth and Mantle."

Lovell looks up from her paper. "Mickey, it's too much, all this playing all the time—football, basketball, baseball. That's all you ever do."

"It's all I want to do."

"Look, I'm all in favor of you playing sports. You know that, but you've got to pay more attention to your school stuff. That's important too. You've got to be able to … you've got to have other things to fall back on when the end to playing comes … whenever that is, but it will come."

"Yeah, well that ain't gonna be tomorrow."

"Maybe not."

"Because that's when we start baseball practice."

"Goody, goody."

MUTT'S DREAM: MAKING THE MICK

By the time Mickey leaves early spring baseball practices, the sun is about ready to hide for the night and he has a seven-mile bus trek out to Whitebird. He is often the only passenger. By the time the bus passes the offices of the old Eagle-Picher Mining Company, all the lights have been turned off. On moonless nights, the area is dark and scary.

He has heard the stories about dark murders, about boys lured to their demise by a vicious killer, about boys having limbs lopped off and heads severed. His mother has told him these stories are not true, but maybe she doesn't know what boys in his school do. When the bus drops him off, he runs the mile to his house as fast as he can.

"A four-minute mile," he tells Mosley.

"Not likely."

"Fast, anyway."

"That I can believe."

"What if I spend the nights at your house until it gets … you know, light earlier?"

"Yeah, sure, if your parents let you."

"They will. It's better than getting murdered."

"Oh, I don't know."

"Why, have you ever been?"

"Murdered?"

"Yeah."

"Not yet."

The first game of the Commerce High baseball season is against the Fairland Owls on the Commerce field.

Coach Woolard tells Mickey he's pitching. LeRoy will be his battery mate. In high school ball, the best players often pitch, and when not pitching play shortstop. Mickey will do both this season, and he understands what it means. So does Mutt.

"You got the arm to pitch," Mutt says. "I don't mind you messing around with your pitches, but it's at short where you've gotta work. You gotta work on your footwork and—"

"Don't worry, I'm a shortstop who pitches, not a pitcher who plays short."

In the first inning against Fairland, Frankie Dry slams out a triple and then scores on an error. It is the only hit Mickey surrenders. When he comes up in the bottom of the inning, he laces a home run over the centerfielder's head to tie the score at 1–1.

Commerce adds two more runs in the third, then finishes its scoring with four in the fifth. Three of their runs in the fifth are driven in by LeRoy, who raps out a four-bagger with two men on. Commerce wins the game 7–1. Mickey ends up striking out 14 of the 22 Fairland batters in the seven-inning game. Their Lucky Seven Conference season is off to a good start.

In their second game, Mickey is again the starting pitcher, and for the second straight time pitches a one-hit game. In the seventh inning, with the Tigers holding a 10–1 lead, Mickey is relieved by LeRoy, with Mickey taking his spot at catcher. The Grove Ridgerunners immediately nick LeRoy for three hits, so Coach Woolard switches them back to their original positions. Mickey strikes out the last two men. The only Commerce extra-base hit is a triple legged out by Mickey.

The Tigers then win their third straight Lucky Seven game, beating the Wyandotte Bears 5–1. This time, Mickey gives up two hits while fanning 14. Both he and LeRoy hit home runs.

"You and LeRoy are making one hell of a battery," the coach tells him.

"Don't tell my father that."

"Maybe you should concentrate on your pitching, as you—"

"Nah. Pitching is fun, but I'd rather play short."

"Or catch."

"Short."

"Pitchers can do very well, you know. They can make a lot of money, I mean. In the bigs, they get paid pretty good."

"So do home run hitters."

"True. But Mickey, look at what you're doing on the mound.

You're striking out everybody, for Chrissake."

"I love it, don't get me wrong, but my father would have a conniption fit if I told him I wanted to be a pitcher full-time."

"Why? It's baseball. Isn't that what he wants, you to concentrate on baseball?"

"Yeah, but pitchers to him are the enemy."

"Look, I know you always want to please your father, but you've got to be your own person too."

"I am."

"By the way, you're pitching tomorrow night."

They win their fourth straight conference game by beating Quapaw 21–1. Mickey pitches, gives up three hits in the three innings he is on the mound, and smacks a four-bagger.

People are noticing this promising pitcher.

The Tigers' perfect league record is spoiled when they lose to Chelsea 3–2. Mickey, allowing five hits and striking out nine, pitches the entire game. Down 3–0, Commerce scores their two runs after two outs in the final frame. LeRoy slices a double down the right-field line and scores when Mosley follows with another two-bagger. Mickey then contributes the third straight double to score Mosley.

"The three double kings," LeRoy observes as they are walking off the field.

"Except we lost," Mosley responds.

"Well, if Mickey would have hit a home run instead of copying us with a double, we would have won."

"Yeah, Mickey, what's wrong with you?" Mosley says.

"Don't look at me. I'm just a pitcher. It's not my job to drive you fielders in."

At the end of the season, Commerce is set to play the Picher Gorillas for the league title. Mickey has already struck out more batters than anyone in the league, so naturally he will be on the mound.

The Tigers take the lead in the first inning when they tally three times. Mosley, who starts the game as catcher, smacks a double to knock in two runs and takes third on the throw to the plate. He scores when Mickey flies out to straightaway center.

The last Commerce run comes in the third frame when Mickey doubles, then scores on a single by LeRoy.

Mickey holds the Gorillas hitless until the fifth, when they take advantage of five hits, three walks, and two errors to tally nine runs. Then Mosley takes over on the mound with Mickey moving to shortstop and LeRoy catching. Picher adds two more runs in the sixth inning on a single, three straight walks by Mosley, and an error. The final score: 11–4. Season over.

Chapter 26

There is no one at Commerce High who doesn't know who Mickey and Mosley are. Maybe no one in Commerce. They are the star athletes, and star athletes get noticed. Despite the local recognition, Mickey is still painfully shy, particularly when it comes to girls. Mosley is much more comfortable in social situations. Mosley has a girlfriend; Mickey doesn't.

Sure, Mose has a girlfriend. Linda. He's taller. Some would say better looking, and he's the quarterback. Don't all girls go for the quarterback?

Linda's best friend is a girl named Jeannette Holmes. Mickey is introduced to her one morning in the hall outside his English class. Mickey is nervous. He doesn't know what to say to girls. He's not Mose.

Jeannette is a year younger than Mickey. One of the prettiest girls in school. She has short, curly blonde hair and freckles. A real Becky Thatcher. Her family is better off than most of the miners' families in the area, and she dresses like it, all of which makes Mickey more nervous. Boys like him don't hang out with girls like Jeannette, do they?

"Maybe you two guys would like to double date with us to the movies this Saturday," Mosley says while holding Linda's hand.

Mickey's heart pounds harder than it does when he's pitching to a big hitter, shooting a free throw, or going out for a long pass. Those are all things he's prepared for. Meeting girls isn't.

"What's playing?" he blurts out before realizing how dumb that sounds.

"Who cares?" Mosley says.

"C'mon, Mickey," Linda says. "It'll be fun. Anyway, Jeannette wants you to ask her."

"Linda!" Jeannette says, blushing.

"Well, you do."

"Just say OK, Mickey," Mosley says.

"OK, Mickey."

"I'd love to go with you, Mickey," Jeannette says, flashing an engaging smile.

For Mickey to take a girl to the movies, and a pretty one at that, it will have to be a double date. There is no way he would agree to go on his own. What would he talk about? But Mosley knows how to do these things, so if Mickey gets struck, he can always turn to his friend to bail him out.

On Saturday morning, Mickey gets a pack of gum from Larry, then adds a couple of sticks of his own. Chewing gum will make him look … confident. Come time to meet Mosley and the girls in front of the theater, Mickey thinks of excuses to not go. He feels a cold coming on. His father wants him to stay home and work on his fielding. He needs to mind the twins while everyone else is away. Something he ate for breakfast caused him to get sick to his stomach.

Anyway, why does Jeannette want to go out with him? Maybe she just likes sports and wants to be seen with a three-sport athlete. She is beautiful and vibrant. Every time Mickey has seen her at school, she is surrounded by other girls and sometimes boys. She has to be one of the most popular girls in the entire school. Maybe the most popular. She is not in any of Mickey's classes, but she seems smart. How do you talk to a smart, beautiful, popular girl? And she has a lot more money than he has. At least her family has.

An hour before they are to meet, it starts raining. Then as Mickey is about to leave the house, it starts coming down in buckets. He never uses umbrellas, but maybe he should take one now to cover Jeannette. Isn't that the gentlemanly thing to do? She would expect him to do that, wouldn't she?

"Mom, do you have an umbrella I could borrow?"

MUTT'S DREAM: MAKING THE MICK

"You never use umbrellas."

"Yeah, well ..."

"Dating changes things, doesn't it?"

Mickey has never seen his mother and father demonstrate affection for each other. He doesn't have an older sister he might have observed as she dated. He doesn't have dating advice from an older brother. No, he is on his own to negotiate his way through anxiety-producing encounters with girls with no models to emulate. And always lurking in the background are the memories of the humiliation he suffered at the pleasure of Anna Bea and her diabolic friends.

His inherent shyness in social situations will always be a challenge for Mickey. Maybe a drink will help settle the nerves, but that isn't a viable solution ... yet.

He puts on his flawlessly ironed best shirt, brushes his teeth (twice), takes Lovell's umbrella, and heads out into the rain for ... whatever.

Despite his uneasiness, he gets to the theater early, so he waits under the marquee. The sign says tickets are 35 cents for teenagers, so assuming he should pay for himself and Jeannette, he counts out 70 cents and transfers it to his shirt pocket. What about popcorn and a drink? He hadn't thought about that, but he'll probably have to pay for those too. He's not sure how much that will cost.

Mosley and Linda arrive together. "Waiting long?" Linda asks.

"Just got here."

"Why don't we get the tickets?" Mosley says. "While we're waiting for Jeannette."

Maybe she won't show. Maybe she's changed her mind.

"Hi, guys." Jeannette greets them as they turn back from the ticket window.

"Oh, hi," Mickey says. "We got the tickets."

"Great."

"Man, it's really raining."

"You've noticed."

"Yeah, really hard."

"I'd say."

"Let's go in, so we can get good seats," Mosley says. "You know how it is on a rainy day."

They find seats near the center of the auditorium.

"You like Stan Musial?" Mickey asks Jeannette.

"Who?"

"The baseball player."

"I've never met him."

"No, I know, he plays for the Cardinals."

"The birds or the priests?"

"The baseball team."

"Never heard of them."

"In St. Louis."

"Never heard of that either."

Mosley pops up from his seat, takes Mickey by his arm. "Let's go to the men's room before the films start."

"I don't need to—"

"Yeah, you do. Be right back, girls."

When they get to the lobby, "What the hell are you doing?"

"What do you mean?"

"You don't open the conversation with a pretty girl by asking her about Stan Musial, for Chrissake."

"She doesn't even know who he is, or even St Louis—"

"She's teasing you, you moron."

"Yeah?"

"Look, just be yourself."

"Baseball is myself."

"Skip the baseball and the football and the basketball stuff. Tell her she looks nice, tell her she smells nice, tell her she's got a great smile, ask her about her classes, who her favorite actor is, what type of music she likes, and anything else that isn't Stan Musial."

"Yeah, OK."

"You'll be fine. She likes you."

"Yeah?"

"At least she did before you started the Musial crap."

When they get back to their seats, Mickey learns that Jeannette likes to read.

"I just finished *Hiroshima*," she said. "You read it?"

"Not yet."

"But you're going to."

"Sure."

"Just as soon as the baseball season is over?"

"It's already over."

"You want to borrow my copy?"

"That would be great."

"I mean, it's so relevant these days."

"Yeah."

The first feature is *Intrigue* with George Raft. "Their kiss kindled a wanton love." Tough-guy Raft plays a soldier, who turns to Shanghai's postwar black market after being dishonorably discharged from the Army. June Havoc stars as the boss who runs the criminal empire.

During the film, Mosley puts his arm around Linda's shoulder. Mickey thinks he should do the same, but he's not sure what Jeannette would think. Mose has been going with Linda for some time, so that makes sense. Maybe Jeannette is expecting him to do the same. Or would she think it too pushy? Mickey hesitates for some time before he finally decides to follow Mose's example. He tentatively slides his arm across the back of the seat. Without looking up, she reaches up and takes his hand in hers. Mickey is relieved.

Between films, Mosley and Mickey go to the refreshment stand and buy popcorn.

"Nice move, champ," says Mosley.

"What do you mean?"

"The stealth move."

The second feature sees Joan Bennett in *Secret Beyond the Door* find her dream man—a handsome, mysterious stranger. In a matter of days they are married, but it doesn't take long for Bennett to realize her new husband wants to kill her.

Before the climactic big scene, Mosley leans over and kisses Linda. Mickey doesn't think this is something he should dare at this point. He throws a handful of popcorn into his mouth, as if that will stop him. Having forgotten to remove his gum, he chokes on the mess in his mouth. Linda laughs, but at least it has taken away the thought of any kiss.

After the show, they walk to Pete's Barbecue for hamburgers and Cokes. It's still pouring, so Jeannette puts her arm through Mickey's and moves close to him under the protection of the umbrella.

Mickey likes it.

Chapter 27

The sun is not yet up when Mutt, Mickey, and Nick load up the LaSalle for the 165-mile drive up to Lawrence, Kansas.

Mutt unfolds a big map. "Looks like pretty much a straight shot due north."

"Why don't you let me drive," Mickey says.

"Not a chance."

"At your speed, I'll be too old to play by the time we get there."

"Hold your horses. The tryout isn't till two o'clock."

Barney has told Mutt about the Browns holding an open tryout. This will be Mickey's chance to show what he can do in front of professional baseball men.

"They're not a very good team, are they?" Nick says. "The Browns."

"No, they ain't," Mutt says, "but look, boys, they're a Major League team, and they've got some good players. And Zack Taylor, he knows what he's doing."

"Who's he?" asks Nick.

"The manager. They'll probably have some of their top scouts there too. That's what they do at these things. They bring the scouts in to look at young talent, and if they see someone they like, they may offer you a contract on the spot."

"Really?" Mickey says.

"Sure," says Mutt. "They gotta build up the talent in their system, seeing as how they really need it."

"What do you think they'll ask us to do?" Mickey asks.

"You'll bat, for sure, probably against one of their good pitchers, or maybe a machine, I don't know. Anyway, you'll bat, and you'll take grounders in the infield and shag a little in the outfield."

"How many do you think will be there?" Nick asks.

"Can't say. Maybe a lot, but the good ones will stand out. They always do, and you two will stand out, I know that."

"For sure," Nick says.

"Mickey, you need to make sure they know you can hit from both sides of the plate. Actually, they need to see you hit from both sides. That will make you stand out for sure. Not many other boys will be able to do that as well as you. Hell, there may not be any who even try to do that. You make sure they let you do that, though."

"What if they only have a righty pitcher throwing to us, or just a lefty? What do I do then?"

"You just … I don't know, maybe they'll have a machine and then it don't matter."

Mutt, always a chain smoker, is out-smoking his normal rate. This is a big moment for him. This is something he has been working toward since Mickey was born, and something he has been thinking about since before Mickey was born.

If the Browns are interested in Mickey, where would they start him out? Probably one of their D level minor league teams. Mutt has looked them up. Maybe their team in the Georgia-Alabama League. That is probably their closest affiliate. Or maybe they'd skip the D level altogether and send him to the Muskogee Reds or Hannibal Pilots. If Mickey does as well as he can, slugs the ball all over the place, shows off his arm and his speed, is it possible he would start with the Springfield Browns or the Wichita Falls Spudders in B ball? It would be great if he plays for a team near enough for the family to drive to see him play. He probably wouldn't stay there long, anyway. He's too good.

The only thing that could hold him back, Mutt believes, is a loss of confidence in himself. He's not usually comfortable around people he doesn't know. He's not good at small talk. He'd rather smile with a nod than engage strangers in conversations. Mutt understands that, because he is similar. Still, Mickey has gotten so many compliments about his playing that he should know in his heart he has the skills necessary to make it as a professional baseball player. But does he?

He also has good qualities that will stand him in good stead. He is polite, although sometimes his shyness is seen by others as rudeness. He demonstrates good manners, does not try to take advantage of weaker people. The Browns will see that.

On the drive Mutt engages the boys by talking about the Major League Baseball season—the Cardinals in particular. He hopes that taking the boys' minds off the tryout will keep them from being as anxious as he is.

Nothing, however, is going to calm Mickey's nerves on this day. What if he does something stupid? Asks a dumb question or something. What if he can't get a ball out of the infield because he's swinging too hard and topping everything? What if he misjudges fly balls or bobbles grounders? He's done that before. What if they don't pay any attention to him because he's the youngest boy there?

Worst of all, though, is the thought that he will let his father down. If his father is disappointed in him, it will be terrible. His father has been working toward this day for so long. Mickey has to deliver a good tryout, and therein comes the pressure. And pressure can make for indecision, tight muscles ... foolish mistakes.

When they finally get near Garnett, Kansas, it begins to lightly rain. The closer they get to Lawrence, the more Mickey's stomach tightens. He tries a new stick of peppermint gum. By the time they get to the field where the tryout is to be held, it is raining more heavily.

"Remember to take a few pitches first," Mutt says. "Get a feel for the field and the pitcher ... and the hitting background. You can swing away later. And be careful when you're running if the field is still wet. Don't cut too hard if they have you run around the bases. Be smart, both of you. You'll be just fine.

When they get to the field, there is only one person there—a man who tells them that because of the rain the tryout has been cancelled. He doesn't know when or if it will be rescheduled. Dream deferred. Although he doesn't admit it, Mickey is relieved. There will be other opportunities when he will be more prepared.

Mickey is back playing with the Whiz Kids. The previous summer, he had mostly played second for Barney.

"You're wasting your arm at second, Mickey," Barney tells him on the first day of summer practice. "I'm going to have you play short this season. You played there some at school, didn't you?"

"Some, yeah. Mostly, I pitched."

"Well, now you're a full-time shortstop. At least with us."

Making up for lost time during his bout with osteomyelitis, his body has filled out even more. It is obvious to everyone that Mickey has become their most improved and most important player. He still makes his share of miscues in the field, but seldom does a game go by that he doesn't hit the ball hard. Often over the fence.

On several occasions, someone tells him in awed tones that a big-league scout is watching him. They are obviously impressed with his physical tools. Strong thrower, fast runner, powerful hitter from either side of the plate. Perhaps just as importantly, they are impressed with his attitude and approach to the game. He plays hard all the time and doesn't make excuses, although he beats himself up when he makes a bad throw or strikes out. Those things can be corrected, however, if he plays professionally and is coached by professionals.

He has gotten better at charging ground balls, and he gets his throws off in a hurry, if not always accurately. The balls that give him the most trouble at short are the balls hit directly at him. Sometimes he isn't sure whether to come in or back off, letting the ball play him.

In a game against a club from Topeka, a ground ball takes a bad hop and hits him in the mouth. For days he has a fat lip that makes it hard for him to be understood. As a result, for the next few games, he backs away from hard-hit grounders.

"Stop backing off," Mutt barks at him. "You ain't no sissy. Fat lips are part of playing short. Get used to it. And stop trying to show off your arm. You're throwing too many away because you're throwing too hard. Throw hard enough to get a runner, not harder. Didn't I teach you anything?"

Mickey has learned to get himself out of the few batting slumps into which he falls by cutting down on his swing for a couple of at-bats. As with so many young batters, he hits fastballs better than curves.

"You don't want to be like me, Mickey," Barney tells Mickey when he senses the young man's self-doubts. "I was a good player. Well, a decent player anyway, and I had dreams of playing in the Majors just like you do. But I never made it, so it was a life down in the mines for me. Oh, I got as far as the Three-I League, but that was it. I could have gone further. I know that now, but I didn't have … OK, I'll admit it … I didn't have the courage. I was hesitant to throw myself all-out into competition with players, some of who were better than me. So rather than fail, I left, went down in the mines. That was easier than trying and risking failure. So, if I have anything to teach you, that's it. Don't give up. The time will come when you won't be able to play baseball at a high level, but until then, you need to be brave. Don't be afraid to push yourself. Don't be afraid to fail, and only then will you be able to succeed. Playing against better players is the only way you'll reach your full potential. Jump in the deep end."

"I can't swim."

"Really?

"Really."

"OK, bad analogy, but the point is worth remembering. Challenge yourself. It's all right to be frightened, but do it anyway, because you can. They'll say you are not big enough, that you're from nowhere, that you shouldn't dream so big. But I believe in you. I see greatness. Lecture over."

There is no doubt, however, that if there are scouts watching, they are there to see how far and often he can launch a baseball.

Among the Major League scouts who work the area, there are several who think Mickey might have enough potential to be worth a detour in their travels to catch one of his Whiz Kids games. Not all come away thinking they should recommend he be signed.

This is Commerce, Oklahoma, hardly the hotbed of baseball talent, and hardly an area that boasts a high enough level of competition to draw conclusions about Mickey's abilities. A number of scouts think he looks like a decent player but nothing special. A lot of big farm kids and tough miners' sons look good playing sports against inferior competition, but take these hicks to a crowded Major League city, and they'll wilt like flowers in the dust belt.

Joe Pollock, a former Ban Johnson League player who had played against Mickey, recommends to "Hoot" Gibson, president of the Miami Owls, that the Owls sign Mickey to play for them since he is developing a good following in nearby Commerce, which ought to swell the gate. Gibson says he doesn't think Mickey is good enough to play professionally.

Throughout the summer they play all over northeast Oklahoma and up into Kansas and Missouri at Joplin, Seneca, Alba, and Carl Junction. They are baseball gypsies. Sometimes they travel by car, sometimes they hitchhike.

Mickey hits well but he bobbles lots of grounders, and in his rush to make up for them he throws too many balls away at first.

When Mutt suggests to Barney that maybe Mickey should play someplace else, Barney won't hear of it. "You know, Mutt, the thing I like best is that he never gives up on a ball, never quits going after it. He takes a bobbled ball personally."

"Yeah, and then throws it away."

"Like he's pissed at the ball. He'll get it. The more he plays there, the better he'll get."

Mutt rolls his eyes as if to say that's too easy of an answer.

Mickey continues to improve at the plate. His swing is becoming more comfortable and freer. He is getting better at running the bases and being more consistent at clipping the base on the inside. He is learning to read pitchers more accurately. With his speed, he could become a proficient base stealer. Maybe a great base stealer.

They play their games midweek, but sometimes on the weekends, Barney matches up his kids against minor league teams in the Tri-State district. This gives Mickey the chance to bat against older, more experienced hurlers. If he feels nervous about going up against them, he doesn't show it. He is gaining confidence as a hitter all the time.

Barney still thinks it would be better if Mickey dropped switch-hitting, but knowing that Mutt would likely pull Mickey if he did, he never pushes the idea.

Despite his troubles at short, Mickey continues to get noticed. The *Joplin Globe* covers the Whiz Kids' games and remarks frequently about his hitting.

Nick and LeRoy have been playing for a league team in Webb City, Missouri. But when Barney asks them to join the Whiz Kids, they jump at the chance. Now the three friends are playing together again. They have played together for so long that they feel comfortable being on the same team. They honed their abilities at the Mantles' with Mutt and Charlie pitching to them. They played together on the alkali and in various pastures, backyards, sandlots, and school yards. They played in Spavinaw, and in just about every other small town within a 25-mile radius.

Before one game, Willy Pitts, a regular centerfielder for the Whiz Kids, asks Mickey to switch positions with him. `

"I'll play short; you can take center," Willy says.

"That's up to Barney."

Willy talks Barney into it. The result is a calamity. Willy nearly kills the first baseman with his errant throws, which are even wilder than Mickey's. In the outfield, Mickey misplays numerous balls.

"Switch back," Barney says, "before somebody gets hurt … if they haven't already."

It is Mickey's first-time playing center on an organized team, and it offers no reason to think it is a position he will eventually play more than 1,700 times in the Major Leagues.

After the game, he goes with Nick and LeRoy to the Black Cat for a hamburger.

"What do you guys want to do tomorrow?" Nick asks. "There won't be many more before we head back to prison."

"I got a job for a couple of weeks," Mickey says, "so I can't—"

"You got what?" Nick says.

"A job. You know, where they pay you money."

"Yeah, I know what a job is. What are you going to do, dig in the mines?"

"You're gonna laugh when I tell you," Mickey says.

"Try me."

"I'm gonna fill in for a while as a lifeguard at the pool."

"Mickey, for Chrissake, you can't even swim."

"Yeah, but they don't know that."

"You told them you can swim?"

"Nobody asked."

"What the hell are you going to do if somebody is drowning?"

"Throw them a life preserver."

"And if you fall in, then what?"

"Yell for help."

"This is great, Mickey," says Nick. "It's a perfect job for you. You're completely unqualified, untrained, and unexperienced."

"It's your future, Mickey," LeRoy says. "It's absolutely what you were made to do. If no one will pay you to play ball, you can be paid to be a lifeguard who can't guard his lunch much less a drowning kid."

"That's always been my dream job."

With that, they all start laughing so hard they can't eat.

One night as the Mantles are finishing dinner, they hear a knock on their front door. Mutt gets up to see who it is.

"Hello, I'm Runt Marr," says a short man extending his hand.

"Mutt Mantle," says Mutt, taking his hand.

"I'm a scout for the Cards."

"Oh yeah?"

"Can I come in?"

"Sure. We're just eating. Would you like some—"

"Oh, I'm sorry. I can come back later."

"Have something to eat?"

"No, thanks. I've already eaten."

"Coffee."

"If you're sure—"

Lovell gets up to get the coffee. "No Major League scout is going to get out of this house without our hospitality."

"Thank you kindly, Mrs. Mantle. You probably have an idea why I'm here."

"Well, it's not because you're hungry, anyway."

Mickey feels the blood rushing from his head. A Major League scout has made the effort to track him down, but now what? Maybe he's come to say they're not interested in him. Maybe because Mickey plays relatively near them, they feel an obligation to talk to local players even if they don't want them. But no, it's more likely he brings good news.

"Mickey, I've seen you play," Marr says, "and I think you have potential. Look, I played a lot of minor league ball, never made it to the majors, but I think I know what it takes, and it don't take someone like me at five foot five inches. But you got strong shoulders, quick wrists, a good arm, and fast feet. You got a chance. It's only a chance, mind you. Most strong, fast kids, no matter what size, never make it. Maybe you won't either. You'd have a lot of work ahead of you, a lot of things to work on ... to get better at. I wouldn't say you're a complete shortstop yet, but you got potential."

Mickey is beaming. This is the first time he has heard such things from a professional baseball player. "Yeah, I hope so. Thanks."

Lovell hands him the promised cup of coffee. "Fixins are on the table there."

Mutt, who is as excited as Mickey, asks Marr what he has in mind to offer.

"Offer? Well we're not there yet, Mr. Mantle."

"Mutt."

"Mutt, we're not ready for that yet. But here's what I'd like you to do. I'd like you to promise me you won't sign with anybody else until I can get back to you with an offer. Mickey, you'd like to play for the Cardinals one day, wouldn't you?"

"You know it."

"You'd have to work your way up through our minor league affiliates, but once you did and made the big club, well, you'd be playing close enough to here that your folks could come up and see you. Oh, and your brothers and sister, too. That would be great, right? Playing for St. Louis."

"Yeah, that would be really great."

"So, can I count on you to not do anything before I get back with a true offer? See, that's the way it works. A scout finds somebody they want to sign, and then they got to get the bigwigs who run the club to agree to cut the check. That's the way it's done. I played a long time in the minors, so I know how it's done."

"How long are we talking about here before we see an offer?" Mutt asks.

"Oh, not long. A matter of a few days. A week maybe. Why? Nobody else has been here, have they?"

"No, you're the first, but we expect more. Mickey is getting a lot of attention."

"I'm sure."

Mutt tells the diminutive scout that they won't do anything for the time being, suggesting that it is only a matter of time before other scouts come knocking. Marr shakes his hand and departs.

The Cardinals are interested in Mickey. It doesn't get any better than that. Now all they have to do is wait for the contract. Mutt will handle the details when the offer comes through.

The wait is filled with both elation and anxiety. The thought of Mickey playing on the same team as Marty Marion, Red Schoendienst, Stan Musial, and Enos Slaughter is hard for them to take in.

"Where do you think I'll start?" Mickey asks Mutt. "Where will they send me?"

"Probably at the D level. That's where they usually start guys. Maybe C, though. Maybe even B if they've seen how hard you can smack a ball."

"I hope it's D."

"You want to start as high as you can, so that you can get to the bigs sooner."

"I'd rather start at D and then work—"

"You've got to be more confident, Mickey. You know how to play the game. Don't ever forget that."

"I know, but the players at C, they'll be older."

"So what? You'll be as good as any of them. Better, probably."

"I'm not sure—"

"C'mon, Mickey, let's go celebrate."

"No, Mutt," Lovell says.

"We won't be long," Mutt says, grabbing his jacket.

"This is not a good idea."

"Back in an hour. I'm going for a quick drink with a professional baseball player. Let's go, Mickey."

Mickey isn't sure if he should mention the contract to anyone until it's signed, but he decides to tell Jeannette.

"Mickey, that's wonderful," she tells him before landing a kiss on his cheek.

"I know, but …"

"But, what?"

"I'm not sure I can … you know, I've never lived away from this area, and they're probably going to send me to the other side of the country where I won't know anybody."

"You'll do fine. It's the realization of your lifelong dreams."

"As long as it doesn't turn into a nightmare."

"It won't. Why would it? You're the best player around here, aren't you?"

"I don't know."

"Well, I do. What's bothering you? That you won't make it to the Majors?"

"I don't want to let my father down."

"Mickey, you need to pay more attention to satisfying yourself, not your father."

"It's the same thing."

"It's not, actually, but OK."

"When will you leave, do you know?"

"We have to wait for the contract. It should be any day now."

They never hear from Runt Marr again. Mickey is not totally disappointed.

Chapter 28

Tom Greenwade had been a pitcher and manager in minor league baseball when he contracted typhoid fever and nearly died. When he recovered, he spent a couple years away from baseball, working for the Internal Revenue Service, and then returned to the game as a scout. First for the Browns, then the Dodgers. Now he's scouting for the Yankees.

Greenwade is one-quarter Cherokee, which, according to him, gives him the ability to spot baseball talent where other scouts can't. Always an extremely frugal man, his one splurge is a big black Cadillac, which he drives from one small town to another while looking for talent.

One day, he shows up at a game at the Baxter Springs ballpark. Despite what others will later write, he is here to see Mickey Mantle. In fact, he's been tracking Mickey's progress for a while.

During a cloudburst, everyone heads for their cars to wait out the rain.

"There's a fella here dying to meet you," Mutt tells Mickey.

Greenwade flashes a friendly smile and asks Mickey if he thinks he's ready to play for the Yankees.

Mickey stands there getting wet but too stunned to respond.

"Well, I can't talk to you officially because you're still in high school. Now, don't sign with anyone else because on the day you graduate, I'll be back."

"With an offer?" Mutt says.

"We'll see what we can do."

From Whitebird to New York? From the dust bowl to the Big

Apple. How could he possibly deal with living in New York City? Commerce is the biggest town he's ever lived in. And the Yankees! That means Yogi Berra, Phil Rizzuto, Hank Bauer, Johnny Mize, and Joe DiMaggio. What would he even say to DiMaggio? Thoughts of playing for the Yankees are overwhelming. He had always thought about playing for the Cardinals or the Browns, never the Yankees.

Lovell doesn't want to put a damper on Mickey's prospects, but she worries that a small-town boy from the mining district of Oklahoma will get eaten alive by the sharks of New York. She tells Mutt that if the Yankee offer really does come through, they need to reject it.

"Something else will come along," she insists. "Something closer to home."

"The Yankees," says Mutt, "they're the greatest baseball franchise in history. They're Babe Ruth, Lou Gehrig, Joe DiMaggio. They're Yankee Stadium."

"Yeah, and none of them came from around here. Mutt, he's just turning 17 years old. What would a 17-year-old do by himself in New York City? He don't know nobody there."

"Don't matter."

"Wouldn't it be better if he starts, you know, someplace smaller, then maybe someday think about the Yankees?"

"Except you know damn well it don't work that way."

"You can't breathe in places like New York."

"You know that because you've been there?"

"I know that because I know that."

"He'll learn. He'll adjust."

"I don't like it."

"Well, he don't have a contract, anyway, just the promise of one. We'll see, we'll see."

Lovell glares at Mutt. "If the Yankee scout thinks Mickey's good enough for them, then other teams will, too."

"Then we'll deal with them when they come."

Mutt figures that if the Yankees do sign him, Mickey will likely start with the Independence Yankees in the Kansas-Oklahoma-Missouri League. That would be good. They could go to his games.

"This is what we've been working for all these years, isn't it? A professional contract."

"Not to play in New York."

The thought that Greenwade will return with contract in hand, as he says he will at the end of the academic calendar, brings both excitement and trepidation, which hang over Mickey's head all year.

"Jesus Christ, Mickey, the Yankees!" Mosley says as they sit in the bleachers.

"I know."

"Who's their shortstop now?"

"Phil Rizzuto."

"How old is he?"

"I don't know."

"But he's been around for a while."

"Yeah, I guess."

"So, they're thinking you could replace him."

"Man, I don't know. Replacing Rizzuto, I don't think I could—"

"Not now, maybe, but in a couple of years."

"Yeah, maybe like 10."

"You never know."

"New York, that never entered my mind at all. It's like on another planet or something. It's a different world."

"But you know it's always 90 feet between bases no matter where."

"Except on the alkali. There it's always 30 paces."

"Ninety feet more or less."

"I keep thinking about meeting Joe DiMaggio. What the hell would I say to him?"

"Do you need anything, Mr. DiMaggio, sir? Can I get you coffee or something? A shot of whiskey, maybe?"

"I read someplace he's not the nicest guy who ever put on a uniform."

"Yeah, a nasty son of a bitch."

"At night, I close my eyes and try to picture myself at short in Yankee Stadium. Snuffy Stirnweiss is at second, Bobby Brown at third, Tommy Henrich playing first. From pictures in the baseball magazines, I sort of know what they look like, so I can see them crouching in position to gobble up ground balls. But I can't see me. I'm invisible. Nobody can see me. Thousands of people in the stands look out to short, and nobody's there."

"Just nerves, Mickey, you'll be fine."

"I don't know anybody in New York City. I don't know anybody in the whole state or any state near New York, and you know, I'm not always so good at meeting new people."

"Don't worry, you play well, and they'll all want to meet you."

"Anyway, I don't know why I'm even thinking about this. Just because Mr. Greenwade said he's coming back with a contract, don't mean he will. We'll probably never see him again."

"I wouldn't be too sure."

"In the meantime, I don't even want to think about New York."

"Well, if they do sign you, it'll be a few years before you get to New York."

"That would be good."

"In the meantime, let's have fun this year."

"Don't we always?"

"More fun."

With Mickey, Nick, and LeRoy leading the way, the Whiz Kids run away with the league. Although they don't talk about it, they can sense that it won't be long before their lives change. High school will be over after next year, and they will have to face whatever comes next. Of course, they dream of playing professional baseball, getting married, getting rich, but these are still fuzzy dreams. Reality will soon be upon them.

Mickey and Nick are scouring the area under the stands along the right-field line. Mickey had two hits on the field for the Whiz Kids the night before. Sometimes, they can find things they can sell or bottles they can return for the deposits. Occasionally, they find a ball that has been missed. Barney always pays 50 cents for those.

On this day, they come up with two balls.

"What do you say we go to the fair tonight?" Nick says.

"After the game?"

"Why not? Jim Kenaga's got his father's car—a spanking brand-new Plymouth with these new low-pressure tires."

"What are they supposed to do?"

"Damned if I know."

The game that night is against the team from Columbus, Kansas. Mickey hits a home run, the Whiz Kids win, and the league championship is theirs.

The celebratory trip to the Cherokee County Fair is on.

The Plymouth is jammed well beyond its intended limit. Since there is no shower or dressing rooms at the field, the boys are still wearing their uniforms. People know the uniform, know they are the Whiz Kids, know they are among the top players in the area. Without any local professional teams or even any top college teams, they are treated as minor celebrities. They lean out of the car windows and wave at passing motorists, many of whom wave back. Some drivers honk their horns when they see the boys in uniform.

As they near Columbus, Jim takes a turn, making the low-pressure tires squeal. The boys think that is funny; the Columbus policeman sitting nearby in his car doesn't.

Jim insists he wasn't speeding. "It's just these new tires," he tells the officer.

"Speeding tires."

"No, I wasn't really."

"I'm going to write you a ticket for $10 anyway."

"Ten dollars?"

"Payable to me."

"I don't have $10."

"Then you're not going anyplace. Not in this car, anyway."

"But it was the tires."

"It's still $10."

"I've only got five."

"I got three," says Nick.

"Mickey?"

"I can come up with two in change."

"You're the kid hitting all them home runs," the officer says when he recognizes Mickey.

"We just won the league championship."

"Yeah, I seen you boys play pretty good."

"So, you don't want to give the champions a ticket, do you?" Nick asks.

"Oh, you want special treatment because you're big shots? Ain't gonna happen, boys."

"What about a Whiz Kids cap?"

"Ten bucks."

Mickey will come to expect special treatment because of his skills, but not on this day.

So, the money they had brought to enjoy the fair went to a policeman who thought squealing tires meant speeding tires. They turned around and headed home, disappointed and penniless.

Chapter 29

In the fall of his senior year, Mickey signs up for home economics and shop to round out his schedule. No reason not to take the easiest classes he can. His mind is on sports and not, despite his teacher's best efforts, Emily Dickinson. He frequently sits in class and stares out the window, seeing himself scoring dazzling touchdowns, hitting home runs, sinking long set shots.

Seeing his wandering attention span, his English teacher, Mrs. Jacoby, makes Mickey memorize Joyce Kilmer's "Trees" and recite it to the class.

Mickey tries to convince her this is a bad idea, but she persists.

On the day of the dreaded recital, Mickey stands in front of the class. He would prefer to strike out looking rather than deliver poetry in front of a class. A big jock reciting mushy verse.

"I think I shall never see / A poem lovely as a tree."

This draws laughs. Mickey, the football/basketball/baseball star, reciting corny poetry is as funny to the class as it is to Mickey, who can't stop giggling when the laughter begins.

"A tree whose hungry mouth is prest / Against the earth's sweet flowing breast."

Complete hysterics follow. Even Mrs. Jacoby has to suppress a chuckle.

"A tree that looks at God all day, / And lifts his leafy arms to pray ... That's all I remember," Mickey says.

"It's *her* arms, not *his* arms," Mrs. Jacoby corrects.

"Oh yeah, I forgot."

"OK, that's enough. Now that wasn't so hard, was it?"

Mickey can't get back to his seat fast enough. It's one thing to play in front of a couple hundred fans, but it's quite another to be embarrassed in front of your schoolmates.

"What is this I'm reading?" Lovell asks between sips of coffee.

"A newspaper," Mickey says, mixing milk with his coffee.

"This article says your school is putting in an engineering classroom and beginning a pre-engineering class."

"It must be so if it's in the paper."

"And it says you and Mosley are among the eight students in the class."

"It must be so if it's in the paper."

"You in a pre-engineering class?"

"Yep."

"How did that happen?"

"It wasn't my idea."

"Yeah, whose was it?"

"The teacher's."

"What good is that gonna do you?"

"Damned if I know."

"You're not in there because that girl you've been seeing is in the class, are you?"

"Nah, they don't let girls take engineering."

"Didn't you tell them you don't want to take engineering?"

"I told them I wanted to take shop."

"Might be more valuable."

"Wait till you hear what else I'm doing at school."

"I can hardly wait."

"Drama."

"What are you talking about?"

"We're doing a play called *Little Nell*, and I'm in it."

"What do you mean 'in it'?"

"Acting."

"You are not."

"I'm an off-stage character, but I've got a bunch of lines."

"Since when are you interested in drama?"

"Since my teacher told me I had to be in it. Mrs. Campbell. She's the director, too."

"This is ridiculous."

"Yeah, so is the play."

"What do you know about acting?"

"I know how to act by making it look to the umpire that I caught a ball on the fly when it really hit the ground first."

"That's not the same thing."

"We all have to be in it because it's supposed to be a letterman's thing. Everybody in it is a school athletic letter winner."

"Who is everybody?"

"Well, Donnie Dodd is Nell Wilkins and—"

"Donnie is supposed to be a girl?"

"Yeah, so is LeRoy Trask. He's playing Donnie's mother."

"That sounds pretty stupid."

"It's supposed to be pretty funny."

"You're not wearing a dress, are you?"

"Nope. Neither is Mosley."

"Don't tell me—"

"Yep, except he's the handsome, dashing hero, Hector Skyscraper."

"And what exactly is your part in all this?"

"I'm called the prompter, and I shout out things from off the stage. The good part about it is that I don't have to try to memorize all those words. I can just read them from my script."

Mickey gets his script and reads: "'Places! Hey, places! Stop that pounding; the audience is waiting! Sure that wig will stay on, Nell?' Then she says it will because it's just like her own hair. 'See that it does! Last night it fell off four times. Places! Hey, Ma, straighten your hair. You look like *The Last of the Mohicans*' mother. Ready? All right, Let 'er rip.'"

"Who woulda thought it? Mickey Mantle, the actor."

"Mrs. Campbell wanted me to do one of the other characters, but I told her no way. She wasn't going to get me out there no matter how much she asked. That's when she said I wouldn't have to go on stage. Seeing as how I have more letters than anyone other than Mose, it would look like I was a spoilsport coward if I wasn't in it."

"So, all you jocks—"

"Do me one favor, though?"

"What's that?"

"Don't come and don't even tell Dad I'm doing it."

His senior year in high school is a busy time for Mickey. In addition to his athletic activities on the court, the field, and the diamond, he is sports editor of the yearbook, an assistant editor of the school newspaper, a member of the pre-engineer program, and a cast member in another class play.

He also remains popular among his classmates. He may be a star on the athletic field, but he remains shy, deferential, and courteous. In the yearbook, he is listed as most popular. Under his picture it reads, "They're great pals, he and his baseball jacket."

Mickey will soon either live up to his father's expectations or he won't. Ever since he was a little boy, to maintain his father's approval, he had to love what his father loved, behave as his father wanted him to behave, live his young life as his father prescribed. Pleasing his father is always uppermost in his mind. He has to be what his father wants him to be. And he is. It is a mask he wears. Mutt Mantle's prodigy. His sense of worth comes from his father's expectations, and maybe in the process he has lost something of himself. If he has, he doesn't complain about it. He needs his father's approval more than he needs his own. Nothing would be worse than not being good enough in Mutt's eyes.

There is little more that Mutt can do with Mickey. He has taught him everything he knows about the game, watched him develop into a power-hitting switch-hitter. He's still not the biggest player around, but he has strong shoulders and quick wrists, and he can run as fast as anyone he has ever seen on a ball field.

Now it's just a matter of somebody from professional ball actually offering a contract. The Tri-State district may not be known as fertile ground for professional baseball players, but Barney knows people who know people who scout for the pros. And then maybe Greenwade will get back to them during the school year to reaffirm the Yankee's interest. But he doesn't.

Mutt and Ox sit in the top row of the bleachers, watching Commerce play Chelsea in a tight basketball game. As usual, Mosley and Mickey are leading the Tigers' attack.

"He looks good," Ox says. "Mickey, he looks like he knows what to do on a basketball court."

"He's grown into it," Mutt says. "Gotten better each season."

"Without you on his back."

"It's basketball. Who cares?"

The two men are quiet for some time as they take in the game. Lovell, sitting down front, lets the officials have it when they miss what she thinks should be a foul on Mickey's layup attempt.

"Well, she does, anyway," Ox says. "Lovell cares."

"Yeah, loudly."

"I understand Mickey's gotten interested in girls."

"As long as he ain't too interested."

"Mutt, what are you going to do after this year? After Mickey graduates?"

"I'm hoping he gets a pro contract."

"What if he does? You've spent so much of your life working with him, what the hell is it going to be like for you without him around? If he does sign a pro contract, you're gonna be … I don't know, like a ship out of water or something."

Although Mutt doesn't acknowledge it, he has had less and less time with Mickey as Mickey has gotten older. Mickey has his friends, his teammates, his schoolmates. That's the way it is with teenagers. So, Mutt has mixed feelings. Sure, he wants Mickey to go off and be successful, but at the same time, there would be benefits for Mutt if he didn't. Mickey is his best friend, and he Mickey's. He's certain of that. When a best friend is no longer there every day, it is bound to leave a hole.

"I'll be fine," Mutt says.

"You'll have to work your ass off if you wanna come here," Darrell Royal says.

The Sooners' star player is showing Mickey around the Oklahoma University football facilities. "Nobody'll hand you anything. You gotta earn it. If not, you'll plant your ass on the bench, collecting splinters for four years."

"What do you play?"

"Me? Defensive back mostly and some quarterback. More and more, I'm quarterbacking, though. You're a running back, I hear."

"Yeah."

"I gotta say, Nicky, you're not the biggest running back I ever saw. You must be pretty fast."

"Yeah, I guess so."

"Well, you'd better be because up here, the defensive lines, they're pretty big, and they ain't slow either. Not like in high school. Nothing like high school. Think you're up to it?"

"I don't know."

"Well, if you're not sure, you're gonna get killed. You gotta believe you can go all the way every time you touch the ball. You gotta have moxie, you gotta have confidence, or else coach ain't gonna play you. You got that?"

"I guess so, yeah."

"Not good enough."

"I've scored a lot of touchdowns."

"In high school. This ain't high school. This is big-time football."

When they walk into the football stadium, Mickey is stunned by the size. "How many people—"

"I'm not sure exactly," Royal says. "They just added more seats. Now over 50,000, I think. And you can see there are three more practice fields over there."

"Is that a baseball field over there, too?"

"Yeah, but the outfield runs into one of the practice fields.

What a pain in the ass that is. Nobody cares about baseball around here. Nobody goes to the games. This is football country, make no mistake about that. People live for football."

"I never seen anything like this stadium. It's pretty …"

"Big?"

"Yeah."

"You met Coach yet?"

"Uh-uh."

"You'd better be straight with him. He don't take kindly to … waffling. You want to play football at the University of Oklahoma, you tell him that in no uncertain terms. You tell him you're the best damn running back in the state, and if he don't offer you a scholarship, he'll be missing out on greatness, and you'll go play for Texas or some other big school. You gotta be strong with him."

"OK."

"Oh, and one other thing, how are you in the classroom?"

"Not as good as I could be."

"Well, you won't have to worry about that. If you're on the football team, you'll be well looked after. You'll be taken care of, if you know what I mean."

"Yeah."

"Nicky, I gotta run. Time to do some lifting, but it's been nice talking to you. Coach's office is over there," he says, pointing to a low row of offices next to the stadium. "I'd suggest you call him Mr. Wilkinson. Once you're on the team, you can call him Coach, but I wouldn't do it now."

Mickey never meets Bud Wilkinson.

When he gets home, Mosley asks him how it went on the trip.

"I don't think it's gonna work out."

"Do you really want it to?"

"Not really."

"It was fun, though, being treated like a …"

"Darrell Royal showed me around, and he couldn't even remember my name."

"I guess that says it all."

"Except you should've been up there, not me."

"Maybe I'll get a call."

"Yeah, you should."

Mutt sits on the loose wooden step outside the front door looking up at the starlit night sky. He sips from a pint of bourbon between cigarette drags. Everyone else is asleep. He is there for the best part of an hour before Lovell comes out.

"You coming to bed?" she asks.

"In a bit, yeah."

"Why so glum?"

"It looks like we're going out again."

"Another strike?"

"Eagle-Picher is … I don't know … management is arguing mostly about seniority rights."

"Does it mean you all have to go out?"

"Yeah."

"Even if you don't belong to the union?"

"That don't matter."

"What about a pay raise? Aren't you gonna ask for that?"

"We're asking for a 48-cent-an-hour increase. They're offering four."

"Any idea how long it might last?"

"Not really. Mr. Maybon, he represents the company, and he can be real stubborn, that son of a bitch. It don't matter to him how long we're shut down. He probably makes a bundle anyway, so what does he care?"

"Maybe it's time to go back to the farm?"

"Oh, I think about it once in a while, but how much more reliable would that be, what with the floods and droughts and tornadoes and all?"

"The cows don't go on strike."

Chapter 30

When he's not playing one game or another, Mickey begins spending more time with Jeannette. Off the field and away from his buddies, he is quiet and reserved, qualities that Jeannette appreciates.

On weekend nights they go to the movies or parties, but usually leave after one dance or sometimes before the dancing begins. They might drink a little beer, but not much. Mickey shows no signs of the heavy drinker he will become.

"Mickey Charles, how come you move around the baseball field like you're a dancer and around the dance floor like you're a baseball player?"

"I dunno, I just don't have the … the coordination to dance, I guess."

"That so? How do you hit a baseball if you're so uncoordinated?"

"Pure luck."

"You're worse at lying than you are at dancing."

She recognizes that Mickey can't stand to be embarrassed in front of his friends. How can he act so confident on the athletic fields and so insecure off it? He is often quiet, sometimes dark. This is what she finds puzzling but loveable.

Often, they double date with Mosley or another of his friends. Mickey likes having others carry on conversations when he can't think of what to say next.

Sometimes Jeannette does his homework for him.

"So, what's on the menu tonight?" she asks every day as they meet in the hall after the last class.

Sometimes he hands her a paper with a group of math problems to solve.

"Geometry?" she asks.

"Yeah, useless stuff that will never be any good to me ever."

Jeannette looks over the paper. "All I see here is a baseball field."

"I think you need glasses."

"What is a rhomboid?"

"Sounds like a disease."

"The shape of a baseball diamond. What is a pentagon?"

"A big military building in Washington."

"Home plate."

"Why is that like a military building?"

"It's not. It's a five-sided figure, sort of like a triangle on top of a square or rectangle with the point facing out toward the pitcher."

"Is this going to help me become a better batter or not, knowing the plate's a pentagon?"

"Or get better swinging at a sphere."

"Pitchers don't throw spheres," Mickey laughs. "They throw breaking balls that just manage to catch the corner of the pentagon."

"See how much you've learned already?"

"I feel better."

"Wait till you get to octahedrons with eight faces."

"What is that on a baseball field?"

"No idea. I'm just showing off."

"So, you'll do the homework?"

"Maybe."

"If what?"

"A kiss."

After looking around to see who might be watching, Mickey obliges.

One Saturday night, they are at a party where a ping-pong table is set up. Mickey challenges Jeannette to a game. With his lightning-quick reflexes, he can easily beat her. Early on, he lobs only soft shots over the net. When Jeannette starts returning them hard, Mickey responds by smashing every ball as hard as he can. Maybe too hard, because she beats him 21–19.

"Let's do another," she says.

"This is not my game, ping-pong."

Jeannette quickly realizes beating Mickey was a mistake. He's in a sour mood the rest of the night, and nothing Jeannette says to him lightens his mood.

"Gosh, he's moody," Linda says to Jeannette when they are away from the boys.

"He hates to lose. I should have thought about that."

"You know, I think all these jocks hate to lose even more than they love to win."

"That's hardly rational."

"Who says athletes are rational? They're like little boys."

"I think Mickey gets that from his father. He pushes him so hard to win all the time."

Mickey would disagree. His father never pushes him to win. Encourages, yes; pushes, no. He pushes him to be the best ballplayer he can—win, lose, or draw.

Jeannette, like the other girls her age in Commerce, lacks the outlets to fill her spare time that the boys enjoy. They have their sports and games and pool hall. The girls have none of that. They spend much of their leisure time walking to one another's houses, looking in shop windows, talking about boys. What is ahead of them is marriage and children. Their future is day-to-day with not much promise for more. The dreams of those like Mutt and Mickey do not come to them, so if Jeannette can share in Mickey's dreams, so much the better.

Mutt worries that Mickey is getting too serious about Jeannette. What if she cons him into marriage? That would spoil everything. His focus would be split between ball playing and family.

"You like her, don't you?" he asks Mickey.

"Yeah, she's neat."

"You're not going to do anything … stupid, are you?"

Mickey understands what his father means, and it embarrasses him. Mutt would never dare talk to his son—or anybody else, for that matter—about sex, and Mickey certainly wouldn't ask him. What he knows about sex comes from his friends, some of whom are apparently rather knowledgeable about the subject.

"No! I gotta go. I don't want to be late for school."

"Since when does that bother you?" Lovell asks.

"Bye."

Everyone in school has heard the stories about the "Spooklight." This strange light occurs in a field outside of Quapaw. According to the legend, the light was first seen by Indians as they travelled along the Trail of Tears in 1836, while being displaced from their homelands in the southeast United States.

Plenty of people have seen it. Stories about it have been printed in the papers. Reports vary, describing it from as small as a baseball to as large as a basketball. It seems to arise out of nothing, then dances and spins, circles at high speeds, and disappears as suddenly as it emerges. Some observers claim it swings from side to side, as if it were a lantern carried by some invisible force. These stories aren't new. They've been around for more than 100 years.

Many theories have been proposed to explain why this mysterious light appears. One of the oldest is that it comes from the spirit of two young Quapaw Indians who died there many years ago. Another story links it to the spirit of an Osage Indian chief who was beheaded there. The light is said to be coming from his torch as he searches for his missing head. Still another story claims it is the lantern light of a miner looking for his children who had been kidnapped by Indians.

Other more scientifically influenced explanations include swamp gas, will-o'-the-wisp caused by decaying wood and organic materials, a glow coming from minerals in the area, earthquake fault lines, and electrical fields. What is clear, however, is that it does exist. Many people have seen it; some have photographed it. A few have fired shotguns at it.

"You have to be there between 10 o'clock and midnight," Nick assures them. "That's the only time when you can see it. Oh, and it shies away from big crowds and loud noises. So we've got to be careful."

"How do you know all this?" LeRoy asks.

"I've got a cousin who's seen it, and I read about it too, someplace," Nick tells him.

They all pile into Mosley's borrowed car. Mosley and Linda in the front seats, and Mickey and Jeannette, Nick, LeRoy, and their dates stacked in the back.

"It don't come out every night," Nick says from the bottom of the back seat pile.

"Now you tell us," LeRoy says.

"When you see it, stay in the car, 'cause soon as someone gets out, it goes away—poof."

"Spooky," says Linda.

"Like it's alive or something," Nick says. "Like it's intelligent."

"How would you know anything about intelligence?" LeRoy says.

"I know I get better grades than you," Nick says.

"In your dreams."

This is fun. Jeannette sits on Mickey's lap. They are all laughing, joking, enjoying the adventure.

"You know, they call this area the Devil's Promenade," Nick says.

"You mean we're gonna see the Devil too?" Linda says.

Nick screws his face into his impression of the devil's. "Sure, who do you think is holding the light?"

"Martians," Jeannette says.

"Nobody calls it the Martian's Promenade, do they?" says Nick.

"Sure, they do."

"Yeah, who?"

"I just did, didn't I?"

"What are you gonna do if you see the Devil?"

"Hide behind Mickey."

"I'll be running like hell," Mickey says.

"You're not gonna protect little ol' me?"

"Sure, if you can keep up with me."

"Has anybody ever been hurt by it?" Nick's date asks.

"Uh, yeah," says Nick. "Some people have dropped dead when they stared directly at it for too long. Lots of people, actually."

"Is that true?"

"Absolutely."

"That's BS," LeRoy says.

"What I've heard."

"People make up all sorts of things."

"How do you know it ain't true?"

"I know."

"Oh, that settles it, then."

When they arrive in the area of the sightings, Mosley pulls the car off the side of the road. The laughing and chatter stop. This is serious now. It is an overcast night, which if anything exaggerates the unnerving feeling they are experiencing.

They peer out through the windshield. A light wind is blowing the branches next to the car, so that they are scraping the fenders.

"What is that?" Linda asks.

"The Devil's fingernails," Nick says.

They are there for some minutes without anyone saying anything.

Then they see it: an orangish light directly in front of them, pulsing in intensity and then splitting into two, one orb hovering above the other.

"Jesus H!" says Nick. "Look at that!"

The mysterious light rises up high, bobs and weaves right and left.

They are all transfixed by what they are seeing … and a little scared.

Mosley opens his door and steps out of the car. "Man, that is—"

"Get back in the car," Linda screams.

"—definitely weird."

"Is it coming toward us?" LeRoy asks.

"Get in, Mose," Linda says again.

"Hey, Mickey, you go chase it. You're the fastest," Nick says.

"Yeah, and what do I do if I catch it?"

"Call for Mose."

Mosley reaches down, picks up a stone, and throws it toward the dancing light. "Oh my God, it's coming after us," Nick yells.

Mosley, feigning terror, jumps back in the car.

"Let's get out of here quick!" Nick shouts.

Mosley starts the car, pulls back onto the road, and amidst shouting and laughter makes an abrupt U-turn, then speeds down the road away from the light.

"It's following us. Faster, Mose!" Linda shrieks.

"Oh my God, oh my God, it's catching up," Nick keeps calling.

Mickey is laughing so hard that tears roll down his cheeks.

As they near home, a certain melancholy emerges. They all sense the same thing. A phase in their lives is nearing its completion, and there won't be many more nights like this. It won't be long before they graduate and take on the next stage. This may be one of the last times they are together. The future, whatever it holds, will likely separate them, maybe forever. Either that or the boys will end up in the mines, and the girls—miners' housewives.

Now in their final year of high school, Mickey and Mosley are receiving a lot of attention, including from papers out of the immediate area. They are both popular and have pretty girlfriends.

Around school they are regarded as the big-shot athletes, but neither Mickey nor Mosley act like cocky ingrates. Mickey is the more reserved and doesn't act like he deserves special attention because of what he can do on the court, diamond, or field. In games, Mickey never criticizes other players when they make mistakes, but gets down on himself when he makes one. Other players see this and appreciate it.

When they walk down the school halls, Mickey and Mosley are treated as stars. The most recognizable students in the school. They are also both on the staff of the school paper *Tiger Chat,* to which they contribute brief reports on the doings of the sports teams. LeRoy and Jeannette also work on the paper.

For the Lucky Seven Scholastic Meet, Mickey's English teacher enters him in the competition for the journalism award. In the event, held at the Northeastern Oklahoma A&M College in Miami, he comes in second and wins a plaque.

He takes Jeannette to the senior prom, but they leave before the dancing begins.

"It's almost that time, isn't it?" Jeannette says as they walk back to her house.

"What do you mean?"

"The end of all of this. I think that's a little scary, don't you?"

"A little, maybe, yeah."

"But you've always had something to look forward to."

"You mean baseball?"

"Or football or basketball or—"

"No 'ors' about it. Only baseball."

"Because of your father?"

"Not only. I like it best, and if I can play professionally, well honestly, you can't make so much playing football or basketball."

"You want to get rich or something?"

"I wouldn't mind, but mostly I'd like to make enough to, you know, stay out of the mines. What about you? You've got dreams, too."

"I was thinking about signing to play shortstop for the Cardinals."

"Oh, were you?"

"I've seen you throw the ball away at first enough to know they can't count on you there."

"But they could you?"

"How hard could it be? It's a little ball, doesn't weigh much."

Mickey takes a ball from his pocket. "Well, you'll have to show me then."

"What in the world are you doing with a baseball in your pocket at the prom?"

"I struck out 12 batters in one game with this ball. It's my lucky charm."

"You think you need luck tonight?"

"Maybe. Here, I'll throw you a couple of grounders, and you can fire them back to me like I was the first baseman."

"Oh phooey, I left my glove at home."

"Do you even have a glove?"

"Do I have a glove? What kind of shortstop do you think I am?"

"A gloveless one."

"OK, go ahead and take your best shot at getting a grounder past me."

Mickey moves a few steps ahead of her and tosses a bouncing ball her way. She manages to stop it and throw it back to Mickey, but it bounces before it gets to him.

"Marty Marion you're not."

"Who's that?"

"The Cardinals shortstop."

"Someone needs to tell him I'm coming to take his job."

"I'll be sure he gets the message. Seriously, though, do you know what you're going to do after school?"

"I'd like to go to college. Maybe become a teacher."

"Good. We could use some better ones."

"Your father, has he always forced you into—"

"It's not that way. He has never forced me. He's encouraged me, but nobody could have made me do all that practicing and playing if I didn't want to."

"OK."

"I choose to do it," he says so forcefully that Jeannette thinks he sounds overly defensive.

"How sure are you that you're … you know, good enough to play for the Cardinals, or any other professional team for that matter?"

"No one can be sure about things like that."

"I'd have to think confidence plays a big part in who makes it in sports."

"I know."

"So, be confident, Mickey Charles."

"Sure."

"But what if, despite that, you don't make it?"

"I'll be in the same boat as everyone else around here. I'll be a miner's son looking for work."

"That may not be what you want, but it's not the worst thing in the world. You make an honest living, stay out of the rain …"

"And end up with miner's disease."

"Life ain't perfect, is it?"

Mickey puts his arm around Jeannette's shoulder. "Guess not."

Mutt's work khakis are hanging looser and looser on his frame. Mickey doesn't notice. All he thinks about these days is graduation and what will come after. Despite all the years of dreaming and looking forward to this time in his life, he is anxious. Despite the advice of others, he is still filled with doubts. Maybe he won't be offered a professional contract. If he is, maybe he won't be good enough to make it out of the lowest rungs on the minor league ladder. If he does, maybe he won't have what it takes to stick.

Chapter 31

As the school year progresses without further contacts from scouts, Mutt becomes increasingly concerned. Surely, anyone paying attention knows Mickey is worthy of signing a professional contract. Even if they just read the local papers, they'd know of Mickey's exploits. And if they saw him play, well, they couldn't miss the combination of his speed and power from both sides of the plate. So why aren't they knocking down his door?

Mickey may harbor doubts about his ability to play at the highest levels of professional baseball, but Mutt never does. He knows that if Mickey commits himself fully, he can play professionally. But to do that, he has to get the chance. If he played elsewhere in the country, his chances might be better. Still, there have been players from Oklahoma to make it to the majors—Johnny Goodell, Earl Huckleberry, Ben Hunt, Roy Jarvis, Paddy Mayes, Euel Moore, Red Phillips, Jim Shilling, Hal Spindel, among others. None had exceptional careers, however. Two who did are the Waner brothers – Lloyd "Little Poison" and Paul "Big Poison." Both will one day be enshrined in the Baseball Hall of Fame.

All baseball fans in the area know the Waners grew up on a farm outside of Oklahoma City. Lloyd was only five foot nine and Paul five foot eight, but both forged brilliant careers, mostly with Pittsburgh.

"If they could make it like they did, Mickey sure as hell can, too," Mutt tells Lovell.

"Pittsburgh ain't New York," she reminds him.

"Yeah, and it ain't Commerce, either."

Unbeknownst to Mutt, some scouts do come to watch Mickey play. They sit attentively in the stands, watch, take notes, pass them on to their superiors.

Scouting report: Mickey Mantle
Pos: SS
Height: 5-11
Weight: 175
Throws: R
Hits: R & L
Hitting ability, speed, etc.: Great Hitter – very fast
Fielding ability, arm, etc.: Fair fielder – good arm
Attitude and disposition: Good
Future possibilities (for what class): M
General Remarks: Is not now a good shortstop—good enough as a hitter to enter A. Don't believe he is capable of playing short in A. If he must play shortstop, would recommend Class C—possibly B.

The rules of professional baseball make it inappropriate for scouts to talk with young men while they are still in high school, so none contact Mickey. Mutt's anxiety grows.

⸻

Mickey is sitting with Nick in the otherwise empty bleachers of the Commerce High football field.

"I'm thinking of becoming a musician," Mickey says.

"Why would you want to do that? You stink at music."

"No, I don't, I just don't have the training. I need lessons."

"As I recall, you were going to but spent all your money at the pool hall."

"True enough."

"Forget music, Mickey. You hit a ball a helluva lot better than you strum a guitar."

"I know, but ... I don't see a lot of offers coming my way to continue playing."

"Oh, but you're getting offers to play guitar professionally?"

MUTT'S DREAM: MAKING THE MICK

"I like country music."

"Forget it."

One day, Mickey, knowing Bob Wills and the Texas Playboys would be playing in Joplin, manages to see them while they are stopped at a gas station in town. When Wills sees the red-haired, freckle-faced kid staring at them, he asks Mickey if he wants an autograph. Mickey says he does. Normally too shy to talk with strangers, he musters enough courage to ask if he can go along with them to Joplin.

"You get your parents' permission," Wills tells him, "and next time we're through this way, we'll take you."

Mickey does, and Wills, true to his word, stops when they see Mickey waiting for them at the station, and takes him along as their guest.

Being a professional musician is a great life, Mickey thinks. You get to travel, meet girls. You make people happy with your music. Bob Wills has it made.

Where's that girl with the red dress on?
Some folks call her Dinah
Stole my heart away from me
Way down in Louisiana.

The next day, Mickey asks Mutt about maybe doing some work in the mines, so he can earn some money for guitar lessons.

"No, but if you want maybe some money for a new glove—"

"I don't need a new glove."

"And you don't need guitar lessons either."

———

Tom Greenwade sits in the top row of the damp bleachers at the field in Coffeyville. The Whiz Kids are playing the local team. He doesn't care about their players. He is here to see Mickey.

Mickey is excused from his commencement so that he can play in front of Greenwade, who is now able to talk to the high school graduate. In the first inning Mickey comes up hitting right-handed.

He hits a home run. In the second, he bats left-handed. He hits a home run.

"A true switch-hitter with power," Greenwade mumbles to himself. Unlike most scouts, he doesn't take written notes, but he can't ever remember seeing someone so young hitting with such skill from both sides of the plate. He returns a few days later to watch Mickey in Baxter Springs.

What he thinks: the kid's unique. A can't-miss prospect. A switch-hitter with power, speed, and a strong arm.

What he tells Mutt: "I think there is serious doubt that he could ever make it to the majors. Right now, I'd have to rate him as a lousy shortstop. Sloppy. Erratic arm. And he's small. Get him in front of really strong pitching, and … well, it's a gamble. I doubt if he can make it, but I'm willing to give him the chance."

"A contract?"

"$130 a month to finish out the season with our team in Independence, Kansas. Class D in the KOM League."

"$130! He can make that much playing semipro ball and working in the mines."

"If that's what he wants."

This is how the game is played. Mutt may not have experience dealing with Major League teams, but he understands Greenwade is negotiating. How far Mutt can push him he doesn't know, but he does know he would be thought a fool if he just accepted whatever Greenwade first asked for.

"How about a bonus? What kind of bonus will you offer?"

"Bonus?"

"Yeah, a signing bonus." This is what Barney told him to ask for.

"I don't know—"

"$5,000."

Greenwade had slept little the night before. He was too worried someone else would offer Mickey more than he had permission to offer. He's never signed someone with the potential he sees in Mickey.

MUTT'S DREAM: MAKING THE MICK

Mutt hadn't slept much either. He was too worried Greenwade either wouldn't offer a contract or would make an offer so low he would be embarrassed to accept it.

"Mr. Mantle, that's out of the question. I don't think even DiMaggio got that much."

"Then $4,000. At least four."

Greenwade looks away for several moments, then turns back to Mutt. "I shouldn't do this. The Yankees will probably have my hide, but since I've come all the way down here, I think I might be able to get them to spring for $1,000."

Mutt knows he's dealing with something with which he has no experience, and it is making him very tense. Greenwade could walk away at any point if he pushes too hard. Still, this is potentially the culmination of the last 18 years of his life's work. If he handles it right, his longed-for dream will become reality.

"What about $2,000?"

Greenwade sighs. "OK, look. Here is the very best I can do. $1,100."

"$1,150," Mutt says, wanting to show he is a good negotiator on his son's behalf.

Greenwade laughs, "OK, you've got a deal. A signing bonus of $1,150 and a salary of $130 a month to finish the season at Independence."

"How about a salary of $140?"

"I suppose an extra $10 a month won't send the Yankees to the poorhouse."

Greenwade has just agreed to a contract with the best prospect he has ever seen, and Mutt has agreed to a contract making Mickey a professional baseball player. No matter what else happens, Mickey will at least be able to say he was a pro.

Greenwade is thrilled not only to have signed Mickey, but to have signed him for peanuts. Around the country, other "bonus babies" are signing for as much as $75,000 to $100,000. He feels a little guilty about taking advantage of such an unsophisticated father. Of course, he could have gone much higher with the bonus, but as it is, if he is right about Mickey, the Yankees will have to acknowledge his scouting savvy and negotiating prowess.

Greenwade shakes Mutt's hand. "You'll get the contract and bonus check in the mail in a couple of weeks. Since Mickey is not yet 18, you'll have to sign the contract."

"Just tell me where."

Mickey scours the house looking for that scorecard from the first Major League game he saw with his father. The one with Stan Musial, Red Schoendienst, Enos Slaughter, Dick Sisler, and Marty Marion on it. The one he said he would keep forever. He wants to put the contract with it. Two life-changing documents.

He can't find the scorecard.

As Greenwade has promised, a check paid by the Independence Baseball Club arrives in the mail, made payable to Mickey Mantle for $1,150. He is a professional baseball player. It is justification of everything Mutt has wanted, but it is bittersweet, too. Soon Mickey will be off to whatever his future holds. It is difficult for Mutt to imagine his life without Mickey. Mutt is both contented and melancholy. His best friend is leaving. What could possibly fill the void? Mutt, making sure no one sees it, wipes away a tear.

For the first time, the full force of Mickey leaving home strikes Mutt. He feels stunned.

Many people will say or think that Mutt pushed Mickey into living Mutt's dream at the cost of his own, but Mutt prefers to see it as encouraging, motivating, nursing—rather than pushing. Mutt wants to ask Mickey if he feels trapped by what Mutt has wanted him to become. But he bites his tongue. Perhaps he doesn't want to know the answer. Perhaps he's afraid the answer is yes.

Mickey can't recall discussing much with his father other than baseball. It's all he has in common with Mutt. Did they ever discuss other things, things most people would say were more important? Did they talk about politics or the war or federal farm policies? Not that he remembers. They did talk about Musial going from first to third when he should have been out at second.

Mickey is lost in these memories, but fearful that whatever lies ahead for him will make him lose them. He closes his eyes hard, forcing the lids down with purpose. Maybe he can press the memories permanently into his brain. Maybe.

Now he bats in an airy game. Mutt urges him on as he smacks home run after home run, all the balls sailing up and away until they are nothing but little dots of memory. As long as he can stay at bat, the game will be endless. Time will be shattered.

When he opens his eyes, there's the rusty old barn where his father first pitched tennis balls softly to him. The barn looks rustier than it was back then, the weeds in front look bigger. It starts to rain.

In the morning, the miner and the miner's son will make the 70-mile trip up to Independence, Kansas, where Mickey will report to the Independence Yankees in the Class D Kansas-Oklahoma-Missouri League.

Now in the early evening dusk, Mutt and Mickey are walking the alkali fields where once they played in the sun.

They see an unsmiling landscape, dusty, flat, barren, parched with only the chat piles breaking up the monotony.

"It's going to be ..." Mutt searches for the right word, but all he can up with is "interesting."

"Yeah."

"You'll be in New York in no time. I know it, and I think you do, too."

"Yeah," Mickey says without much conviction. "Can't wait."

Is there any place farther away from Commerce than New York? It might as well be on another planet. Not only have they never been there, but they don't even know anyone who has.

"When you get to the Yankees, look who you'll be playing with—Yogi Berra, Tommy Henrich, Phil Rizzuto, Hank Bauer—"

"Joe DiMaggio."

"Of course."

"That's ... that's hard for me to ... I don't know, even think about it."

"You'll be OK."

"I can't even imagine talking to him. Forget about playing next to him."

"Someday he'll brag about playing with Mickey Mantle."

"I doubt that."

"Anyway, it's good you're starting in a place we can come and see you play—up in Independence."

"Yeah, I hope you can."

"You know we will. Harry Craft, a good ol' southern boy from Mississippi, is the manager. Now the Yankees, they got Casey Stengel as manager. Know where he's from?"

"I don't know."

"Our neck of the woods. Kansas City."

They walk for a while in silence. This is an exciting stage in the life of a lead miner and the miner's son. But it is also ominous. Mutt can barely remember a time when he wasn't playing or talking with Mickey about baseball, or thinking about Mickey's future or dreaming about what Mickey's life will be ... without him. Is Mickey facing a challenge or a threat? Mutt doesn't now, nor has he ever questioned what happens when a dream is realized.

"Just remember this," Mutt says as he picks up a small stone and throws it like he is a catcher trying to nail a runner at second. "The most important thing is to always do your best. No matter what happens, the good and the bad, you won't have no regrets if you know you did your best. Know what I mean?"

"Yeah."

"Nothing else matters."

"Yeah."

They walk on, stepping across shadows in the dust.

What lies behind Mickey and what lies before him is less important than what lies within him, but neither Mutt nor Mickey is capable of acknowledging that. Mutt sees Mickey lofting majestic flies over the iconic frieze of Yankee Stadium that he has seen only in pictures; striding across the greenest grass in the world while tracking down a line drive; stealing home. He can hear the raucous cheering crowd and the voice of the umpire.

Mickey suddenly stops walking. "What if I don't?"

"Don't what?"

"You know, make it."

"Don't even think like that. That's what gets people in trouble—not having the confidence to do what they damn well know they can do. You can do it. Don't be a baby."

"I'm not. It's just—"

"No 'justs' about it. You are a damn good baseball player and that's all you need. Be yourself and that'll be fine. You'll be better than fine. You'll be great. Mickey Charles Mantle, the professional baseball player. Sounds good, don't it? What are you worried about?"

Mickey takes a deep breath deciding whether or not to say what is really bothering him. He's never admitted this to his father before. "I can't help it," he says finally. "I'm worried about letting you down. I know how hard you've—"

"You won't."

"What if I do?"

"You can't. I'll always be proud of you no matter what happens."

"Even if I fail?"

"Stop that talk. Mom's got dinner on, so we should probably head back."

"I'm not hungry."

"You should eat. Gotta keep your strength up."

Mickey will be away from home for the first time, but he isn't thinking about picking up the spin of a curveball or hitting the cutoff man. He is thinking about where he will sleep and whether he will wet his bed. He is thinking about where he will take his meals and what he should wear when he is not in uniform. He's wondering whether he should call the manager "Mr. Craft," or "Harry." He's concerned about how the other players will treat him. He knows he's not always comfortable with people he doesn't know, so he's worried he won't make new friends. He's afraid he won't be able to handle failure.

What is making him most anxious, however, is the nagging feeling that maybe he really isn't good enough to have a career as a professional baseball player. Oh sure, he'd outdistanced the other kids with whom he played, but now everything was changing. The competition would be stronger, the crowds bigger, the demands greater. Everyone else he'll be playing with on the Independence team was probably also the best on his local team.

What if he fails? He'll be embarrassed, disappointed, but his father will be devastated. What then? He can always come back and work in the mines. It's a steady, reliable occupation, and it would allow him to continue playing in local amateur games. He's already proven he can do that well. He'd be a local star. Maybe that's good enough.

"Let's go back and put your things in the LaSalle," Mutt says. "I want to get an early start in the morning."

"Yeah, ok."

A restless wind kicks up and shrouds the landscape in a gloomy ochre veil of dust. Mutt hardly notices. In the green field of his mind Mickey is at the plate, tense and waiting. The pitcher winds like a clock ...

Afterword

No one—**Mickey** included—was surprised that the transition to big-time baseball presented challenges for the wide-eyed young man from Oklahoma. He was away from home, away from his friends and family, away from the scenes of his achievements. Without Mutt's guidance, he quickly became discouraged. His father had always been there when he needed pumping up, when he needed a boost to his fluctuating self-confidence.

After earning a spot on the 1951 Major League roster in spring training, Mickey suffered through a mid-season slump and was sent to the Yankees' AAA farm team, the Kansas City Blues. There he continued to slump – on the field and at bat. His natural rhythm was off. He was frustrated, so he did what he knew best to do in such situations—he called his father.

"I can't do it anymore. I'm going to quit," he said, choking back tears.

"The hell you are. Where are you?"

Mickey gave him the name of the hotel where the team was staying.

"Don't leave." Mutt told him. "And don't do anything you'll regret. I'm on my way."

If Mutt ever drove too fast, this was the time. He made the trip from Commerce to Kansas City in three-and-a-half hours.

When Mickey answered the knock on his door, there was Mutt, eyes raging, looking drained from the long drive.

"I thought I raised a man, not a coward!" he said.

"You don't know what it's like—"

"Pack your things. We're going home. I'll get you a job in the mines."

"It's just I can't hit anymore. No matter what I try—"

"What the hell did you expect? Of course, you're gonna have slumps. Everybody does. It's about how you deal with it that matters. You can fight through it or you can quit. You wanna quit, OK, then quit, but don't look back. You've got your chance. If you want to throw that away, that's up to you. Now get your things together fast. It's a long drive home."

Whether it was his despair at disappointing his father or fear of spending a life below ground, Mickey listened to his father and finally agreed to stay and give baseball another try.

The "try" turned into a career among the greatest of any player ever. The Mick became a legend. Mutt never got to see it. Within a year of convincing his son to continue his career, he died of Hodgkin's disease. He was 40, Mickey 20.

Despite his success (or maybe because of it), Mickey became overwhelmed by the challenge of being The Mick. He didn't have the emotional tools. Fueled by alcohol, his shyness turned to rudeness. He became bellicose, coarse, and loud.

Mutt may have pushed Mickey into baseball, but Mickey chose to be The Mick, chose how to respond to pressure, chose how to treat others.

Lovell remained in the area all her life. She died five months before Mickey. She was 91.

LeRoy Bennet received an appointment to the U.S. Naval Academy, and went on to earn an advanced degree in electrical engineering from the Massachusetts Institute of Technology.

Nick Ferguson received an offer to try out for the Pittsburgh Pirates. Instead, he moved to Southern California. He worked in the aircraft industry for a time, then for the U.S. Postal Service.

Bill Mosley played college football in Kansas at Fort Scott Community College and at Kansas State Teachers College in Pittsburg. He served in the Korean War, and then earned a master's degree from Washburn University. He began his coaching career in Fort Scott, and later became a successful football coach at Seaman High School in Topeka.

Today, many of the chat piles in the Tri-State district remain, as if monuments to another world, another time, but most of the hardpacked diamonds on which Mickey played are long gone. Under leaden skies, the area looks desolate, forgotten, a graveyard of rocks, stunted trees, and earth as dry as a bone.

Acknowledgements

All the stories portrayed here are true—or at least they were claimed to be true by Mickey, or his family and friends, or were related as true by the press. Some dialogue is word-for-word accurate as recorded; some has been invented but it is always consistent with the reality of the situation.

There are quite a number of books about Mickey. Most concentrate on his Major League Baseball career. Some delve into his public life after he left the game. Not a great deal has been written about the years before he became a professional. There are snippets here and there in various books, including some written (or ghosted) by Mickey himself, including: *The Education of a Baseball Player*; *The Mickey Mantle Story*, as told to Ben Epstein; and *Mickey Mantle: The American Dream Comes to Life*, co-authored by Lewis Early.

John G. Hall's *Mickey Mantle Before the Glory* was a valuable resource for this book. It takes Mickey up through his early years as a professional.

Thanks to the relatively new availability of online digitized newspaper archives, I was able to access hundreds of mentions of Mickey in *The Miami Daily Record*, *The Ottawa County Beacon*, and *The Ponca City News*. I also accessed the Commerce High yearbooks that supplied considerable information about Mickey's experiences as a football and basketball player, as well as some details on his other interests while a student there.

Jane Leavy's *The Last Boy: Mickey Mantle and the End of America's Childhood* mostly covers Mickey's professional career, but did include some references to the earlier years. Other books that provided a few insights into his life before he turned pro included: *Mickey Mantle: America's Prodigal Son,* by Tony Castro; *The Last Hero: The Life of Mickey Mantle,* by David Falkner; *A Hero All his Life: A Memoir by the Mantle Family,* by Merlyn, Mickey Jr., David, and Dan Mantle; *Mickey Mantle: Stories and Memorabilia from a Lifetime with The Mick,* by Mickey Herskowitz with Danny and David Mantle; and *Memories of Mickey Mantle: My Very Best Friend,* by Marshall Smith & John Rohde.

Also of help in setting the scene in Oklahoma during the years when Mickey was growing up were *Wilderness Bonanza: The Tri-State District of Missouri, Kansas, and Oklahoma,* by Arrell M. Gibson, and *Union Busting In The Tri-State: Oklahoma, Kansas, and Missouri Metal Workers Strike of 1935,* by George G. Suggs.

The Oklahoma Historical Society archives provided additional information about life in Oklahoma during the 1930s and '40s, as did scores of online sources—the most valuable of which was *Cardin Kids,* which provided valuable insight into Mickey's earliest years.

For the first section that deals with Mickey as a cancer patient in the Baylor University Medical Center, I am indebted to *Raising the Dead: Organ Transplants, Ethics, and Society,* by Ronald Munson.

The Baseball Hall of Fame researched and found the scouting report of young Mickey Mantle as he was about to turn professional.

About the Author

Howard Burman was born in Brooklyn. Occasionally in the summer his father would take him to Ebbets Field to see the Dodgers. His love of baseball, reflected in some of the books and plays he has written, began there.

Burman attended Wilmington College in Ohio and later transferred to The Ohio State University, where he received his B.A. and remained to earn his Ph.D. He later helped form Cameo Entertainments, and toured productions with television and film stars such as Valerie Harper, Roscoe Lee Browne, Lee Meredith, Michael Learned, and Roy Dotrice. He also produced an off-Broadway show in New York, *Behind the Broken Words*. Burman moved on to become Artistic Producing Director of the Hilberry Theatre in Detroit and the Chair of the Theatre Department at Wayne State University, where he produced some 35 shows, including two that were nominated for a national critics award.

He returned to California to start the California Repertory Company, and chaired the department of Theatre Arts at California State University, Long Beach. There he produced more than 150 shows, including 23 which he wrote. Among the most successful were *Article 24, The Boys of Summer, The Puccini Project, The Third Lie, The Miracle of Piaf, On the Beach,* and *Willie, Mickey & The Duke.* He is the author of *The Iliad Was Either Homer or Somebody Else of the Same Name,* a novel, *A Story Told by Two Liars,* and several baseball books, including *A Man Called Shoeless,* which relates the life story of the enigmatic Joe Jackson.

Burman has traveled extensively in Europe and Asia and

has been a Fulbright scholar in Taiwan. He lived part-time in Switzerland and then for a few years in Ireland. He and his wife, Karen, currently reside in Felton, California—a small town in the mountains of Santa Cruz County south of San Francisco. Their son, Ty, daughter, Kerry, and granddaughters, Gabrielle and Lucy, live nearby.